MY ADVENTURES
WITH
YOUR MONEY

ALSO BY T. D. THORNTON

Not by a Long Shot: A Season at a Hard-Luck Horse Track

MY ADVENTURES
WITH
YOUR MONEY

George Graham Rice and
the Golden Age of the Con Artist

T. D. THORNTON

St. Martin's Press
New York

www.stmartins.com

Library of Congress Cataloging-in-Publication Data

Thornton, T. D., author.
   My adventures with your money : George Graham Rice and the golden age of the con artist / by T. D. Thornton.
       pages   cm
   ISBN 978-1-250-05437-1 (hardcover)
   ISBN 978-1-4668-8697-1 (e-book)
   1. Rice, George Graham.   2. Swindlers and swindling—United States—Biography.
3. Speculation—United States—History—20th century.   4. Finance—United States—History—20th century.   I. Title.
   HV6692.R53T46 2015
   364.16'3092—dc23
   [B]   2015029683

Our books may be purchased in bulk for promotional, educational, or business use. Please contact your local bookseller or the Macmillan Corporate and Premium Sales Department at (800) 221-7945, extension 5442, or by e-mail at MacmillanSpecialMarkets@macmillan.com.

First Edition: November 2015

10 9 8 7 6 5 4 3 2 1

CONTENTS

To The American Damphool Speculator, surnamed the American
Sucker, otherwise described herein as The Thinker Who Thinks
He Knows But Doesn't—greetings! This book is for you!
Read as you run, and may you run as you read.

—G. G. R. , NEW YORK, MARCH 15, 1913
(GEORGE GRAHAM RICE'S ORIGINAL INTRODUCTION
TO HIS 1913 AUTOBIOGRAPHY, *MY ADVENTURES
WITH YOUR MONEY*)

CONFIDENCE MAN

After six months of shifting and grifting between crooked card games, poolrooms, and horse tracks without a real job, George Graham Rice crisply aligned the brim of his derby with the top of his smart-looking spectacles and edged into the seven-story shadow of the Metropolitan Opera House, calmly but keenly observing New York's urban blur from the yellow-bricked street corner of Fortieth and Broadway. Maintaining a countenance of congeniality, Rice shrewdly scanned the slushy chaos of foot, trolley, and carriage traffic, sizing up faces with a feral inner cunning his thirty years had honed to a sharp tool of self-preservation. Because the $7.30 tucked tightly into the pants pocket of his one good suit represented Rice's entire net worth on this first Tuesday of March 1901, George was instinctively—but with casual, cultured dignity—on the hustle for marks who looked ripe to be suckered.

Amid the swirl of strangers, Rice recognized an old racetrack chum. Although George was a man of many acquaintances, he steered clear of true friendships based on mutual trust. Rice could play the part of a witty, charming ringleader when he chose, but he valued his charismatic personality more as an asset that afforded him an edge in social manipulation.

As the man from the track approached, George clicked into intuitive overdrive, calculating the costs and benefits of extended conversation. Without missing a beat, Rice beamed a phosphorescent smile and reached out to heartily shake Dave Campbell's outstretched hand, even though he knew in his gut the gent's too-robust greeting belied the desperation of a struggling soul down on his luck.

"Buy me a drink?" Campbell rasped as soon as pleasantries were out of the way.

Rice didn't consider Campbell a sucker he'd fleece. But he was willing to speculate on the chance that Dave might be harboring some nugget of useful information worth extracting.

George wasn't much of a drinker—the occasional silver gin fizz or flute of fine champagne—but he did have a weakness for good cigars. At a café table, Rice lit up a twenty-five-cent perfecto and set up Dave with a nickel beer. Over by the lunch counter, a regulation news ticker chattered away, spitting out a continuous tape of stock quotes and racetrack results.

"Still bet on the horses?" Campbell asked.

"No," Rice replied, exhaling a plume. His unflinching blue eyes squarely met Dave's. "Haven't had a bet down in more than a year."

This was an outright lie. Yet the man telling it possessed a most persuasive way of making even the most outlandish distortions of reality seem wholly convincing and plausible.

Although it was technically true there had been recent periods when George did not set foot in any gambling establishment, that's only because those abstentions coincided with stints behind bars for stealing. For two and a half years at Elmira Reformatory, Rice was known as inmate No. 4018. Serving a six-and-a-half-year forgery sentence at Sing Sing, George was prisoner B-516. Prior to incarceration, he had abandoned his birth name, Jacob Simon Herzig, in favor of multiple aliases, trying out and discarding names—Abram Herzog, Joseph Hart, Jack

Hornaday—as they suited his convenience. Rice's current nom de plume—liberated from a deceased reform school inmate—had been his preferred moniker since he first tried to use it to win a short story contest. Around the gritty Tenderloin district, they knew him as GG. In racetrack betting rings, bookies dubbed him Ricecakes. His first wife called him Jock. His second bride probably had a nickname for him too, although Rice took great pains to ensure neither spouse became aware of the other's existence.

As the twentieth century opened, Rice had not yet settled into the nebulously mysterious role of con artist. But he had tried it out, just like the various aliases, and would have bristled at the notion that anyone considered him a thief because of the series of—as he preferred to term them—"youthful indiscretions" that landed him in jail. George cultivated a literary style while incarcerated, reading voraciously, improving his manners, and earning early release. Now, back on the street, he could pass for a college graduate. Except his education took the form of the dark, nuanced art of swindling.

After Sing Sing, Rice hooked on as a newspaperman with the New Orleans *Times-Democrat*. He happened to be in Galveston, Texas, on September 8, 1900, in the hurricane eye of America's most deadly natural disaster. His firsthand stories of carnage and courage made headlines nationwide, but conflicting accounts arose over whether Rice's writing was more fiction than fact: One self-styled tale had George stealing a horse to escape the flood before heroically meeting a supply train to lead the relief expedition. A separate version asserted he was run out of town by colleagues for selling stories to rival papers and double billing expenses. Yet another contended the military ordered Rice out of Texas for spreading false panic. Now, back in New York, the only certainty about George was that whatever sensational tale he spun, it was bound to be brimming with the allure of tantalizing possibility. He didn't care that he was broke and jobless; Galveston had sparked a brainstorm about the sensational selling power of a well-crafted story.

Campbell was cagey enough to know you didn't get something for nothing from GG, not even a five-cent mug of suds. He followed his opening gambit about the racetrack by producing correspondence from a notorious horse hustler, the only item of value Dave had in his possession.

"Here's a letter I just received from Frank Mead at New Orleans," Campbell said, sliding a folded slip across the table. "It ought to make you some money."

Mead wrote a racing column for the New Orleans *States-Item* under the pen name Foxy Grandpa and recorded bets as a sheet writer for a Crescent City bookmaking firm known as the Big Store. He also moonlighted as a night-shift croupier at a clandestine casino, and his unique combination of quasi-legal gambling gigs meant Mead frequently brushed up against inside information in horse racing's premier winter betting market. The letter told Campbell to keep an eye out for a precocious colt named Silver Coin: Held back by his jockey the last few races to make the fast horse appear talentless, Silver Coin would be unleashed to run to his true potential next time out. Those in the know would bet big, presumably burning bookies at odds as high as ten to one.

Rice was quick to compute how to best leverage this edge. If he bet his last $7, it would net him $70 if Silver Coin won at ten to one—a decent return, but not the huge, breakthrough score GG was gunning for. If he was going to risk every last cent in his pocket, George wanted a gamble that paid off in life-altering terms.

Lost in a swirl of cigar wisps, he began sketching the outline of a scheme on a scrap of paper.

The ticker awoke with a clatter. Campbell idly went to unravel the jumble, then exclaimed when he read the tape: Silver Coin was entered to race the very next afternoon in New Orleans.

Rice sparked into action.

Grabbing the sketch, he hustled two blocks north to the classified office of *The Morning Telegraph* at 140 West Forty-Second Street. He pushed his entire bankroll across the counter to the cashier. Seven dollars bought a sliver of advertising space, a four-inch, one-column next-

day placement in the nation's most widely circulated horse-racing paper
that read:

Bet Your Last Dollar On
SILVER COIN
To—Day
At New Orleans
He Will Win At 10 to 1

In fine print, the ad explained that this sure thing was the first and
last free horse from a bold new "turf advisory bureau." After Silver Coin
proved the accuracy and veracity of the inside information, anyone who
wanted the bureau's best bets would have to subscribe to a $5 daily
tipping service.

Rice christened his newly minted firm Maxim & Gay after glimps-
ing the regal-sounding stallion name St. Maxim on a racing sheet and
coupling it with sporty-sounding "gay" for a euphonic pairing. George
then leased a closet-sized walk-up at 1410 Broadway, secured secondhand furniture, and had tin signs painted to advertise Maxim & Gay—
all, of course, on credit.

Campbell tagged along but didn't really understand what Ricecakes
was up to.

The next afternoon, March 6, 1901, Rice and Campbell went to the
Gallagher & Collins poolroom on Sands Street in Brooklyn to learn the
results of the second race at New Orleans. At the turn of the twentieth
century, "poolrooms" in America had nothing to do with billiards. They
were openly illegal gambling establishments where bookmakers offered
wagering pools on horse races. The nation was zany over horse betting,
and big-city poolrooms like Gallagher & Collins were equipped with
cutting-edge technology that catered to the craze. Because it was imperative for bookies to have access to the order of finish before anyone
else—lest they risk being "past-posted" by bettors who attempted to
wager with advance knowledge of race results—top-notch poolrooms

utilized clandestine telegraphy to receive cipher wired from racetrack spies. After being decoded in a back office, the results were chalked on a board in the gamblers' lounge for all to see. An eager mob always hovered around the blackboards because the poolroom payouts were quicker than the "official" transmissions that went out on delay to the general public.

Waiting for the race to go off, George riffled through his *Telegraph* for the umpteenth time to check his ad. Buried at the bottom of a back page, its fifty-six agate lines disappointed him. "It looked puny," he thought. "Would people notice it?"

At higher-class poolrooms, races were re-created by a back-room announcer narrating the running order off a ticker tape, embellishing the call with theatrical flourishes. If Silver Coin's race was one of those performed aloud, the announcer had plenty of drama to work with: Careening into the turn, Silver Coin got cut off by a rival. Nearly whipsawed off the horse's back, the jockey had no choice but to yank Silver Coin back to last and try to circle the field. Rallying from far behind, the colt stormed down the stretch and lunged ahead in the shadow of the winning post, nailing the favorite, Sarilla, to prevail by a nose.

When the prices were chalked up, the cheering was more boisterous than Rice and Campbell expected, considering the favorite had lost. By the time they crossed the East River back to Manhattan, the Tenderloin was abuzz with how bookies had been burned by some mystery horse out of New Orleans. Silver Coin had gone off at eight to one at the track in Louisiana, but an unexpected swell of action was so heavy in New York that the best price you could find in any East Coast poolroom was six to one.

Even though he hadn't backed the horse himself, George got to feeling euphoric. He told Dave with an opportunistic glint that Silver Coin's win was sure to snare Maxim & Gay at least ten solid subscribers to get the venture off and running.

The next morning, Campbell woke Rice with news of another telegram from Mead. This one advised to bet a hot horse named Annie

Lauretta in Friday's first race. The betting line in New Orleans was an astronomical forty to one.

When Rice and Campbell arrived on Broadway, they were confounded by a throng in the street, with half a dozen policemen attempting to corral the herd into some sort of line.

"What theater has a sale on seats today?" Dave wondered aloud.

George didn't know. But when he turned the corner to climb the rickety stairs of their office building, he was startled to see the line traced straight up to the locked front door of Maxim & Gay.

Keeping their mouths shut, Rice and Campbell marched up the narrow stairway past an impatient file of customers. George turned the key, the two stepped in, and Rice re-bolted the door, bracing it with his back.

"What have we done?" he gasped.

The first order of business was deciding what to do about Friday's best bet. Even GG was unsure about the audacity of selling a tip on a forty-to-one long shot. But the vision of all those $5 bills thrust at him by race-mad disciples assuaged any such concerns. The next dilemma was how to convey this hot horse into merchantable form. George sent for a typist from the Hotel Marlborough across the way.

The girl probably thought it was a peculiar assignment to be asked to strike the name "Annie Lauretta" hundreds of times on small slips of paper while Rice and Campbell sealed them in tall stacks of envelopes.

Keep typing, George urged the girl between tastes of envelope glue. Dave craned his neck out the window and saw the line snaked down Broadway for a block and a half.

They made the transactions as efficient as possible, with Dave handing out envelopes as each man handed George five bucks. Rice stuffed the cash into the right-hand drawer of his desk. When it became clogged, he crammed it into the left drawer. "Finally, the money came so thick and fast that I picked up the waste-paper basket from the floor, lifted it to the top of the desk and asked the buyers to throw their money into the receptacle," George would later reminisce. "When a man wanted change, I let him help himself."

The procession moved steadily for two and a half hours. By the time the race was about to go off, Maxim & Gay had sold 551 tips on Annie Lauretta, raking in $2,755—roughly $75,000 in 2015 dollars.

Rice and Campbell didn't have time to make it to a poolroom, so they scurried to a neighborhood spa where a news ticker would discharge the New Orleans results thirty minutes after the race became official. The wait was excruciating.

Ticka, ticka, ticka . . . NEW ORLEANS . . . FIRST RACE . . . *Ticka, ticka, ticka* . . . WEATHER CLEAR . . . TRACK FAST . . . *Ticka, ticka, ticka* . . .

Finally, here it came.

Ticka, ticka, ticka . . .

The first letter was *F.*

Instantly, they knew their horse had lost. It was Free Hand. Free Hand won the race.

"Grim silence" was how George described it. He didn't bother to watch the rest of the result sputter out of the machine.

Ticka, ticka, ticka . . .

"Here she is!" bellowed Campbell.

Annie Lauretta had just missed, finishing second at huge odds.

Any customer who had backed up win wagers with "across the board" place and show bets for finishing second or third was about to be rewarded with a twenty-to-one return. From a pure publicity perspective, GG knew giving out a narrowly defeated long shot would prove many times more profitable than if Maxim & Gay had tipped the actual winner of the race at much shorter odds.

George now had more cash in his pocket than he was accustomed to earning in a year.

Ricecakes asked his pal how much it might cost to keep him in beer money while helping to run Maxim & Gay. Campbell proposed a $10 daily salary. GG stripped a sawbuck off his wad and slapped it into his partner's palm. Dave laughed that it was more money than he had touched in a month.

George hopped aboard a streetcar and rode down to the stately marble Stewart Building at Broadway and Chambers. He peeled off more bills and rented an office suite of "sober magnificence" commensurate with the status he wanted to project upon Maxim & Gay. Then he hightailed it back to *The Telegraph* and ordered a "flaring full-page ad" that unabashedly called attention to the bookie-busting success with Silver Coin and Annie Lauretta while announcing the firm was open for business at a swank new address.

After a sumptuous dinner—George relished the three-finger steaks and clubby "no women allowed" atmosphere at Browne's Chop House— he wired Mead, empowering his man in New Orleans to spare no expense in setting up the best staff of "clockers, figurators and toxicologists" money could buy. In return for a sizable salary, Mead was to distill his racetrack intelligence into the form of a single wagering proposition each day, which he would then wire to the home office so George could trumpet the horse's name nationwide as Maxim & Gay's "One Best Bet."

By the end of the spring season, New York's most sought-after horse advisory bureau would be soaring toward its first million in profits. Yet George Graham Rice did not make a dime of this money by selling winners to gamblers.

Instead, he got rich peddling confidence to suckers.

Jacob Simon Herzig was born in Manhattan's Lower East Side on June 18, 1870, on the cusp of a searing, rain-starved summer that no one yet recognized as the sultry, pulsating dawn of America's golden age of con artistry.

During that same hazy time frame, a bold swindler known as the King of the Fakirs was tearing across upstate New York in a high-wheeled carriage drawn by a spanking team of horses. The grifter was William B. Moreau, but the French-Canadian hustler used a different alias everywhere he went and traveled fast enough to outdistance warnings of his broad-daylight rip-offs. Village by village, Moreau pillaged the countryside, working the Bohemian oats hoax here and the bogus diamond dodge there. After a successful run with the liver-pad racket and toothache fake in Dunkirk, the slick, mustachioed pitchman zeroed in on the sleepy hamlet of Fredonia, which he thought would be ripe for a nervy new fraud he had cooked up but not yet tried—the "giving away dollars" gimmick.

Moreau made a spectacle of his arrival, touring Barker Common with harness bells jangling, setting out placards announcing a free show. Although each swindle was different, the fundamentals were always the same. If people questioned him, Moreau breezily suggested they telegraph his good friend, police chief so-and-so, in the town he just came from, but no one ever bothered because Moreau seemed so avuncular and trustworthy. As he entertained a growing crowd with witty small talk and prepared to launch into a spirited performance, Moreau eloquently underscored to the townsfolk that he was there not for his own health or amusement but to make money.

With a flourish, Moreau produced a case of worthless goods. Usually, it was some defective tool he had liberated in bulk. He started in with his showman's patter, but no one was willing to part with a dollar for a hunk of junk. So Moreau started giving the tools away, and at that price a few halfhearted cheapskates stepped up. Then Moreau started tossing fistfuls of coins into the crowd, cackling when boys scrambled after them. "I said I had no use for such stuff, and if I was crazy, as people generally said I was, I couldn't help it."

At this point, a man came forward and actually purchased one of the faulty items, paying with a $5 bill and getting back change. The unassuming gent tried to slip back into the crowd, but Moreau called for him to halt.

"What did I give you besides the purchase?" the pitchman demanded.

"Four dollars," the man stammered, acting perplexed. He had arrived in town just before Moreau, but no one recognized him as the show's hired "capper," or planted accomplice.

"This is wrong!" Moreau boomed. "Here is your other dollar, and one of mine, too!"

A few stragglers, picking up the scent of something for nothing, suddenly wanted in on the deal. They too bought the worthless tool and triumphantly got what they paid back, plus a buck or two extra. Farmers, tradesmen, business leaders, bankers, schoolteachers, and church elders all queued up to the wagon, jostling for position. "The money rolled up in a blind stream, the fake article being handed out in each case," Moreau later recalled. "Some dollars had to be reached over the heads of the excited people."

He congratulated the sharp-witted townsfolk for knowing how to spot a bargain and hinted that it would be wise for them to stick around; the biggest surprise was yet to come.

After handing out $50 or $60 in this fashion, the swindler switched into deal-closing mode.

"Now, gentlemen, I have given away a good many dollars to-night," Moreau called out to the eager swarm, switching his tone from conversational to conspiratorial. "I am a stranger in a strange land. Is there a man here who thinks enough of me to give me a dollar?"

Believing the fool was about to launch into another streak of irrational charity, men thrust bills at the showman. Those who had skeptically sat on the sidelines during the first part of the pitch were now fearful of missing out, and they too advanced, digging into their billfolds. Moreau patiently waited until every last sucker who wanted to had forked over cash.

Clutching $188 in his fist, Moreau stood tall, raised the bankroll over his head, and addressed the expectant horde. "I have some money here. If you were me, what would you do with it?"

If no smart aleck in the crowd had the presence of mind to wisecrack, "Keep it!" then it was the capper's job to make exactly that suggestion, loud and clear.

"That seems to be good advice," Moreau called back, pretending to mull it over. Then he nodded decisively and slipped the bankroll into his pocket. "I believe I'll take it!"

None of the entranced locals had noticed the pitchman packing up while he distracted them with his spiel, and now Moreau closed with a hurried apology; usually, he said, he liked to end his shows with a festive song.

"But as I am a little hoarse to-night, I will simply give you a little advice."

Moreau paused, eyes agleam, smiling down from his coachman's seat at the bewildered villagers. Then he flicked the shiny leather reins at his muscular team of horses.

"No I won't, either," the King of the Fakirs declared, tipping his hat and waving cavalierly, clopping briskly out of town. "You wouldn't take it."

When the Austrian immigrants Simon and Anna Herzig settled in Manhattan's Jewish ghetto in the decade after the U.S. Civil War to trade furs and raise a family, they didn't have to worry about getting fleeced by traveling charlatans giving away dollars. Their own lawless neighborhood was teeming with the Lower East Side's uniquely territorial cast of thieves, thugs, and ethnic gangs, and con artists like Moreau who relied on slick talk in the open country knew it would be ludicrous—if not fatal—to drive a fancy carriage into a maze of tenements to hustle up a swindle. Even though petty vice was rampant right outside the Herzigs' front door, actual violence against ghetto residents was low so long as you banded together with your own kind and minded your own business. In this respect, the shadowy alleys of Ward 14 were comparatively safe for the Herzig clan. The family had no way of knowing it, but its greatest risk of ruin was festering from within.

Jacob was the third of five kids, four boys and a girl, born five years after Simon and his brother Philip opened a New York fur shop that did steady business at the busy intersection of the Bowery and Grand Street.

Simon had been well educated in Europe and was fluent in German, French, and English, and when large-scale manufacturing took off, Herzig Brothers Furriers seized the opportunity to supply the nation's hat and overcoat factories with imported pelts, skins, and feathers. The firm expanded to 133 Mercer Street, and the ensuing windfall meant an upward move for the family, to 147 East Forty-Ninth Street. By the time Jacob was ten, in 1880, the Herzigs had broken free from tenement squalor, with all five children away at school and a live-in Irish servant keeping house in their sprawling uptown apartment.

Jacob was undersized and scrawny, and his formative years spent avoiding ghetto pummelings taught him to rely on brains rather than brawn. As a schoolboy, he stood off to the side and observed older men cheating at street corner dice and card games, then adapted those techniques to gaining an edge at winning marbles. After liberating coveted marbles from older kids, Jacob frequently had to use his wits to talk his way out of beatings. He had been blessed with extraordinary intellect, but school bored him, and Jacob was not so much ambitious as aloof about being able to accomplish whatever he set his mind to—if he felt like doing it. He gravitated to stories about underdogs and entertained penmanship teachers with an uncanny ability to copy signatures. Even after the family moved uptown, adolescent Jacob still felt a pull to the seamy gambling haunts of his old neighborhood, yielding to the allure of illicit adventure as his psyche jelled around a core concept that honesty was dull and provided zero thrills.

Two of Jacob's brothers, George and Leo, were being groomed to run the family fur business. George would turn out to be a South American pelt expert known as the "Chinchilla King," leading years-long expeditions into the Andes Mountains. Leo rose to executive level at the company's New York headquarters and gained sporting-class status as an international yacht racer. Their younger sibling Charles aspired to get into Columbia University's prestigious School of Mines and would blossom into a world-renowned geological engineer, developing landmark mines on six continents.

Simon encouraged his four boys to go to college, join fraternal orga- nizations, and pursue enterprise (his daughter, Helen, was expected to marry well). But by age eighteen, Jacob wanted no part of convention- ality. He stole from the family fur business to pay horse-racing debts, and his father had him arrested. But instead of pressing charges, Simon took custody of his son and forced him aboard a boat to Europe, believ- ing a temporary exile would sever the boy's ties to bad influences.

Jacob treated his "punishment" like a holiday abroad, carousing across the Continent as if he had hit the number in the Lower East Side lottery. After a few months, Simon summoned him to return, confident the boy had learned his lesson. In a leap-of-faith placement, Simon set Jacob up with a job on the company accounting staff. Jacob still spent more time with bookmakers than with bookkeepers.

On one occasion shortly after returning home, Jacob took off on a whim to see the heavyweight champ John L. Sullivan spar in a boxing exhibition. The rural Vermont match was part of a barnstorming tour and meaningless in terms of the title, but Jacob got to see America's first true sports superstar from a behind-the-scenes perspective. He would recall the experience for decades as a galvanizing lesson in showmanship.

A boisterous crowd had lined up to greet the champ at the small-town train station, and Herzig watched intently as Sullivan disembarked from his private car. It was neither raining nor blazingly sunny, but the boxer's manager scurried in front of John L. to shield him with an umbrella. When the imposing fighter clambered into a waiting carriage, another handler immediately drew the blinds at all the windows. At the hotel, the coachman was instructed to divert to a side entrance, and the man- ager again hid the champ behind the umbrella and whisked him straight up to a guarded suite. Sullivan was similarly cloistered whenever he ventured from his rooms. His manager seemed intent on not letting a single soul glimpse the Boston Strong Boy before he appeared onstage in his customary woolen fighting breeches—the distinctively long, formfitting knickers that would come to be known for generations in his honor as long johns.

After Sullivan's crowd-wowing display of fistic discipline, Herzig worked up his courage and approached the manager, who seemed less uptight with the rake from the gate tucked in his vest pocket. Jacob asked him why, if the purpose of the tour was to drum up publicity, such secretive measures had been taken to keep the champ hidden.

The showman sized up the plucky teenager and gave Jacob a straightforward answer.

"If the public thought John L. was just an ordinary human being with black mustaches and a florid Celtic face," the manager scoffed, "they wouldn't go to see him. The public demand that they be mystified, and to have shown people off the stage that Mr. Sullivan is just a plain, ordinary mortal would disillusion them and keep money out of the house."

For Jacob, that explanation resonated as a truism of influence. It was as if a magician had revealed the simple secret behind an intricate trick.

By 1889, Jacob had begun to infuse a bit of mystery into his own life, experimenting with aliases and settling for a time on Joseph Hart. He fancied himself a dandy who liked to impress girls by spending big and moved into a ritzy apartment his $1,000 annual accountant's salary doubtfully afforded. At five feet seven and a quarter inches tall and a slender 134 pounds, Jacob was budding into a magnetic charmer, with wavy light brown hair and a faint, intriguing scar at his left temple. His trustworthy face was framed by round ears, a narrow upper lip, and gold spectacles that adorned azure eyes. Not so much handsome as persuasive, Jacob had the ability to illuminate his expression at will with a broad, beaming smile—even if inwardly seething with rage. He sometimes changed tailor-made suits four times a day, and although his shoulders were stooped, Jacob carried his head high and topped it with the season's most stylish hats. Strolling Broadway wielding an ornate ram's head walking stick, Herzig was not yet an aristocrat grifter but grandly aspired to play the part.

A few months after his European sojourn, Jacob bolted to the West

Coast, financing an eight-month betting binge by forging Herzig Brothers Furriers bank drafts. The amount Jacob stole was in excess of $500,000 in today's dollars, but his father remained adamant about saving the family from embarrassment. Once again he honored the checks and once again had his son arrested. But this time Simon insisted that Jacob be committed to Elmira Reformatory, the nation's first adult psychological institution based on rehabilitation rather than punishment.

The "Elmira system" had been the 1876 brainchild of the institution's superintendent, Zebulon Brockway, and his model of reform was hailed worldwide as a visionary penal experiment. Male first-time offenders between the ages of sixteen and thirty were committed to open-ended sentences. Their actual lengths of jail time were calculated by a complex grading system based on performance in vocational training and military discipline. At Brockway's insistence, attendance was required at brass band practice, ethics lessons, and regimented gymnasium calisthenics. The goal was to "correct the roots of deviance" and churn out sin-free, God-fearing gentlemen who would know their place in society when finally granted freedom. But when the erudite, white-bearded Brockway tried to apply his high-minded theories to hardened criminals who had conned their way into his reformatory solely to escape the horrors of New York State's more barbaric lockups, the results proved more brutal than benevolent.

By the time Jacob was committed to Elmira for second-degree larceny on April 30, 1890, Brockway's vision had been consumed by chaos. "Escapes, violence, gangs, drugs, predatory sex, arson and suicides were persistent problems," one historian wrote. Another described sixty-three-year-old Brockway as a master of rhetoric who knew how to cast sadistic degradation in a progressive, forward-thinking light. Resistant inmates at his "college on the hill" were treated with "positive extraneous assistance" (lashings with a leather strap), "quickening slaps" (punches to the face), and "rest cures" (bread-and-water dungeon confinement). Brockway defended a regimen of "scientific whipping" as a component of reform, testifying that "patients" often thanked him after they had time to reflect on their course of treatment. "They come to me at interview very often, the very next evening or the same week, and we have a pleasant, friendly and social chat," Brockway explained when state officials showed up to investigate complaints of cruelty. "A prisoner usually overestimates the treatment he receives. . . . I will state that no blow has been inflicted upon the spinal cord; it is protected by the protuberance of the buttock."

Jacob's handwritten intake record described him as "bad with gamblers" and noted he suffered from "simple venereal disease." Brockway, who personally evaluated every incoming prisoner, budgeted a five-year plan for inmate No. 4018, mandating vocational rigor based on stenography so Herzig could aspire to a lifetime of clerical work. Jacob bought into the program—spitefully—only because he was shrewd enough to realize cooperation was his only chance at early parole.

Herzig marched in formation, kept his sky-blue uniform impeccably starched, and whizzed through Brockway's requirements in half the time. But what Jacob truly learned at Elmira was how to assemble a nefarious swindling repertoire that would one day rival the most seasoned and brilliant charlatans on the planet.

D id twenty-year-old Jacob absorb tricks of the trade from con artists while locked up at Elmira? The answer is certainly yes, but Herzig would not have known or referred to his criminal tutors by that name. Neither would anyone else in 1890s America, because even though swindlers known as confidence men had been bilking suckers blind for as long as anyone could remember, their racket would not be elevated to the level of artistry for another twenty-five years. The term "con artist" would sweep into vogue around 1915, with Jacob at the vanguard of get-rich-quick profiteering, feasting on a nation of gullible prey.

Crimes of deception—as opposed to outright, smash-and-grab stealing—are as old as human nature. Medieval folktales from the tenth century celebrated Reynard the Fox, a sly cheater whose weapons were guile and trickery. In 1592, the British essayist Robert Greene authored a series of tawdry pamphlets portraying street grifting as "coney catching" (the Elizabethan term for taming a wild rabbit you later plan on eating). Colonial America was fraught with economic misrepresentation. "To make one's way through the nineteenth-century marketplace required constant scrutiny of goods," wrote one scholar of fraud. "Individuals and firms who did not remain vigilant soon found themselves saddled with dubious patent medicines, uncollectible debts owed by merchants who had misrepresented their financial conditions, stock certificates from fake life-insurance and mining companies, and counterfeit banknotes."

In 1839, *The Hand-Book of Swindling* was published in London, based on an unfinished manuscript discovered after the death of Captain Barabbas Whitefeather, who billed himself as "Knight of Every Order of the Fleece, Scamp and Cur." Whitefeather did not impart actual secrets of deception in his book, but instead aimed to guide aspiring fraudsters on the finer points of duplicity, outlining practical tips in sections titled "Blushing Fatal to Swindling," "Difficulty of Choosing a Name," and "The Use and Abuse of Mustachios." It would be another ten years before cheats who fostered trust for the sole purpose of exploiting it got their own specific term in the American vernacular, when the actions of one Samuel (William) Thompson were reported in the July 8, 1849, *New York Herald* under the headline "Arrest of the Confidence Man":

> For the last few months a man has been traveling about the city, known as the "Confidence Man," that is, he would go up to a perfect stranger in the street, and being a man of genteel appearance, would easily command an interview. Upon this interview he would say after some little conversation, "have you confidence in me to trust me with your watch until to-morrow;" the stranger at this novel request, supposing him to be some old acquaintance not at that moment recollected, allows him to take the watch, thus placing "confidence" in the honesty of the stranger, who walks off laughing and the other supposing it to be a joke allows him so to do. In this

way many have been duped, and the last that we recollect was a Mr. Thomas McDonald, of No. 276 Madison Street, who, on the 12th of May last, was met by this "Confidence Man" in William Street, who, in the manner as above described, took from him a gold lever watch valued at $110.

The police apprehended Thompson several weeks later when he had the misfortune to cross paths with his victim on the street. After a brief scuffle and an appearance before a judge who recognized him as a repeat offender, New York's first documented confidence criminal was locked away in the city's hellacious Tombs prison.

It's easy to snicker at nineteenth-century chumps for being gullible enough to hand over valuables to strangers, but one constant of con artistry is how potential marks never think they'll get suckered themselves. Confidence swindlers—then and now—are the magicians of thievery. They rank at the top of the grifting hierarchy and take aristocratic pride in their craft, operating with a gentle touch and avoiding brutality. Truly fluid confidence men even evoke a twinge of admiration from impartial observers when they skillfully turn a con, because when suckers don't get (physically) hurt and the swindles are compellingly clever, tales morph into lore and beg repeating.

Edgar Allan Poe's 1843 essay "Diddling" examined popular scams of the day, postulating that conning others (diddling) is an inherent human trait: "A crow thieves; a fox cheats; a weasel outwits; a man diddles. To diddle is his destiny." By the time Herman Melville published *The Confidence-Man: His Masquerade* in 1857 about a costumed fraud who sneaks aboard a Mississippi riverboat on April Fools' Day, the "gold brick swindle" had left countless Americans holding gilt-leaved hunks of lead, and the "green goods game" had tricked innumerable aspiring counterfeiters into forking over real money in return for meticulously packaged bundles of sawdust.

In the goldbrick and green goods swindles, marks are led to believe they are getting the upper hand in a too-good-to-be-true transaction, yet their own willingness to be complicit in a shady deal is what sends them smack into a setup. In the first example, suckers are offered a suspiciously low price on "stolen" goldbricks, only later to discover that the doctored metal is neither stolen nor precious (the only actual gold being a wafer-thin veneer and tiny center core the victim is allowed to sample). In the second swindle, would-be conspirators are offered a chance to buy "green goods" (counterfeit money) at a fraction of their face value. The victims turn over real cash and are shown high-denomination bogus bills, but during a distraction the funny money is switched for tightly wrapped sawdust parcels that mimic the heft of banknotes. The marks are instructed not to open the bank bag until they reach a safe place, which of course means "safe" for the con artist, who will be long gone by the time the victim realizes he has been ripped off.

In order for these types of scams to be successful, con men insist that victims have a touch of larceny in their own hearts. Grifters bleed suckers dry by milking greed as soon as they tap into it, stoking traces of avarice from flickering latency into fully engulfed lust. The lawman Allan Pinkerton, founder of the high-profile Pinkerton's National Detective Agency in 1850, wrote that the green goods game was safer for nineteenth-century criminals than almost any other fraud, because it was only practiced upon men "whose cupidity overcomes their judgment, and who in their desire to swindle others, become dupes themselves." Victims rarely reported goldbrick and sawdust rip-offs to police, because doing so compelled them to acknowledge their own dishonesty. "As a natural consequence the swindled customers of these sharpers prefer to quietly submit to their losses," Pinkerton wrote, "rather than to advertise themselves in the doubtful light which would follow any attempt to punish the offenders."

An 1860 survey of New York police officers estimated one out of every ten city criminals was a confidence man. Around this same time, the idiom "There's a sucker born every minute" was widely being misattributed to the pitchman extraordinaire P. T. Barnum (Barnum was a master hoaxer, but for the most part he sent people away satisfied they had gotten their money's worth). It's not that Americans were more naïve back then; they weren't. It's just that the truth about the most legitimate investments was never so tantalizing as the made-up deceptions of con men.

"Why, it would just make you giddy to read the evidence in some cases brought to our attention," said one nineteenth-century antifraud official. "It almost makes a man want to quit work and get into the business of separating the gullible from their money. Get-rich-quick concerns, firms offering something for nothing, and companies guaranteeing attractive prizes at little or no risk . . . insert their advertisements in the newspapers, and the 'suckers' do the rest."

By 1880, popular publications were jammed with blind ads promising dubious solutions to everyday problems. Dupes who sent fifty cents to a sham exterminator for "a sure way to get rid of rats" got a postcard with the obvious advice "Catch and kill them." The same four bits got you a "cure for the liquor habit" ("Stop drinking"), the "best way to raise potatoes" ("With fork, at table"), and the secret of "how to break a kicking cow" ("Sell her to a butcher"). Newlyweds who mailed $1.25 for a "fine set of parlor furniture" got tables, chairs, and a sofa barely big enough for a dollhouse. Housewives unable to resist the dazzling ad for a "sewing machine for $2.00" were crestfallen to receive only an envelope containing a darning needle.

Spinsters who swooned at the prospect of their own Angora kitten did indeed receive a feline, but the yowling stray in a filthy box was hardly the silky, purring beauty they expected. "What they were Heaven only knows," one investigator confided. "We discovered in this particular case that the man who offered the 'Angoras' did not breed the animals at all. When he got an order he roamed around the neighborhood, and the next day it was reported to the police that a household pet had disappeared during the night."

But blind-reply magazine frauds were pocket change compared with the highly structured wave of con artistry that was just beginning to crest in America. By the early 1890s, mechanisms for ripping people off had begun to mirror the complexities of the country's booming industrialism, and high-volume expansion of securities markets provided anonymity and liquidity for swindlers who branched into stock frauds. Discerning grifters began to differentiate between "small cons" (street corner hustles designed to clean out whatever was in a man's pocket) and "big cons" (elaborately staged rackets that carved huge chunks of capital out of high-net-worth individuals). Swindlers were aligning in a new hierarchy, with the con men who could orchestrate elaborate rip-offs ascending to the top of grifting's totem pole. Jacob Herzig would emerge from Elmira Reformatory just as American fraud was undergoing this grand metamorphosis, from hit-and-run pillaging to high-stakes coups of dizzying deception.

As America's swindling landscape shifted, even the master pitchman William Moreau found it difficult to earn a living pillaging villages in the bold, high-carriage fashion he pioneered in the 1870s. After four decades on the road finally wore him out, the giving-away-dollars grifter began compiling an autobiography titled *Swindling Exposed* that he hoped to pawn off on some publisher before he died. Moreau took a dim view of low-level hustlers who didn't respect the so-called code of confidence swindling, and when he wrote of his particular distaste for forgers—who occupied a lower, less honorable rung on the underworld class ladder—the King of the Fakirs might as well have been describing young Jacob's career arc, even though the two never met:

> *The kindergarten of the forger is his early tendency to deception, lying, shifting responsibility and making things appear in a false light. . . . The forger and check raiser usually is known (before he is found out) as a gentleman, and associates with the upper crust of society. . . . A "Jim the Penman" does not associate with the toiling*

*masses, for his aim is to gain recognition. . . . He makes a business
of it, and takes chances of long terms in prison. With him life
means desperation and no law is too severe in giving him his just
deserts.*

In contrast to common forgers, noble practitioners of the con in the
1890s adhered to a methodical framework that progressed through rec-
ognizable stages. Similar to the magicians' code of honor, these secrets
were only passed down from one con man to another. Although popular literature of the 1890s tried to illuminate snippets of this clandestine subculture, it would be another fifty years—when the golden age of
hustling was sinking into its murky twilight—before the sociology of
confidence swindling was codified in depth. Oddly enough, this fundamental blueprint came about entirely by accident, when a University of
Louisville linguist undertaking a study of underworld dialects became
sidetracked by the entrancing folklore of con artistry.

David W. Maurer's *The Big Con: The Story of the Confidence Man*
came out in 1940, and no historical record—published before or since—
captures the sordid aura of swindling with such matter-of-fact detail,
sly humor, and chilling appreciation. "The methods by which I collected
my material were not in any way bizarre or unusual," Maurer explained
in the book's introduction. "I did not resort to false whiskers. . . . I did not
try to join any mobs incognito. I simply talked to confidence men,
who, little by little, supplied the necessary facts, facts which were not
available in libraries or police records, facts which could come only from
the criminals themselves." It helped that many of the old-time rogues
Maurer got access to—Yellow Kid Weil, the High Ass Kid, Brickyard
Jimmy, Limehouse Chappie—were well into the autumn stages of their
swindling careers by the time the professor interviewed them. Perhaps
sensing that grifting was mired in a post-Depression ebb and knowing
there were too few aspiring inside men to prosper from their knowledge,
these kingpins of confidence reversed the traditional flow of trust late
in their lives and, somewhat surprisingly, opened up to Maurer.

Maurer had compiled thousands of index cards referencing low-life slang and the intricate taxonomy of swindling. "The impetus for [*The Big Con*] came from the half-humorous suggestion of a confidence man who was going through my files," Maurer wrote. "The execution of it was made possible only by the cooperation of competent professionals." Emphasizing that there are many offshoots and variations to core swindles, Maurer was the first researcher to paint a vivid, behind-the-scenes picture of American confidence artistry at its zenith, because the way he wrote it in 1940 was based on the collective intelligence of grifters who had risen to peak prowess in the final decade of the nineteenth century—exactly when Herzig was becoming acquainted with some of these same specialized secrets at Elmira.

True confidence swindlers, according to Maurer, take time to research both victims and potential markets. Once contact has been initiated (seemingly random to the victim), swindlers establish a focal point of trust that will later justify shared immoral behavior (psychologists have since dubbed this moral licensing). The process of reeling in the catch begins by dangling the irresistible lure of easy (or illicit) riches, often in the form of a too-good-to-be-true proposition. At this point, the deception might detour to allow the sucker to make a small amount of teaser profit ("giving him the convincer") before determining exactly how much money the mark needs to invest for the whole shebang to succeed ("giving him the breakdown"). Blinded by gluttony, the victim rationalizes away any misgivings about being involved in a shady endeavor, oblivious to the fact that *he* is the actual intended target of the rip-off.

The deal is sealed by getting the mark to hand over cash in some highly scripted fashion ("taking off the touch"). Once the quarry has been ensnared and it becomes apparent to the victim that he isn't going to get rich quick, the con artist either tries to "blow him off" by getting him to go away quietly or—better yet—"cools him out" to lay the groundwork for a future fleecing. The holy grail of grifting is a mark who can be talked into thinking it was his own fault or incompetence that botched the caper and in order to recoup losses will willingly go "on the send" to scrape together more cash to make up for his mistake. (You might recognize this as the basic plot from the 1973 Academy Award–winning grifter movie *The Sting*. Maurer did too. In 1974, seven years before his death, he filed a $10 million lawsuit against the studio, alleging that his description of the "wire" horse-racing scam had been lifted nearly verbatim. He received an undisclosed, out-of-court settlement.)

If the victim hollers for the law, the swindler can always call in the "fixer" (the underworld expert in every town who gets bribes to the proper officials) or get the case dropped by offering a partial return of money. A refund usually satisfies suckers but frustrates police and prosecutors who invest time building cases only to have to drop them (which further disincentivizes lawmen to pursue future frauds). But most of the time these final steps aren't necessary, because marks are so embarrassed about being taken that they never report the crimes.

In the aftermath of a successfully turned con, swindlers feel zero remorse, rationalizing that marks motivated by greed get exactly what they deserve. Yet at the same time, they harbor no individual malice toward victims. In the worldview of a seasoned hustler, taking off a touch is strictly business, nothing personal, and—when suckers are so obviously ripe to be had—more of an inevitability of *when* they'll be conned than *if*.

"Confidence games are cyclic phenomena," Maurer emphasized. "They rise to a peak of effectiveness, then drop into obscurity. But they have yet to disappear altogether. Sooner or later they are revived, refurbished to fit the times, and used to trim some sucker who has never heard of them."

That logic helps explain why low-level hustles like three-card monte are as productive today as the nearly identical shell game that rooked gullible unfortunates hundreds of years ago. Similarly, it's why the Spanish Prisoner postal scam of the nineteenth century—in which a "foreign dignitary" solicits financial assistance to get out of a nonexistent jail by vowing an extravagant, nonexistent reward—is mirrored by the proliferation of spam that plagues twenty-first-century e-mail users (often taking the form of a deposed Nigerian prince seeking up-front funding or the use of your bank account to help sneak an "inheritance" out of his country).

The most enduring example of multigenerational repurposed swindling traces to the 1844 Charles Dickens novel, *The Life and Adventures of Martin Chuzzlewit*. In the book, a devious character cooks up a multilevel investment scam that promises extraordinary (but unsustainable) returns to early participants by paying them with premiums from subsequent recruits. The story was well-known in its day, but seventy-five years later no one recognized this "pyramid" scheme when the Boston businessman Charles Ponzi amplified the same fraud. He too delivered astronomical returns at first, but his top-heavy pyramid collapsed in 1920, burying speculators and landing Ponzi in jail for five years. Yet in *another* seventy-five years, money-hungry investors were equally oblivious when the Wall Street asset manager Bernard Madoff perpetuated similar deceptions. His highly complex, decades-long $65 billion swindle, exposed in 2008, is considered the largest financial hoax in history. Despite massive media attention and a hefty 150-year prison sentence imposed on Madoff, don't bet on a nation of suckers being able to resist the next incarnation of a similarly styled great get-rich-quick craze.

"Confidence men trade upon certain weaknesses in human nature," Maurer summed in the final paragraph of *The Big Con*. "Hence until human nature changes perceptibly there is little possibility that there will be a shortage of marks for con games."

Just before his Elmira stint was up, Herzig struck up a jailhouse kinship with an eloquent older forger named Willie Graham Rice. The two shared an affinity for fast racehorses and faster women and passed time comparing notes on financial fakery. Willie was a newspaper reporter who had been convicted of falsifying banknotes against his employer, and he regaled Jacob with stories about the sensationalized nature of 1890s journalism. The wily, articulate Rice was probably the closest thing Herzig ever had to a mentor. At some point, Willie impressed upon

Jacob how anyone with a flair for exaggeration would never go hungry in America.

The twenty-two-year-old soaked up the wiseguy guidance, but what especially captivated Jacob was the hustler's ultra-persuasive way with words. When Willie first arrived at Elmira, his grifter's sixth sense had sized up Zebulon Brockway as a malleable mark. After waxing passionately at interview sessions about his (totally false) zeal for martial training, Willie talked Brockway into granting him a free pass and $200 in spending money so he could travel to a prestigious military academy (most likely West Point) to learn how to organize a disciplined regiment back at the reformatory.

Willie, of course, disappeared as soon as he strode outside Elmira's front gate. He bolted for Boston, landed work on another newspaper, and tried to keep a low profile.

Brockway took Willie's vanishing as an act of extreme disrespect. He ordered his henchmen to spare no expense in hunting him down.

A short time after being forcibly escorted back to Elmira, Willie Graham Rice died in his cell under murky circumstances.

What happened was never clearly documented. But betting men inside the reformatory would have laid short odds that Willie's demise was related to a vengeful frenzy of "rehabilitation" involving a notorious nail-studded cudgel that had earned the superintendent the derisive nickname "Paddler Brockway."

If Herzig mourned for his mentor, it was not for long. Jacob seized upon Willie's departure as an opportunity to create a new identity, or at least two-thirds of one.

As an aspiring writer, Jacob had been contemplating entering a short story contest in *The Youth's Companion*. But because the nation's most popular weekly magazine published only wholesome, benevolent stories that "warned against the ways of transgression," Herzig knew his entry stood little chance considering the submission would be postmarked with the return address of Elmira Reformatory.

Having demonstrated ample chutzpah in stealing signatures,

Herzig appropriated "Graham Rice" and experimented with a multitude of prefixes. Had he been alive to witness this pilfering of his persona, Willie might even have approved—or at least understood from the standpoint of practical con artistry.

Under his new pen name, Herzig decided to enter the contest, perhaps thinking that masquerading as a newspaperman might augment his chances. His story did not win, but Herzig's nom de plume caught the eye of Brockway as the superintendent censored the outgoing mail. Shortly before Jacob's release, Brockway affixed an "Alias" notation in regal, flowing penmanship to the upper left-hand corner of inmate No. 4018's case file—the first known documentation of the swindler who would bilk suckers blind for the next fifty years as "George Graham Rice."

Herzig walked out of Elmira on December 24, 1892, having achieved special parole contingent on eight months of probation to monitor his transition back into society.

Because he needed to replenish his bankroll, the first thing Jacob intended to do was get back into his father's good graces. The next important item on Herzig's to-do list—settling the score with the tyrant whose sadistic whims had consumed two and a half years of his life—would have to wait a few months until his penal paperwork was finalized.

Superintendent Brockway, it seems, sent Herzig home with a cranial souvenir of his stay at Elmira: a disfigurement at the base of his skull consistent with the type of injury that results from an untreated blow to the head. Jacob was so self-conscious of the lump that he began slicking his hair back to cover it, cultivating a style noticeably longer than the clipped-and-oiled, center-parted men's standard of the day.

On July 17, 1893, Brockway summoned Herzig to Elmira for his final probation meeting, at which Brockway wrote he was "absolutely released." Even as the ink was drying on his release, Jacob was scheming to lash back.

Within weeks, every sizable newspaper in New York state had been anonymously tipped off to the hellish cruelties at Elmira.

By September, journalistic exposés had so stirred public sentiment that Governor Roswell Pettibone Flower was demanding a sweeping investigation into the reformatory by the State Board of Charities.

It's not clear if Herzig was able to orchestrate such a systematic exposure of Brockway's oppression by himself or if he was part of a broader network of whistle-blowers. But the seeds for being able to pull off this sort of character assassination had almost certainly been planted by Herzig's old pal Willie, who managed before his death to impress upon Jacob that a whiff of scandal was the best accelerant for igniting the press into a firestorm.

A special committee sat for twenty-five days, read nine hundred complaint letters, and heard testimony from two hundred former detainees. Inmate after inmate described patterns of "unlawful, unjust, cruel, brutal, inhumane, degrading, excessive and unusual punishment . . . frequently causing permanent injuries and disfigurements." It was revealed that nine-foot iron hooks, seared in a furnace until glowing red, were used to yank reluctant prisoners out of cells. Guards would then string the men up by their thumbs in a bathroom to be whipped and flogged by Brockway, who only stopped when flesh resembled "raw liver." After such beatings, the superintendent ordered convicts chained to the floors of dark detention cells, where they languished for days without medical attention. When returned to the general population, some abused prisoners were described as "gibbering idiots" who resorted to suicide to avoid repeat beatings.

Newspapers sensationalized the violence in macabre detail, with headlines shouting, "Shocking Brutality," "Inmates Tell of Barbarous Punishments," and "Brockway's Paddle Must Go." Once the stories had gained enough traction to achieve front-page status, a dapper Jacob S. Herzig came forward to make sure reporters knew to identify him as "one of the principal witnesses" to the ceaseless savagery.

Despite daunting evidence and damning testimony, reforming the reformatory proved an exasperating task. The committee took months to produce a twenty-four-hundred-page report that condemned both Brockway and the institution. The legislature then debated for a year over what (if any) action it should take. Brockway's attorneys argued two contradictory defenses: first that Elmira was not a prison (and thus not subject to corporal punishment laws); then that Elmira was indeed a prison (and not subject to oversight by the State Board of Charities).

Eighteen months into the investigation, Elmira's board of managers passed a toothless resolution forbidding paddling "until further orders." But before the decree could go into effect, the reformatory and its officers were fully exonerated. The ruling dismissed the hundreds of documented cruelty charges as "distortions of fact," adding that Brockway's violence was justifiable because "there is a percentage of criminals so hardened and morally so abnormal that reformation cannot be begun with them except for the infliction of bodily pain."

Paddler Brockway ruled for five more years, then retired to write an autobiography titled *Fifty Years of Prison Service*. He was so popular that the locals elected him mayor of Elmira.

For Jacob, it was back to the family fur emporium and the raffish gambling salons of New York City's loud and lurid Tenderloin district.

Herzig had failed to topple Brockway. But during the process, he did acquire a taste for bucking the system. Jacob savored the rush he got from making authority figures squirm on the witness stand, and it dawned on him that he might have the unique talent it takes to harness the power of the public against the established order. He might not have yet known what the word "iconoclast" meant. But if it signified a lust for shattering old-boy networks and destabilizing conventionalism, Herzig was all for it.

Sixteen months. That's how long it took Jacob to squander his freedom. Or at least that's how long it took authorities to finally track him down and catch him.

"The young rascal is only twenty-four years of age, yet he has been half-way round the world on the strength of his knack in forging his father's name," the *Philadelphia Record* reported after Herzig's November 8, 1894, arrest for racking up $40,000 in bad debt—the equivalent of $1 million today. "He was no sooner released than he resumed his old life," chided *The New York Times,* painting Jacob as a poster boy for recidivism. "He has traveled from Boston to San Francisco, leaving a trail of forged checks and drafts. . . . The checks were always honored to save the family from disgrace."

What the newspapers *didn't* report was that at the same time Jacob was being pursued by Columbia National Bank, the police, and his father, a furious Canadian minister also wanted a piece of his hide: At the start of his betting binge, Herzig had persuaded the clergyman's sixteen-year-old daughter to run off with him, and the two cavorted across the continent on a spree of debauchery bankrolled by fraudulent flicks of a fountain pen.

In St. Louis, Jacob lost $10,000 at the faro banks, even though—like most gamblers—he knew the wildly popular card game was notorious for being rigged in favor of the house. Kansas City dealers recognized "Joseph Hart" as the compulsive card chaser who burned through $1,000 an hour at their tables. At his arraignment in New York's Tombs Police Court, Herzig/Hart had the audacity to demand $150 for the bank draft he had been trying to cash when apprehended, claiming that without the funds he couldn't afford a lawyer. The judge tersely denied this request, citing the check as evidence of his crimes. Herzig shot back that the money had indeed been stolen—from him—by the corrupt arresting detective.

Jacob's family had finally had enough. Living in sin with a teenage girl outside the Jewish faith was in some ways worse than the stealing. His parents and siblings disowned him, and no one was willing to post his $15,000 bail. The judicial docket was backlogged until spring, so Herzig was shackled and marched across the Tombs' infamous "Bridge of Sighs," a long gated passageway that connected the court complex with the dank, foreboding cesspool where New York's most deviant thieves, hooligans, cutthroats, dope fiends, and murderers awaited their days of reckoning.

Erected in the style of an Egyptian mausoleum atop a sludge pond contaminated by decades of slaughterhouse offal, the original 1838 version of the Tombs encompassed an entire city block of imposing granite in lower central Manhattan. Twenty-two hours a day, Herzig was confined to a lightless ten-by-six-foot box that contained a filthy straw mattress and a noxious open drinking spout whose basin doubled as his toilet. It's likely Jacob had to share this cell with two or three other prisoners, because right around the time he was locked up, the state senate was in the midst of a full-blown investigation into overcrowding at the jail. "Such treatment of dogs would be gross cruelty," one report recommending closure concluded. "The Tombs prison, as it has existed for years past, is a disgrace to the city of New York. It ought to be immediately demolished. It cannot be made decent."

Herzig languished in the Tombs until March 7, 1895, when he was roused to testify in his own defense. The only person who showed up to support him was the brown-eyed beauty who had been his companion on the cross-country check-kiting binge. The teenager's presence piqued the interest of the crime beat reporters, so Jacob made a show of having the minister's daughter pin a handful of white flowers to the lapel of his gray ulster overcoat. When the courtroom hacks clamored to learn the girl's name, Herzig forbade her to give it.

The next-day newspapers focused more on the mystery of the "strange young woman" than the trial itself, which was fine by Herzig, who had little to say under oath anyway. He politely declined to answer specifics about his signature while under cross-examination and appeared beset by forgetfulness when peppered with questions about checks he had endorsed in the names of his father and uncle. "I know that I am under indictment for some forgery," Jacob repeated, blinking quizzically. "That is all I do know about it."

No one bought the amnesia act, except maybe Herzig's swooning sweetie, who fainted and had to be carried out of the courtroom when the jury returned in less than an hour with guilty verdicts on all five forgery counts.

At his sentencing six weeks later, the presiding judge, John W. Goff, laced into Jacob with a severe scolding that explained why he would be ignoring the jury's specific recommendation for a merciful penalty.

"An educated criminal is the most vicious member of society," Goff spat in his excoriating Irish brogue. "This young man has had all the advantages of education and good social surroundings, and he has brought disgrace upon his family. . . . It is not his first offense. . . . He deliberately and systematically applied his talents for the purpose of swindling these banks, and obtained, according to his own testimony, some thousands of dollars, which he lost in speculation. . . . It would defeat the ends of justice if this prisoner did not meet with substantial justice for his crime. . . . I would be derelict in my duty if I did not give him a substantial remembrance."

With a slam of his gavel, Goff condemned Jacob to six years and six months in Sing Sing.

Even if he had steeled himself for the worst, Jacob must have gone weak in the knees upon hearing his fate: Sing Sing owned a soul-crushing reputation as America's most dehumanizing prison, an emasculating institution whose keepers took an iron-fisted pride in stripping away all traces of individuality.

Sing Sing prisoners—among the first to be outfitted in black-and-white-striped uniforms that would become emblematic of jailbirds everywhere—were forced to shuffle as anonymous units in shackled lockstep, from the mess hall to the slop toilets to the dreaded workhouse: right arms out straight, open palms tucked into the armpit of the man in front, eyes always riveted on the guards. Rigid, mind-numbing adherence to the "Auburn system" mandated strict silence and docile herd obedience, and convicts were driven beyond exhaustion by a slavish regimen of repetitive labor. Deviance from exacting standards resulted in punishments designed to inflict maximum psychological humiliation, and Sing Sing's abnormally high suicide rate was rivaled only by what was then called its "insanity rate."

It was common to hear of despondent inmates plunging their hands into molten metal in the smelting shop, self-amputating digits in the brickworks, or diving headlong from cell-block towers to the rocky Hudson riverbank hundreds of feet below. Sing Sing "represented all that was vile in American penology," one criminologist would write in 1919. "The very site of the prison breathed physical as well as moral contagion. . . . In general, the population was the most terrifying to the conventional mind that could be found anywhere."

Sing Sing's mechanization was so ruthlessly efficient that its overseers had ample time to pursue rampant profiteering. Prisoners toiled night and day mining a distinctive local stone known as Sing Sing marble from the on-site quarry so jailhouse bigwigs could sell the bluish-gray slabs to builders of High Victorian mansions. Large-scale contract manufacturing was solicited for the prison's various factories, with kickbacks buying private firms the right to beat inmates who failed to meet impossible quotas. But pervasive corruption cut both ways: Convicts who had a source of funding from an outside accomplice could funnel money into the paws of crooked officials to "shoot the curves," which was 1890s prison parlance for buying one's way into doing easier time.

At the extreme end of the scale, the wealthiest criminals could arrange for "escapes" guaranteed never to be solved. But most everyday Sing Sing graft involved upgrades to better cells or getting assigned to easier work crews. The prison also supported a robust underground economy, in which convicts established not-so-secret accounts with guards to procure contraband like candy, fruits, nuts, tinned meats, tobacco, the occasional jug of stout, or even fixes of morphine and opium

to slake narcotic cravings. Because valuables and currency were confis-
cated upon incarceration, an outside "sponsor" was imperative. Without a flow of fresh cash, inmates slid to the bottom of the human slag
heap, where they suffered in intensified misery as the most wretched
subclass of Sing Sing society.

Jacob's narrow window of opportunity between sentencing and the
trip to prison was about to slam shut. Within an hour of being condemned by Judge Goff, he was to be part of a chain gang herded aboard
the 2:05 P.M. Hudson River Railroad local chugging north to Sing Sing.
The thirty-two-mile riverside journey was one of the most scenic rail
trips out of Manhattan, but the ride was so infamously dreaded by
those about to be imprisoned that the euphemism for it—"going up the
river"—would soon become the colloquial catchphrase for going to jail
anywhere in America, regardless of proximity to a waterway.

Herzig, uncharacteristically, sought the help of a man of the cloth.
The Reverend William Lindsay was the chaplain of the Bleecker Street
mission for "fallen women" and also volunteered his time to detainees at
the Tombs who were about to be sent to Sing Sing. In just a few moments
of hushed conversation inside his holding cell, Jacob managed to arrange
for a bizarre last-minute blessing. The vicar didn't know it, but Herzig
had twisted the sympathetic minister's confidence to his advantage.

The grim procession to the train station was nearly always the same:
A horse-drawn van backed up to the waiting room entrance at Grand
Central Depot and disgorged a motley collection of cuffed convicts.
Deputy sheriffs and Pinkerton guards barked to get the prisoners in line
and keep them moving, but unless a hysterical inmate refused to walk,
displays of force were largely for show. And "show" was the key word,
because the morbidly curious crowds at America's busiest train station
reveled in these daily parades of malaise, jeering and pointing as if the
jailbirds' walk of shame were a bonus included in the price of a train
ticket.

As the chain gang threaded its way through the mob, taunts and heckling led to hats getting knocked off prisoners' heads and shirt collars being ripped off their necks. Newsboys and bootblacks crouched at the front of an ever-tightening circle to be within prime spitting and stone-throwing range, and the pitying glances from factory girls were almost as unbearable as the abuse from the workingmen. To all but the most hardened criminals, the hostility was a kaleidoscope of fear and confusion—exactly the sort of atmosphere the lawmen wanted to create before moving on to the crucial phase of the transport.

Once on board, inmates were corralled into the smoking car. Guards chatted with passengers but did not allow anyone to converse with the convicts. When the train began rolling, a deputy broke out a bottle of whiskey (rotgut, for certain) and cigars (lung-searing cheap ones) and let the prisoners drink and smoke as they pleased. Then the lawmen began to brace up the inmates by imparting "inside" knowledge about Sing Sing, reassuring the felons that if they were tough enough, they could reasonably handle doing time there.

Having fostered a degree of trust, the keepers then made the rounds: Guards homed in on convicts who seemed overly fearful, offering to put in a good word with the jailers in exchange for cash (a scam that left convicts feeling damned if they participated and doomed if they didn't). If Jacob was still wearing his good ulster overcoat or had a bundle of personal items, a deputy would explain how the penitentiary was going to take away everything upon arrival. But if Herzig handed his items over *right now,* the man promised to send them to a friend or relative for safekeeping. Inmates who fell for this ruse never saw their belongings again, even if they additionally parted with their last few dollars to ensure "express delivery." Prisoners who refused to hand over anything would get another chance at being rooked, because the same false promises and confidences (minus the whiskey and cigars) were sure to be repeated by the more forceful guards who took them in at Sing Sing.

Jacob must have slipped a little something extra to the deputy sheriff Joseph Burke, the lawman in charge, because just as the train pulled out of Grand Central, Herzig was uncuffed and whisked back to the baggage car, where a conductor with long white whiskers had been paid to block access to curious passengers. At the rear of the compartment stood the pious reverend Lindsay with a Bible in his hand.

Alongside the clergyman trembled Jacob's dewy-eyed teenage sweetheart, Theramutis Myrtle Ivey.

Among steamer trunks and hat boxes, the deputy gruffly affirmed to the minister that yes, he would vouch for the prisoner as his best man.

By the time the train passed beneath the massive stone arches of the High Bridge aqueduct at 173rd Street, the convicted forger and the runaway schoolgirl were man and wife. With no time to spare en route to prison, Herzig had secured his all-important outside accomplice.

The outlandish news about the jail-bound wedding spread so fast that reporters were on the story even as the train steamed into Sing Sing. Write-ups about the nuptials titillated readers up and down the East Coast and all the way to Ivey's hometown of Jarvis, Ontario. Yellow journalism's standard-bearer, the New York *World,* gave the ceremony prominent play alongside similarly sensationalized articles about an operation on conjoined baby twins and the theft of a prized Great Dane:

> *When the train arrived at Yonkers, the minister dropped off and Herzig and his bride came into the smoking-car and received the congratulations of "Moke" Murray, sentenced to three years and three months, and a tough looking negro to whom "Moke" was handcuffed. When the party left the train at Sing Sing, the woman was sent to a hotel and the prisoners were taken to prison. Burke, the deputy sheriff, denied that any ceremony had taken place, or that he had acted as best man, but the story was fully corroborated by train hands.*

In the days to come, reporters hounded the teenage bride for details. *The Norfolk Virginian* ran an exclusive that emphasized the couple's impulsivity, going so far as to suggest in its headline that the girl had been "Svengallied" into marrying the felon:

Hypnotism is said by Theramutis Ivey to have played no small part
in her marriage to Convict Jacob S. Herzig. . . . [The bride] has been
disowned by her parents for the persistency with which she has
clung to Herzig, even after he was convicted. . . . "I had no inten-
tion of getting married when I went to the train to accompany
my lover to Sing Sing. But before I knew it we were standing before
the clergyman, and I became 'Jock's' wife. I must have been
hypnotized. . . . I am not sorry I married him, and yet—and yet—
well, I don't know. It all seems so strange and weird-like. . . ." The
next instant she added: "Well I am glad I did it. I don't believe Jock is
guilty. . . . I love him, and I could never love anyone else. . . . I shall try
to get my husband pardoned. . . . Jock always seemed to have such
an influence over me that he could make me do almost anything."

When the locomotive hissed to a stop at Sing Sing village, the prisoners were marched off the train. The platform was crowded, but unlike at Grand Central the sight of men in cuffs and leg bracelets was too
common for the locals to bother gawking. Even boys shooting marbles
on the sidewalk paid the chain gang no attention. The convicts were
made to zigzag the tracks, dodging departing trains, before being ordered up a rock-strewn bluff to the long, dusty road that led to the hulk-
ing stone penitentiary.

If Herzig looked back, chances are it was not to exchange parting
glances with Theramutis. The grinning deputies and Pinkerton men,
arms laden with overcoats and misbegotten belongings, were what would
have caught Jacob's appreciative eye.

Even while plodding to the slammer, Prisoner B-516 would have
grudgingly admired the thoroughness with which the crooked keepers
had completely fleeced the captive suckers.

It didn't take Jacob long to deduce he had made a mistake in marrying
Ivey, at least from the perspective of banking on a love-struck seventeen-

year-old to negotiate the byzantine appeals process and prison black market on his behalf. Other convicts facing sentences extending into the next century might have done everything they could to hold on to their wives, but it wasn't hard for Jacob to conclude that his bride was a bothersome liability. Getting the annoyingly loyal girl to stay out of his life for good was what proved exasperatingly difficult.

Herzig first tried black humor. Didn't she understand the ceremony had been an elaborate practical joke? Then he tried a made-up legal angle: Their marriage was not lawful because it occurred while he was in custody. In the end, Jacob figured caustic honesty would do the trick. When Ivey called one afternoon during visiting hours—she had secured a job as a dressmaker's assistant and was trying to funnel a trickle of money into the jail on his behalf—Herzig made it clear that unless she could provide for him in significantly better fashion, he had zero use for her. Choosing words that stung like acid, Jacob ordered the girl to go away and never come back.

The cruelty worked. But for Herzig, it wasn't enough.

Jacob talked up Theramutis—muttering out of the corner of his mouth to get around Sing Sing's strict no-speaking rule—to an inmate named John J. Gilmore, a habitual offender who was nearing the end of his prison sentence. Omitting any mention of his marriage, Herzig intimated that he knew of a gullible working girl living alone near the prison. Upon release, Gilmore tracked down the easy target and took her for his wife. After they had been together for a short period, Ivey let it slip that she had already gone through one wedding ceremony with a convict but that of course it didn't count because the groom had not been a free citizen when they exchanged vows. Learning he had been tricked into supporting another man's wife, Gilmore flew into a rage and beat Theramutis so viciously that she lost an eye. This news filtered back to prison, and Jacob seized upon it as his chance to file for an annulment, petitioning the church to void his marriage on the grounds that his bride had abandoned him to live in sin with another man.

It was up to Herzig to fend for himself for the balance of his imprisonment, but no documentation exists as to how he managed to do so. Sing Sing's surviving handwritten records from this era detail minutiae such as Jacob's hat size (7⅜), shoe size (8½), and condition of teeth ("fairly good, some filled with gold") but give no clue as to how he secured a transfer to the less severe Auburn Prison in 1899, where he served as the chaplain's assistant and was the first editor of an inmate newspaper called *Star of Hope*. Sometime in the first few months of 1900, Herzig was granted early release after serving only five years of his six-and-a-half-year sentence.

In the decades to come, Jacob would reveal little about this stint behind bars, hinting only that he read voraciously and tried to stay out of trouble. By the time he got out, he had made up his mind to become a different person—in name if not in deed—and took great pains to obliterate his true identity while embracing life anew as George Graham Rice.

George/Jacob was approaching thirty after having spent the better part of a decade in New York's most debasing jails. Considering the average life expectancy for an American male in 1900 was forty-seven years, it would not have been a stretch to say that Rice/Herzig had blown his opportunity to make a meaningful mark in life. But it's doubtful that George, even with his gambler's sense of probabilities, gave serious consideration to being past his prime. During most of the time he was in prison, America had been struggling to recover from a financial panic that rocked the nation in 1893, and it was not until the country turned the corner into the twentieth century that the economy truly started to regain steam. Rice emerged to a nation that had been made over as the playground of the new rich, and the hallmark of elite status within this exclusive, so-called smart set was the conspicuous ability to burn through fortunes with a lavish hand.

Taking care to avoid anyone who knew him by his former name, Rice

upped his social ante, steering clear of the seedy Tenderloin while infiltrating the mink-and-monocle crowd at fashionable Broadway nightspots. Affable and impeccably mannered, George fit in easily and was
well liked. But how he afforded daily extravagances like high tea in the
Palm Garden of the Waldorf-Astoria or truffled Strasbourg foie gras
in the Gilt Room of the Holland House must have been a bit of a mystery to his new acquaintances, because the outgoing newcomer had no
visible means of support. Unbeknownst to his new circle of socialites,
George viewed mixing with the well-to-do as an occupational prerequisite for tapping into fresh wealth.

Within weeks of hobnobbing with the theater district's in crowd, Rice
became smitten with—or at least pretended to be head over heels in love
with—a matronly leading lady who loved a good splurge and owned an
ample bankroll. A domineering presence both on and off the stage, Frances Drake had been one of the few female newspaper reporters in the
Pacific Northwest during the 1880s (when women were compelled to
write under a pseudonym), but around 1890 she gave up journalism to
make a successful switch to playacting. Exuding confidence, the dark-
haired Drake shone in everything from wistful French monologues to
bawdy vaudeville knee-slappers. But male cast members resented Frances because her strong performances overshadowed theirs, and Drake
routinely clashed with the managers of her various touring troupes. Still,
houses continued to fill, so Drake's queenly tantrums were tolerated, and
in the spring of 1900 she starred in *The Adventures of Lady Ursula*, a
romantic comedy about a bossy heroine disguised in men's clothing who
gets challenged to a duel. After debuting to acclaim in Rochester, the play
got good reviews in New York City and up and down the Eastern Seaboard, including one write-up that noted, "Miss Frances Drake . . . is an
actress of experience and reputation, [who], apart from her histrionic
abilities, is an unusually clever woman."

Drake, in turn, fell for Rice, who—as an actor in his own illicit way—
came across as a cultured wiseguy with a flair for spontaneity. On June
13, 1900, when *Lady Ursula* was on a break between engagements,

Frances and George got hitched in Rochester. Presumably, Rice enjoyed his honeymoon. He certainly didn't find it necessary to spoil the good time by mentioning to his new bride that he already had a wife and—because he had never sought an official divorce—was still legally bound to her.

When the Rices returned from celebrating their nuptials, Frances had a disturbing revelation awaiting. But it didn't come from George, and it had nothing to do with Theramutis Ivey. Among the accumulated wedding cards and notes of congratulations was a letter written by someone Frances did not know—Simon Herzig, a New York City furrier.

The gentleman identified himself as the father of her new husband, wished Frances happiness, and expressed hope that her love was strong enough to enable her to forgive his boy's past errors. Then Mr. Herzig went on to enumerate his wayward son's long list of ethical lapses and legal woes, supplying Frances with details, dates, dollar amounts, penal chronology, and George's full real name.

Confronted with the contents of the letter, Rice figured there was only one thing to do: He got down on his knees and confessed fully—at least according to his prism of reality.

George came clean about his time in Elmira and Sing Sing. Then he laid out *exactly* how he had come to be shamefully branded as a felon—by a scheming father and spiteful uncle who conspired to have their own kin locked away for crimes everyone in the family knew he did not commit.

"I burst into tears," Frances would recall a decade later, "but loved him all the more for telling what I thought then to be the truth."

It is unclear exactly when it dawned on Frances that Simon Herzig's version of events just might be more accurate than her husband's. About a month after their honeymoon would be a good guess, because by then the newlyweds were leading separate lives: Frances was on the road with her theater troupe, while George had skipped town and was off on another cross-country betting bender.

. . .

After who knows how many train stops south from New York, GG found himself in New Orleans by the late summer of 1900. Although it was probably not his original intent to look for a job, he had no choice after the Big Easy's infamous gambling gantlet of racetracks, prizefighting clubs, cockfighting rings, Cajun Bourré parlors, roulette wheels, and faro banks left him high and dry. Somewhere along the line, money wired from Frances had ceased to be an option.

Perhaps presenting himself as the Graham Rice who previously wrote for newspapers in the Northeast, George landed a gig on the staff of the New Orleans *Times-Democrat*. He was assigned to the hotel beat, which meant prowling the lobbies and scanning the registers of lodging establishments to report the comings and goings of influential businessmen and high-ranking socialites. As the new guy on the staff, he had to work Saturdays. George was hardly accustomed to spending his weekends rooting around for breaking news.

The evening of Saturday, September 8, 1900, was tremendously wet and gusty, and Rice took refuge in the lobby of the nearly deserted St. Charles Hotel. He was probably working harder on a La Belle Creole cigar than on meeting his deadline when he overheard a frantic clattering from behind the closed door of the Hyams & Company brokerage suite off the hotel's main corridor. George knew the rudiments of telegraphy from years deciphering race results in poolrooms, and when he paused to eavesdrop on the mechanical sounder, he recognized the urgent dots and dashes as a distress call coming over the Western Union wire from somewhere on the Gulf Coast of Texas.

A devastating tidal wave had just leveled Galveston Island. Capsized ships, washed-out bridges, splintered buildings, uprooted trees, and thousands of livestock, pets, and humans had been swept away in a frothing vortex of death. The entire city was fifteen feet underwater and being battered by hundred-mile-per-hour hurricane winds. Rice recognized the tragedy as his chance to scoop the greatest natural disaster of the new century. He knew the value of a highly saleable human interest catastrophe, and fate had practically gift wrapped this one and dropped it into his lap.

George sprinted four blocks through the pelting rain to his newspaper's business office on Camp Street. He roused the drowsing teller in the cashier's cage and got him to front $500 in expense money and a one-way ticket to Houston on the Texas and Pacific Railroad, insisting he couldn't wait for an editor's permission to chase down the story of a lifetime. This was Rice's chance to be the lone newspaperman rushing into the heart of an epic disaster while everyone else was evacuating away from it.

The overnight train got GG 350 miles west but no farther south because storm surges had already drowned eighty-five passengers in submerged railway cars. Relying on bribed rides aboard mules and in rowboats, George spent another full day negotiating the final fifty miles to Galveston. Arriving Monday at midnight, he was granted a pass by the U.S. Army to report from within the disaster zone. While under escort to view recovery efforts, he was strongly advised to stick to the military's version of events.

Instead, Rice slipped his leash and took liberties with the officially issued reports. By Tuesday morning, he was on the run from military police trying to arrest him for spreading false panic.

"My offense lay in sending out the truth about Galveston," Rice contended, savoring his claim of being the first outside newspaperman to land on the island. "When I first reached there I sent out an estimate of 5,000 killed. The authorities limited the dead to 1,000 then. Since that time they have gradually advanced that number until now Governor [Joseph] Sayers admits 12,000 dead. I believe that 18,000 would be nearer correct. . . . The stench of the city is frightful. [The American Red Cross founder] Clara Barton told me she recognized it—the battlefield smell—while she was on a Southern Pacific train fifteen miles outside of Houston. . . . People with no property interests are making every effort to leave the island. Men who will be ruined unless the city is rebuilt are trying to allay the panic and keep the people there."

While George was journalistically correct to be skeptical of the casualty estimates, he was not so ethical when it came to deciding which newspaper would receive his exclusive reports. Because telegraph wires were down for miles around, Rice knew he was sitting on a big story as soon as he could get off the island to transmit the full-blown version. Even though *The Times-Democrat* had paid his way to Galveston, George didn't see why he should turn over such a sensational scoop to a piddling publication that paid him thirty bucks a week. In fact, before he even left Houston for Galveston, Rice had sparked a bidding war and accepted a $5,000 offer from *The New York Herald* to deliver a first-person feature and follow-up series.

"When my pass was taken up I was in danger of being shot," Rice boasted. "But I smuggled myself through the lines, and by the aid of Captain Rafferty, U.S.A., left the island on a tug. The objection to me was that in my dispatches, I had expressed the opinion that Galveston is irretrievably lost. . . . When I came away we were going through dead bodies [in the water] all the way to Buffalo Bayou, twenty-five miles distant. . . . Before I left there were many cases of what the doctors called malarial fever, and a scourge of yellow fever is feared."

On his way home to New York, Ricecakes gave New Orleans a wide berth, returning north by way of Cincinnati. For a month, he was interviewed as an expert eyewitness about Galveston, feigning modesty while basking in the glow of recognition. "It was a 'beat' and I netted a big sum for a few days' hard work, but the money had all been spent for subsistence," he claimed. Back on Broadway, George embellished his adventures, including one version in which he allegedly stole a horse, raced to meet an onrushing supply train, then heroically led the relief expedition back to Galveston.

In addition to his upgraded social status, Rice now had some capital at his disposal. With part of his $5,000 windfall, he bought a horse-racing sheet called *Spirit of the Times*. George thought he was getting a bargain because the publication was in decline, and he had grand plans for a relaunch. But a printers' strike caused him to miss several issues, and by the time the sheet came out again, its circulation had evaporated. Both Rice and his racing paper were yesterday's news.

George next tried to catch on as a reporter with one of New York City's nine daily newspapers. But even at the zenith of yellow journalism, Rice's editorial credibility was shot because of the backstabbing stunt he had pulled on *The Times-Democrat*. While New York papers had been perfectly willing to bid on his onetime freelance exclusive, none wanted to hire a two-timing reporter as a full-time staffer.

In the first week of November, Rice checked in—alone, no sign of Frances—at the Park Avenue Hotel. He got the hotel beat writer at the *New-York Tribune* to list him as a "prominent arrival" in hopes of drumming up a business venture. Nothing came of it.

By Christmas, George, by his own admission, was "loafing" and quickly going broke.

By March 5, 1901, he had exactly $7.30 to his name and was out of options.

Then Rice spied Dave Campbell trudging in his direction through the slushy intersection of Fortieth and Broadway.

His grifter's intuition picking up a whiff of opportunity, George beamed his phosphorescent smile and gregariously thrust out his hand as if welcoming a long-lost friend.

After making a splash with the big scores by Silver Coin and Annie Lauretta, the Maxim & Gay turf advisory bureau played it safe, selling tips on heavy favorites. Although these horses did not fail to win, their short prices "provoked some sensation of anti-climax among the boobs," who were quick to grouse about forking over five bucks for obvious standouts. Still, the firm managed a winning record through its first four days, impressive for any tout.

Then, on day five, Frank Mead wired the name of a long shot owned by a man known to be "handy with a needle and syringe."

In 1901, performance-enhancing pharmaceuticals were an open secret in American horse racing and not even technically illegal. The practice was so widespread that Maxim & Gay touted Mead's "hop horse," even though Rice knew that the main competitor in the race was also trained by a notorious New Orleans doper.

As one turf columnist described it, this race would be remembered as "a competition in stimulative medication" in which both horses "went to post frothing and preening like unto DeQuincey's opium addict." At the precise moment Mead's eight-to-one tip surged past the winning post to snatch a narrow victory, the winner collapsed to the racecourse, stricken by a drug overdose.

"The success," the scribe wryly pointed out, "under circumstances that denoted Maxim & Gay knew the very stride a horse would drop dead on, appeared symbolic. The high-riding Maxim & Gay people were now in the lap of the gods running before the wind with all sails bellowing." The surprise score put two Herald Square bookies out of business, and the next day Ricecakes raked in $10,000—the firm's highest gross yet.

When the racing swung north in the spring, Rice bought intelligence at the Benning race meet near Washington, D.C., and hired informants at tracks in New York. Walk-in customers were soon outnumbered by subscribers who wanted the establishment's selections wired to them, which was understandable because George had expanded advertising to reach poolroom devotees in San Francisco, Los Angeles, Dallas, New Orleans, Chicago, Detroit, and Toronto.

Rice's monthly budget for newspaper ads soared to $22,000, and the full-page displays ran true to George's insistence that "small type was never intended for commercial uses." Maxim & Gay diversified its product line, expanding from the "One Best Bet" to the "Three-Horse Wire." Occasionally, GG dangled a "$50 Wire Special," demanding ten times the usual rate. When enough rubes bit at that price, Maxim & Gay launched a "$100 Special" that required recipients, in lieu of payment, to make a $100 wager on the firm's behalf. Business was so brisk that the Postal Telegraph Company and Western Union both had to furnish the Stewart Building with direct-loop switching systems to handle the volume of wire traffic.

There were competing tipster services, but early-twentieth-century horse touts were burdened by a shifty stigma. Maxim & Gay, by contrast, published an (allegedly) objective weekly recap of how its selections fared, noting not only winners but losers (with appropriate excuses). Rice wrote one clever "convincer" ad disguised as a letter of apology for "only" earning $540 for customers, berating the firm's own experts for not doing better. By March 1902, Maxim & Gay had sixty-four thousand daily subscribers marching lockstep into poolrooms and bookie joints, laying it in so heavily on George's best bets that every published nudge on a horse set off nationwide odds plunges.

As business grew, Rice realized he was sitting on a wealth of information culled from clients. Although it would be another full century before terms like "customer profiling" and "data mining" entered the lexicon, George was an early pioneer. He instructed his staff to keep meticulous records about individual purchasing patterns, and Maxim & Gay salesmen were among the first to ask "May I have your telephone number?" as part of routine transactions (in 1902, the phone was so newfangled that anyone who could afford one thrilled at the novelty of hearing it jangle). The compilation of this original "sucker list" would be Rice's best long-term investment. Over the next few decades, he would crisscross the continent with it, seducing loyal old saps with newly enticing swindles, fine-tuning and expanding his database of prey by adhering to the time-tested truism "Once a sucker, always a sucker."

Maxim & Gay's success came not so much from *which* horses Rice touted as from *how* he touted them. George didn't just offer the name of a hot horse, but used insider terminology and a cloak of secrecy to weave a compelling narrative. To Rice, it was imperative for clients to feel as if their $5 were buying entry into the exhilarating, behind-the-scenes world of the racetrack. "We used in our big display advertisements a nomenclature of the turf that had never before been heard except in the vicinity of the stables," Rice would explain a decade later in his autobiography, *My Adventures with Your Money*. "It was our aim, in using the language of horsemen, to be technical rather than vulgar, the theory being that, if we could convince professional horsemen that we knew what we were talking about, the general public would quickly fall in line."

As it was for John L. Sullivan's manager, "The public demands to be mystified" became George's mantra. That way, even when people lost a bundle betting on a Maxim & Gay stiff, they were sufficiently intrigued to come back for more.

Rice tried to walk a fine line between enjoying the luxe life his new line of work afforded him and keeping his identity secret from racing's old-boy network. GG relished carousing along Manhattan's Rubberneck Row, picking up checks at swank nightspots like Delmonico's, Sherry's, and Rector's. But he had to keep his mouth shut about Maxim & Gay when deep-pocketed owners of prominent racing stables were around, because some of them forked over ridiculous amounts of money just to make sure they weren't missing inside information about their own horses. Eventually, George cost himself his privacy by being unable to resist a few mocking jabs at a blue-blooded scion of the turf: William Collins Whitney, one of the richest, most powerful men in America.

By 1902, Whitney was in the autumn years of a full life, a retired secretary of the navy who had been legal counsel for Thomas Edison's electric lighting patents. In his dotage, Whitney was co-developing New York's first underground transit system. He owned both a high-class racing stable and a controlling interest in *The Morning Telegraph*, the bible of horse-racing publications.

Whitney owned a talented mare named Smoke who had trounced high-class competition and was then entered to race right back against inferior horses. She figured to dominate, but one of GG's private clockers thought Smoke didn't look quite right in her morning gallops, so he recommended betting against her. In a twist of misdirection, Maxim & Gay took out ads in *The Telegraph* offering this bit of cryptic advice:

Don't bet on Smoke to—day.
She will be favorite, but will not win.

Despite Maxim & Gay's caution, the betting opened hot and heavy on Smoke. Whitney's own wagering commissioners scurried about the bookmaking ring, getting as much money down on the mare as they could.

Then Smoke turned in a lackluster performance, clunking home at the back of the pack. Whitney, spitting mad both at the inexplicable loss and at having been embarrassed in his own newspaper, demanded that officials launch an investigation into whoever tampered with, drugged, or paid a bribe for his horse to lose.

For the first time, the spotlight intensified on Maxim & Gay. George knew the tracks could make trouble for him if they learned of his criminal past, so Rice had his chief clocker write up a report documenting how in his opinion the filly had "soured" after Whitney's trainer left her in the care of a lesser-qualified assistant. This explanation satisfied the stewards but infuriated Whitney. When Maxim & Gay gloated in subsequent ads about knowing more than W. C. Whitney did about his own stable, it constituted a very public and disrespectful slight.

In the aftermath of Rice's exposure, bookies were curious to finally learn the identity of the anonymous insider who had been yanking their betting markets out of whack. When they saw it was some skinny advertising whiz with glasses and a cane, they felt duped. The public, on the other hand, didn't give a hoot who George Graham Rice was so long as Maxim & Gay kept churning out reliable info. One notorious high-stakes plunger, Riley Grannan, befriended George after learning who he was. "Got to hand it to you, kid!" Grannan said, backslapping

Rice. "Any time you can put one over on the Weisenheimers that have been making a living on race-tracks for twenty years you are entitled to medals!"

In the tout biz, when you were on a roll, you were on a roll, and when you weren't, you were due. The following ad, tipping a well-meant horse at Sheepshead Bay in New York, was broadcast to distant cities in the spring of 1902, typifying Maxim & Gay's go-for-broke spirit:

A GIGANTIC HOG—KILLING

We have Inside Information of a Long Shot that

Should Win To—Morrow at 10 to 1

and Put Half of the Book Makers out of Business.

Be Sure to Have a Bet Down on This One

Terms $5

This particular best bet failed to win. Half an hour after the sure thing ran out of the money, the first angry telegrams rained down on Maxim & Gay:

THE HOG-KILLING CAME OFF ON SCHEDULED TIME—HERE IN LOUISVILLE. I WAS THE HOG.

DEAR SIR: YOU HAVE BEEN ADVERTISING FOR SOME DAYS THAT YOU WOULD HAVE A GIGANTIC HOG-KILLING TO-DAY. I WAS TEMPTED BY YOUR ADVERTISING BAIT AND FELL—AND FELL HEAVILY WITH MY ENTIRE BANK ROLL.

PERMIT ME TO STATE, HAVING RECOVERED MY COMPOSURE, THAT ARMOUR OR SWIFT NEED HAVE NO FEAR OF YOU AS A COMPETITOR IN THE PORK-STICKING LINE, FOR FAR FROM MAKING A "HOG-KILLING," YOU DID NOT EVEN CRACK AN EGG.

Rice smirked at the sarcasm. Sore losers were in the minority compared with gamblers who didn't care about blowing a wad so long as they had a rollicking fine time watching it go.

"Good game," wrote one undaunted disciple. "Have sent for more money!"

That summer Maxim & Gay opened a branch in Saratoga Springs, the upstate resort where New York's fashionably wealthy retreated every August to partake of mineral spring baths, no-limit casinos, and elite Thoroughbred racing. Rice siphoned $50,000 from the "smart set" over the course of this three-week spree, and many of his clients were women (ladies, although not permitted inside the betting ring, were allowed to have wagers placed on their behalf by bet runners). George immediately conjured up a separate tip sheet he thought would appeal to the fairer sex, featuring clairvoyant selections from a mystic who claimed to be able to communicate with horses. This "straight from the horse's mouth" angle was a huge hit, but not nearly as profitable as GG's parody of a rival tip sheet.

A tout under the pseudonym Dan Smith had been undercutting Maxim & Gay with a rip-off service that printed glowing predictions of at least five horses in each race. When one of them came in, Smith crowed about "selecting" the winner. In retaliation, Rice launched the "Two Spot" sheet in the same crude vein at a cheaper price. This scheme worked so well that not only was George able to kill off his competitor, but because less astute bettors failed to discern the ploy as a hoax, many actually began to prefer the sham service. "The whole enterprise appeared to me in the light of an experiment—just trying out an idea, and having a lot of fun doing it," George later recalled. "All the pleasure was in the accomplishing."

Rice devised an ingenious hedging system in which Maxim & Gay advertised a refund of $6 if patrons bought a $5 "One Best Bet" that lost. The trick was to only advertise the refund on days when there was a two-horse race. He gave out the favorite as his published pick and bet a portion of gross receipts on the long shot as insurance. If the favorite won, the firm stood to profit from the increased sales, minus the cost of the hedge bet. If the long shot won, Maxim & Gay profited from the hedge bet, even after using part of the winnings to pay refunds on the losing favorite. Either way, Rice made money, customers were happy, and bookmakers couldn't figure out how he did it. "It was taking candy from a baby," George boasted.

But the problem with accumulating so much candy was that Rice had a self-destructive sweet tooth.

When Maxim & Gay first launched, George's ego was so inflated that he insisted on betting his own selections. Then, realizing the power that his opinions had on moving wagering markets, George began intentionally touting horses he didn't like just to drive up the odds on those he intended to bet for himself. By autumn 1902, Rice estimated Maxim & Gay had netted close to $1 million in profits—$28 million by today's standards. But a staggering amount of that revenue had been flushed directly into the pockets of bookmakers.

"Recklessly and improvidently I had let it slip through my fingers," Rice later admitted. "I spent the money as fast as I made it. It was easy come and easy go. The patronage of the bureau fell away to almost nothing."

A change of tactics was in order.

George concocted an initiative to go after tens of thousands of customers right outside the front gates of New York's racetracks, hiring an army of salesmen costumed in khaki military uniforms. His theory was that if he created a clamor over Maxim & Gay's ubiquitous white envelopes, every sucker in the vicinity would flock to the authoritative-looking vendors out of fear of missing out on a sure thing. The Jockey Club, the genteel sanctioning body that governed the races, made it known that it strongly disapproved of such hucksterism. But Rice knew that as long as he kept his sheet sellers off the tracks' private property, there was nothing The Jockey Club could do about it.

On the morning of October 30, 1902, Rice wasn't feeling well and took a rare day off. Had he been at the office, it's likely George would have micromanaged even the stuffing of the salesmen's envelopes, because he was gaining a reputation as an exacting boss who insisted on control over every niggling detail. His minions apparently needed close supervision, though, because the lackey in charge ineptly sent the tip sellers out to Aqueduct with thousands of envelopes that contained blank slips instead of that afternoon's best bet. Irate patrons demanded refunds, and even though the office promised to send a messenger to the track with the correct slips, no one ever arrived, and Maxim & Gay did not issue a single tip that day. When he heard of the debacle, George was livid.

In that afternoon's fifth race, a no-hoper named May J. scored a shocking upset, winning at a hundred to one. "The spectacle of the derided filly finishing first startled the spectators for a few seconds," *The New York Times* reported. "Then the racegoer's sense of the ludicrous asserted itself, and there was such an uproar of laughter and ironic cheering as never before was heard on a New York race track."

The next day, an ecstatic customer showed up at Maxim & Gay, wanting to sign up for an extended subscription. He claimed to be rolling in money and was adamant that the firm had tipped him on May J.

The gentleman insisted he had purchased an envelope from one of the khaki-clad army men outside Aqueduct. Maybe he did, but it certainly hadn't contained the winner. Euphoria had blinded him to the power of suggestion, resulting in a fanatical belief that Maxim & Gay had supplied him with the windfall.

A clerk asked if the gent would mind signing an affidavit acknowledging the firm as the source of his luck. The sucker obliged, and next-day ads ran nationwide featuring the man's sworn statement. "The office was thronged with new customers who enrolled for weekly subscriptions at a rate that put new life back into the business," Rice said, beaming. "Within a month our net earnings had again reached $20,000 per week." (In his autobiography a decade later, Rice would exaggerate the winning price on May J. to two hundred to one and implausibly allege that he fired the clerk who had the affidavit printed because "I could not tolerate misleading advertising.")

With business back on a roll, GG decided to go for the kill. First, he opened new turf bureaus in New Orleans and San Francisco. Three separate tout sheets meant he could cover even more horses in every race, with selections never overlapping.

Through extensive advertising, Rice had drummed up interest in playing the ponies in rural corners of the country. But what good was coast-to-coast coverage if there were no bookies in tiny towns to take people's bets?

To fill this niche, the second part of Rice's plan called for the establishment of mail-order betting. George moved his staff to New Orleans for the start of the 1902–3 winter racing season, renting the entire floor above Crescent Billiard Academy at 928 Canal Street. For six weeks, a thirty-paper nationwide ad blitz klaxoned that Maxim & Gay would hereafter function as a mail-order "commission house." Clients could send in any amount of money, and it would (ostensibly) be kept on account and bet for them in accordance with the firm's selections. For this privilege, customers would be charged $10 weekly—plus a 5 percent commission on winnings.

The final component of George's brainstorm was the boldest: Advertising was the biggest drain on his bankroll. Too much of GG's money was flowing into the pockets of W. C. Whitney in the form of full-page ads in *The Morning Telegraph*. So Rice bought a competing paper that was on the rocks, the *Daily America*. He stoked his sport-and-showbiz sheet by stealing the best writers and encouraging unbridled sensationalism. Once the *Daily America* became an established must read, the plan was for Rice to pull all his advertising out of *The Telegraph*, which he envisioned would be like yanking a very expensive carpet out from under Whitney's feet.

"He became crazed with the megalomania of octopus-like expansion," said Colonel Stingo, a racetrack columnist who admired George. "Not content with selling information, wagering his clients' money, clipping them 5 percent of their winnings, shaving the odds and occasionally slipping them a wrongo, he decided to become a newspaper publisher, run his own ads and make a profit on himself."

On November 25, 1902, two days before the Thanksgiving opening of the Crescent City racing season, George sauntered into a New Orleans post office to claim his mail. The postal clerk was startled when Rice stated his name, gaping as if coming face-to-face with a burglar.

"Wait a minute," he stammered, backing away and scuttling out of sight.

The clerk did not return, but a U.S. deputy marshal did.

"Postmaster wants to see you," the grim-lipped lawman said, clasping Rice above the elbow and escorting him to a chamber deep within the building, where George was given the silent treatment by three glowering men sent to keep him on ice.

"What's the trouble?" GG genially inquired after the postmaster took his time in arriving.

The southerner stared at George, then seethed, finger-pointing in spasms: "You bring us a recommendation as to who you are, and what you are, and all about yourself before we will answer any of your questions as to how much mail there is here for you."

Rice smiled. The advertising about the new betting service was a success, then.

George had prepared for this parry and had a riposte. He knew a network of local fixers from his days at *The Times-Democrat,* so within thirty minutes an attorney and some New Orleans bank men showed up to vouch for his character. Matter settled, Rice decided to leave the 1,650 registered letters and twelve sacks of first-class mail with his postal pals for the time being. He would need a wagon anyway; the envelopes were so bursting with coins and currency that they couldn't be lugged out by hand.

This shakedown clearly came at the behest of W. C. Whitney, who had friends in high federal places and scores to settle with Rice. George had gotten his first taste of the tycoon's influence just prior to Maxim & Gay's moving out of New York. After the Smoke fiasco, he had been called to the Nassau Street chambers of August Belmont Jr., who was Whitney's partner in the city's first subway system and was building the opulent Belmont Park racetrack. Belmont laced into Rice, demanding that he cease advertising Maxim & Gay in his own *Daily America*.

"Why?" George asked. What could possibly be wrong with his *Daily America* ads that was different from, say, the identical ones that used to run in *The Telegraph*?

"They flagrantly call attention to betting on the races!" Belmont roared.

"But you allow betting at the tracks," Rice countered.

"Yes," Belmont huffed. "But public sentiment is being aroused against betting, and an attack is bound to result."

George left and didn't give the matter another thought until a few days later, when he was again summoned before the thundering industrialist.

"If you don't quit advertising the Maxim & Gay company in the *Daily America*, I will see William Travers Jerome, and he will stop you!" Belmont bellowed. Jerome occupied a top spot in horse racing's old-boy network and was then New York County district attorney.

"If Mr. Jerome sends word to me that the Maxim & Gay advertising is illegal, I will discontinue it," Rice replied curtly, walking out.

No directive came down from the DA, but George was just as glad he had decided to move the wager-by-mail part of the operation to New Orleans.

Over the winter, the new commission house raked in $1.3 million. Sometimes Rice invested his clients' money on the firm's selections as promised; often he did not. If the horses won, he pyramided profits on paper. When they lost, he pocketed the thousands he was supposed to have staked and told clients to send more money.

On one occasion, Rice held off betting a ten-to-one shot as advertised. When the horse won, it cost the firm $130,000. Staffers panicked, but Rice waved off concerns. He ordered full-page ads braying about the latest score and wired them to fifty major newspapers (but not *The Morning Telegraph*). "The gain we will reap in prestige and fresh business will repay our loss on the horse," he assured skittish underlings.

Ricecakes was right. Western Union had to scramble to assign extra cashiers to handle the incoming $150,000 wired to Maxim & Gay overnight. New subscribers wanted in on the deal; existing clients wanted to double or triple standing wagers.

The truest measure of Rice's success was the imitation it spawned. By 1903, the tout market was glutted by copycat mail-order bookie shops. Incensed that shoddy imitators would besmirch his company's good name, George took out "warning ads" to differentiate his upstanding firm from the frauds:

Maxim & Gay Co.
Has No Chicago Office!
Any one doing business in Chicago
representing himself to be our agent,
IS A SWINDLER!

A longer-winded version ran nationwide on March 1, 1903:

SPECIAL NOTICE

The Maxim & Gay Company believes it judicious at this stage of its long and useful career to point out to the unsophisticated that there is nothing in common between methods of the Maxim & Gay Company and those of the so-called get-rich-quick turf concerns which recently went to smash and buried their promoters in obloquy. Our methods are strictly honest, are founded on business prin-

ciples, and have long since been endorsed by the most prominent
and influential racing men of the country.

Horse race betting was technically illegal throughout the United
States at the turn of the twentieth century, but bookies circumvented
laws by bribing local authorities. George's wager-by-mail enterprise was
a murkier proposition, because Maxim & Gay was flirting with a litany
of federal offenses for involving the U.S. Postal Service. It wasn't clear
whether the firm was breaking a specific law or even which authorities
had jurisdiction. But the magnitude of Rice's operation made Maxim &
Gay the obvious target for a test case. GG's reaction was to ratchet up
market presence to an even more ostentatious scale.

Rice got major newspapers to extend up to $200,000 in credit, and
he ordered the *Daily America* to run edition after edition of full-page
Maxim & Gay ads without compensating the paper for the space. His
racetrack comrade Colonel Stingo likened George's maniacal marketing to "a dangerous practice if carried to extremes, like continual reli-
ance upon strong stimulants." The entire scheme was complicated by
Rice's inveterate betting, which ravaged both the turf bureau and his
insolvent scandal sheet.

"My exchequer was low," George confided. "Nearly every dollar I had
made in the Maxim & Gay enterprise had been lost by me in plunging
on the races myself."

When the circuit switched to Washington, authorities refused to
hand over mail until the company's ledgers were audited (GG kept a doctored second set of books for this purpose). In New York, George rented
a nondescript apartment at 67 West Forty-sixth Street and had the firm's
correspondence delivered there, establishing a covert basement mail-
room that became Maxim & Gay's new bet-processing center.

After the *Daily America* lost a libel suit in April 1903—an actress
sued Rice because he made up a story about her eye being blackened
by her husband—GG decided to dump the paper. He thought he had a

resourceful plan for getting rid of it, so one spring morning, hat in hand, George called on W. C. Whitney at his Fifth Avenue estate.

After being made to wait through the tycoon's leisurely breakfast, Rice was ushered in for an audience. He should have been on guard when Whitney received him magnanimously. George detailed how he wanted to offer Whitney the *Daily America* for the $60,000 he claimed to have put into it. Whitney quizzed him for an hour before concluding the meeting on an upbeat note, saying he had to cable a distinguished magazine editor in Paris who advised him on all newspaper acquisitions. Rice left confident he had swindled the old man into paying much more than the paper was actually worth.

A week passed without reply.

After ten days, it started to sink in for George that it was he, and not Whitney, whose confidence had been suckered.

"I did not hear from Mr. Whitney again," Rice recounted. "But I did discover that my business manager was in close communication with Mr. Whitney and that the state of my financial condition every evening was being religiously reported to him."

On April 23, 1903, Daily America Publishing Company filed for voluntary dissolution in New York Supreme Court. Whitney swooped in and bought the *Daily America* for pennies on the dollar, cherry-picking the best writers and reassigning them to his *Morning Telegraph*. He let the rest of the staff go and gave strict orders that when Rice came calling, *The Telegraph* was to refuse all advertising from Maxim & Gay.

At the same time, the Feds had begun cracking down on mail-order betting.

"These schemes are always fraudulent," one inspector told *The Washington Times*. "The victims, who number tens of thousands, dare not raise their voices in protest or complaint, knowing full well that they would only be the butt of ridicule in their community." When asked to tick off names, the official listed Maxim & Gay as the nation's most egregious offender.

In June, District Attorney Jerome had an undercover New York detective write a letter to Maxim & Gay inquiring about betting by mail. In return, the cop got the company's prospectus and remitted $30 for a Three-Horse Wire. A stakeout team witnessed his registered letter being signed for by Rice at the back door of the Forty-sixth Street basement office, then burst in and arrested George on charges of violating section 351 of the Penal Code, the law that broadly covered bet taking. George was bailed for $1,000, and it is unclear whether his case ever came up in court. But the arrest drove Maxim & Gay even further underground.

In a last hurrah at New Orleans, GG bled suckers for all he could, pumping up the commission on winnings to an absurd 25 percent. This lasted until just before Christmas 1903, when postal authorities issued a formal fraud order barring Maxim & Gay from operating by mail. Within ninety days, similar raids eradicated every sizable bet-by-mail competitor in the country. Rice had introduced America to grand-scale tipster thievery, and when his empire collapsed, he made sure every copycat con artist got yanked down with him.

"Having lost the *Daily America* and having 'blown' the Maxim & Gay company, I was again broke," George explained. "But my credit was good, particularly among racetrack bookmakers. That summer, 1904, I became a racetrack plunger, first on borrowed money and then on my winnings. By June I had accumulated $100,000. In July I was nearly broke again. In August I was flush once more, having recouped to the extent of about $50,000."

Rice's big-bettor status afforded him a berth aboard the Cavanaugh Special, a private train chartered by bookies to shuttle high rollers back and forth to Saratoga. Its exclusive smoking car is where George made the acquaintance of two members of the New York shadow world who would influence his life in the coming decades: a debonair doctor and mesmerizing confidence swindler named J. Grant Lyman, and a quiet, milk-faced bookie who would grow up to be America's first organized crime boss, Arnold Rothstein.

By September, Rice had sliced his losses to $8,000, but bookies were getting antsy about settling up. "Disgusted with myself, I longed for a change of atmosphere," George said. "I stayed around New York a few days, [yet] the yearning to cut away from my moorings and to rid myself of the fever to gamble became overpowering."

GG impulsively decided to head west and make a fresh start.

"I bought a railroad ticket for California," he explained. "And, with $200 in my clothes, traveled to a ranch within fifty miles of San Francisco, where I hoed potatoes and did other manual labor designed to cure racetrack-itis. In less than six weeks I felt myself a new man, and decided to stick to the simple life forevermore—away from racetracks and other forms of gambling.

"But," George would later write, penning his autobiography from the gloom of yet another prison cell, "I didn't."

2

GOLD WITHOUT DIGGING
FOR IT

The Frisco-bound locomotive chugged west through the late summer stillness. Teeming cities gave way to vast open plains, each middle-of-nowhere water stop more cinder smudged and desolate than the previous. The townsfolk on the fringes of these outposts zoomed by in indistinct blurs, but George Graham Rice could sense they represented a different breed of Americans: rugged, mind-your-own-business westerners who did everything on a grand scale, whether stealing land from Indians to build a transcontinental railroad or inventing a multimillion-dollar monopoly out of something so ingeniously simple as barbed wire.

Rice did not attempt to con any fellow passengers during his four-day train excursion—at least none that he owned up to. But he certainly would have been in prime position to take off a touch or two, because by the first decade of the twentieth century the coast-to-coast conviviality of the nation's well-appointed Pullman cars had gained an underworld reputation as a captive-audience poaching paradise.

George would have been well acquainted with the basics of railroad swindling: Look for a clean-cut man traveling alone. Strike up a conversation in the smoker or lounge car. Be engaging and outgoing, and know how to ferret out answers to important questions (line of work, financial standing) without coming across as intrusive. Hustlers knew never to offer personal, political, or religious views (while constantly validating the mark's), never to boast (while giving marks every opportunity to do so), and to avoid drinking with potential victims (not as a moral concern, but because liquor interfered with control). A sharp con man could be on good terms with any stranger within fifteen minutes and, if the mark looked promising enough, be able to morph into his trusted friend for the duration of the trip. The hallmark of a proficient swindler was his ability to feign rapt fascination in the presence of pompous bluster, so grifters gravitated to blowhards and attached themselves like leeches to know-it-alls and braggarts.

Once a sense of trust was established, swindlers could play marks for any one of a number of colorfully named short cons that happened to be in vogue—the big mitt, the tear up, the cross, the high pitch, the soap game, the shake with the button, the spud, the tip—either before the journey was over or immediately upon arrival in a "right" (meaning crooked) town. These ruses were good for getting whatever money a victim might have on him, but the most adept Pullman con artists did not profit by fleecing travelers firsthand. Rather, these specialized "ropers" rode the rails back and forth across the country for weeks at a time, collecting finder's fees for steering the most lucrative rubes to "inside men" for ensnarement in high-stakes scams. Because well-connected ropers knew an extensive network of big-store swindlers across the nation, operatives were always at the ready, no matter the chump's final destination.

The concept of using an edge to take advantage of others didn't just apply to hustlers ripping off marks on train trips. "Broadly speaking, this philosophy was one of individual opportunity free and untrammelled, based upon the assumed right of the individual to seek his fortune in his own way, without interference, supervision or even question from his government," the financial historian Proctor W. Hansl wrote in his 1935 book *Years of Plunder: A Financial Chronicle of Our Times*. "The name 'American' came to connote a shrewd and often unscrupulous fellow who had lots of money and spent it ostentatiously, without ever arriving at an understanding of the finer things of life. Success—in dollars and cents—was the keynote of this philosophy [and] Uncle Sam became an animated dollar-mark."

Everyday swindling was so topical that George might even have chatted about it while making small talk in the dining car. Newspapers in 1904 were widely reporting Theodore Roosevelt Jr.'s bombastic attacks on "get-rich-quick promoters, watered-stock manipulators, non-dividend-paying securities dealers and wind-enterprise swindlers." Yet that July, even the president's own wife, Edith, was targeted by charity scammers faking the grave illness of a child. Around the same time, gossip was buzzing about one Cassie Chadwick, who for years had managed to defraud Ohio banks out of millions by pretending to be the out-of-wedlock daughter of Andrew Carnegie (her ruse worked because no banker would risk embarrassing the billionaire philanthropist by asking about an illegitimate child). At the midpoint of his journey, Rice's train quite likely sliced through St. Louis, where detectives were busy arresting some five hundred pickpockets, bank sneaks, counterfeiters, hotel cheats, and flimflammers who had descended upon the city for the World's Fair and Summer Olympic Games. Even the scholars who edited that year's *Judicial and Statutory Definitions of Words and Phrases* saw fit to include "confidence man" when they made revisions to the eight-volume tome, establishing that "any person or persons, who shall obtain or procure, or attempt to obtain or procure, from any other persons any money or valuable thing by means of any game or games, or in any fraudulent pretense or pretenses, practice or practices, or any scheme, trick, device or deception, and any person who shall confederate, conspire or combine with any bunko-steerer or any other person or persons . . . shall be deemed a 'confidence man.'"

But one didn't need a legal definition to be in the know about confidence trickery in 1904. References to swindling abounded in magazines and newspapers, like this fictional exchange between "Green" and "Brown" in the funny pages of the *New-York Tribune*:

Green: What's the difference between a confident man and a confidence man?
Brown: Whatever it is, the latter usually gets the difference.

Or this humorous snippet titled "An Ingenious Plea" that ran in a Utah weekly called *The Broad Ax*:

"Your honor," said the confidence man, "the man who tempts another man to do wrong is as bad as the man who does wrong, isn't he?"
    "I believe it has so been held."
    "Well, then, send that hayseed to jail! He's such a fool that he just tempted me to flimflam him!"

On one end of American enterprise existed legitimate business. On the other, outright theft. It had never been difficult to distinguish between these extremes. But as George hurtled west to begin the second act of his swindling career, the shadowy center was increasingly blurry, and this hazy miasma was precisely where Rice aspired to thrive.

As polished and poised as Rice was by age thirty-four, he was still capable of preposterous distortions of truth. George's most audacious claim about his life to this point—that he went west to immerse himself in the morals-cleansing rigor of unskilled farm labor—is laughable.

With his cosmopolitan air and shiny patent-leather shoes, the deposed millionaire would have cut quite an incongruous figure in the dusty potato fields of the San Joaquin valley. Rice, after all, was a man so averse to physical drudgery that he had wheedled his way into a soft job as a chaplain's assistant while imprisoned. If there was ever a con artist who epitomized the old saying "Would rather work twice as hard to steal fifty cents than to earn an honest buck," it was George.

Several independent sources place Rice in California by late summer

1904, but none corroborate his farmhand claim or offer any other explanation for what he was doing there. For the sake of not letting facts get in the way of a good story—the way GG preferred—let's accept Rice's self-centric version with a jaundiced eye and allow him to pick up the tale from just after the autumn harvest, when he found himself with time on his hands and a yearning to move on:

> *I had never visited San Francisco. Being close to the city of the Golden Gate—within fifty miles—I decided to "take a look." So one evening, in the late fall of 1904, I packed my grip and within two hours was comfortably housed in the old Palace Hotel.*
>
> *The first man I met upon entering the lobby was W. J. Arkell, formerly one of the owners of* Frank Leslie's Weekly *and of* Judge.
>
> *"Hello, Bill!" I exclaimed. "What are you doing here?"*
>
> *"Same as you," he answered. "Morse trimmed me in American Ice, and I'm broke. I am in hock to the hotel. They think I am worth $2,000,000. I haven't 20 cents."*

William J. Arkell, forty-eight, was the down-on-his-luck son of an upstate New York manufacturing millionaire who had patented the first paper-bag-making machinery in the 1860s. By the turn of the twentieth century, Bill had burned through his father's fortune by embarking on one failed venture after another, including a disastrous 1890 expedition to Alaska in which several party members perished after the group got hopelessly lost. Although none of his explorers ever set foot in the Klondike region, when the great Alaskan gold rush commenced several years later, Arkell insisted his men had already "discovered" the entire vast swath of Yukon ore fields. His claims were ridiculed, and while 100,000 prospectors stampeded into the Klondike with hopes of getting filthy rich, Arkell was reduced to floating sketchy stock scams and bumming meals from strangers in San Francisco.

At the Palace bar, Arkell plied Rice with cigars, silver gin fizzes, and sincere-sounding condolences about the demise of George's brilliant horse-betting venture. Arkell complimented Rice on his advertising acumen and hinted at how a man as intelligent as GG could make a mint in the Nevada mining boom that was on the brink of exploding into the next big thing.

"Come with me up to Tonopah and be my press agent," Arkell implored. "We'll get a hold of a mining property up there, promote a company and make a barrel of money."

George was skeptical. What did Bill know about mines?

"Well, I've lost enough in 'em to know a great deal," Arkell huffed.

"I don't know a mine from a hole in the ground," Rice admitted. "And I know nothing about the stock brokerage business. So I don't see how I can be of any assistance."

George was attempting to impose logic and reason where Bill felt neither belonged.

"Don't let that bother you," Arkell cajoled. "I'll show you how."

Bill talked Ricecakes into bankrolling 50 percent of the endeavor. After the two shook hands, Arkell revealed he didn't quite have his half of the funds. George agreed to put up $150—all the money he had left—to get them to the mining frontier.

"Suppose we get stranded out there, what will happen?" Rice asked.

"Oh, forget it!" Arkell boomed. "How can a couple of Easterners like us, wide awake and with phosphorous brains, get stranded in a place where they dig gold and silver out of the ground?"

Tonopah ended up being a raw and wintry thirty-six-hour trek across the bleak desert moonscape of central Nevada. The locomotive strained every inch up the six-thousand-foot pass, leaving George chilled and longing for the potato fields of central California. But his spirits began to perk up the last hundred miles or so when he caught sight of train after train hurtling down the mountain from the opposite direction, each and every freight car brimming with freshly excavated ore.

Rice and Arkell arrived after dusk and found the town's deeply rutted main drag teeming with the soldier-of-fortune bustle of an anything-goes mining camp. Work didn't cease when the sun went down in Tonopah, and George and Bill were the only men standing still amid a rush of Stetsons, string ties, and pistols strapped conspicuously to each and every hip. Crossing the street required a bold dodge of wagon traffic—safety was secondary to making sure ore made it onto departing freight cars—and the two newcomers were the only ones who flinched when dynamite blasts rocked the ice-crusted San Antonio Mountains, triggering the competing calls of baleful coyotes. The thin, dry air and constant swirl of dust left the taste of grit in George's teeth, and the entire ramshackle camp reeked of mules, wood smoke, unwashed men, whiskey, and the desperate lust for gold.

George and Bill sought lodging in the only hotel they could find. They were told they could have the last room in the house, except it wasn't really a room and wasn't exactly in the house but in a dubious annex off the back, roughed out with thin pine partitions and a sagging tarp roof. Although they were exhausted, the moldy bedding hardly invited sleep. "The aspect was so inhospitable that Arkell and I decided not to retire for a little while," Rice recalled. "We gravitated out toward the barroom, where the click of a roulette wheel caught our ears."

The Mizpah Bar was jammed with a gruff mix of gamblers, gunmen, speculators, mining engineers, hammer jacks, hoisters, haulers, drillers, and Oriental and American Indian grunt laborers jostling shoulder to shoulder at the overcrowded betting tables. No distinction was made between the classes—all the men craved action—and every put-up-or-shut-up soul in the joint was as willing to chance everything on a roll of the dice as on the random, go-for-broke strike of a pickax. At first, Rice and Arkell just stood in the back and watched. Before long, they were convinced they could discern a pattern in the roulette wheel. They were further emboldened by the reckless play of the inebriated miners. "Soon we were buying stacks of checks and ourselves bucking the tiger excitedly," Rice recollected. Suppressing their giddiness, the partners began placing bets.

It took less than an hour before George and Bill were completely cleaned out.

"The remnants of my $150 passed to the ownership of the man behind the game," Rice lamented. "Arkell had put his last two-bit piece on the black and lost."

Back in the annex sharing a single soiled blanket, George meekly cataloged his possessions: one cane, an umbrella, and three suits of clothes. He wondered if Bill thought they could pawn the belongings to get money for breakfast.

"Oh, come off!" Arkell said, laughing. "Wait till I present my card around this burg in the morning. Then we'll get all the breakfast we want."

Tonopah at daybreak was a stark contrast to George's hazy first impressions from the cover of darkness. The blinding desert sun—merciless even at dawn—glazed the panorama in a white shimmer that distorted all depth and distance. Coarse mountains ringed the horizon like broken teeth, their irregular ledges strewn with rock slides and lightning-singed sagebrush. The skeletal framework of hoists, head frames, and winches zigzagged crazily as far as the eye could see. The more established mines, silhouetted against the glare of a too-turquoise sky, traced the camp's original discovery veins. But with wildcatters now drilling willy-nilly all across the valley based on the hope of random strikes, the juxtaposition of one- and two-man squatter crews toiling alongside towering industrial rigs made the pockmarked hillside resemble a vast, fractured David-versus-Goliath battlefield.

"We awoke hungry, as all men have a habit of doing when they are broke," George later wrote in his memoir. Bill was already up and had scouted out breakfast: A buck anywhere in town got you a salty slab of ham, two runny eggs, and a filthy cup of coffee. Arkell passed on the eats and strolled over to the office of the State Bank and Trust, where he had sent advance word he was coming and wanted to be introduced to the biggest mine broker in the district. Bill had also arranged to have an inside man in New York field phony telegraphs from him and to wire back in response, pretending to be a prestigious banker.

After a brief conversation with Malcolm Macdonald, the local mining monopolist, Arkell asked for permission to send a wire. In return, Macdonald's bank received prompt assurance that Arkell had an unlimited line of credit. This news caused the balding, taciturn Macdonald to turn from skeptical to fawning, and at once he insisted on touring Arkell around the superb properties he had to offer. Arkell halted Macdonald to disclose he had a partner and that the two of them had not eaten since arriving the night before. Bill went to fetch George, and Macdonald fell all over himself arranging the most sumptuous home-cooked spread he could rustle up on short notice.

After breakfast, which consisted of mountain trout, the flavor of which was more delicious than anything I had tasted in many years," Rice recalled, "we returned to the office of the bank. There Arkell explained to Mr. Macdonald that he wanted 'a big mining proposition or nothing.' He said that he represented big Eastern capital, and that he was prepared to pay from one to three million for the right kind of property."

Macdonald made a show of looking pained to come up with a list of mines he would consider letting go for under $3 million—the equivalent of roughly $80 million in 2015 dollars. Nevada mining was cresting an unexpected boom after a long period of decline, and Tonopah was decidedly a sellers' market.

The Comstock Lode rush of 1859 had produced the most significant silver discovery in U.S. history, drawing sixty thousand opportunists to the territory and establishing Nevada as a state. Profits from the monumental strike were so widespread that the Comstock Lode was instrumental in financing the winning Union effort in the Civil War. But the mines bottomed out within fifteen years, and the region spiraled into an economic abyss.

By the 1890s, statewide population had dwindled to forty thousand, and newspaper editorials back east were arguing for revocation of Nevada's statehood on the grounds that a handful of cowboys in 110,000 square miles of wasteland had more per capita congressional representation than any other state in the Union. Still, a scattering of grizzled prospectors continued to scour the desert, determined—or desperate—to get lucky.

On May 19, 1900, one such prospector, Jim Butler, was exploring the desolate western edge of Nye County some 225 miles south of Reno. Butler was fluent in the Shoshone dialect, and local Indians had directed him to Sawtooth Pass because it offered the easiest crossing through the San Antonio Mountains and a *tonopah* (hidden spring) to water his animals. Knowing Butler was looking for mineral deposits, the Indians suggested he check out a three-hundred-square-yard black quartz outcropping visible through the pass from three miles away. Butler camped at the *tonopah,* but sometime during the night one of his burros wandered off. The next morning, when he finally found the stray out near the distinctive black ledge, legend has it Butler was so angry that he picked up a rock to hurl at the beast—then stopped in mid-heave, because the strangely dark stone was unusually dense and heavy for its size.

Butler collected samples and brought them to Reno. He was broke, so he offered an assayer a share of his discovery in exchange for testing its value. The assayer replied he "would not give a dollar for a thousand tons of such stuff" and tossed the samples on a slag heap. Butler dejectedly retrieved his rocks and showed them to other experts who similarly scoffed. For years, ranchers had ridden through Sawtooth Pass and noticed that same black outcropping, but dark rock was common in southern Nevada and generally attributed to iron compounds. It took another week for Butler to find someone who would test his samples on spec. By then, his enthusiasm had ebbed, and he forgot about the rocks soon after sending them off.

Three weeks passed while Butler returned to his ranch to cut hay—oblivious that the assayer had dispatched an Indian runner into the wilds of Nye County to track him down. It turned out that the odd coloring was due to magnesium compounded with high concentrations of silver, and the samples were valued at $600 per ton. Word of the discovery got around, and a mad rush was under way at what would come to be called Tonopah Springs. But only Butler knew the exact spot of his strike. He made six official claims and posted location notices, naming one of his mines Burro in honor of the stray that had sparked the second-richest silver strike in Nevada history.

The quality of the camp's silver (and later gold, copper, and lead) deposits was indisputable, but it was a challenge to get these metals out of the ground in a cost-effective manner. Tonopah in 1900 was located in the most inaccessible region of America's third-largest county land-wise. The nearest railroad, sixty-three miles west at Sodaville, was a narrow gauge that ran only three times a week. With rainfall averaging less than five inches per year, water was beyond scarce; to support any sort of labor force, it would have to be hauled down from the mountains. Trees were also in short supply, and both mature timber (for underground staging) and scrub (for fuel) were necessities for large-scale mining. Not only was geography against Tonopah, but geologists were pessimistic too: Eons of seismic disturbance had badly fragmented Nevada's mineral veins. What were once even striations of high-character ore were now deeply shattered filaments impossible to trace with any reliability.

Butler and other early claimants cooked up ingenious work-arounds to Tonopah's shortcomings. For starters, they made sure only to send out the best mineral samples for assaying. That way, when consistently glowing test results came back, the news was sure to entice eastern capitalists, who provided money for development by buying shares of incorporated mines. And rather than mine these disrupted veins themselves, owners got prospectors to pay *them* to work the claims under a system that was mining's equivalent to sharecropping: Anyone who could afford a $10 prospector's permit could lease a fifty-by-one-hundred-foot length of ground and harvest as much ore as he could within a six-month period. These "grubstakers" were paid on a sliding scale based on the quality of the ore they dug up and were sometimes advanced supplies and dynamite to expedite their work. In exchange, property owners took 25 percent of the haul. If a vein proved productive, owners could elect not to renew the lease, kick out the grubstakers, and continue to develop the claim themselves without sharing its bounty.

By the spring of 1901, one hundred such grubstake leases had been granted in Tonopah. In 1902, a major gold strike on nearby Columbia Mountain solidified Nye County as the most lucrative mining outpost in the West. When another rich strike in January 1904 "created an explosion of excitement reminiscent of the earlier Comstock rush," asking prices for mining properties—*any* mine in the district—soared.

This was why Macdonald, with a straight face, was able to offer Arkell and Rice his five-acre Simmerone property for $1 million, just to see if they'd blink.

Simmerone had only been developed six feet deep. But because of the "extreme richness of the ore that had been opened at [the] grass-roots [level]," Macdonald claimed he had been forced to erect a stockade to keep out poachers.

Arkell knew Macdonald's first pitch was bound to be a bluff, so he respectfully passed. (Later, Bill and George would learn that Macdonald had paid only $32,000 for Simmerone and that at the time of his offer the mine was neither being worked nor believed capable of production.)

Next up were a leadworks at Reveille and a silver mine at Tybo. These too Macdonald dangled for $1 million each, selectively omitting that both camps had long ago gone bust and were now considered ghost towns.

Again, Arkell declined.

Macdonald got down to business.

He showered praise on the two sharp easterners for knowing that anyone arriving this late in the boom cycle would only be clawing after expensive scraps. But what about something farther out on the fringes? The inside scoop was that Goldfield, twenty-eight miles south, was in line to be the next Tonopah—bigger, even. Macdonald had control over some promising claims that had yet to hit the open market. Did they want to take a look? Macdonald wanted to drive them to Goldfield in his newfangled Simplex automobile—an exciting opportunity in and of itself, because travel across the desert by horseless carriage was a novelty in 1904.

Arkell was won over by the prospect of the free motorcar ride. Rice wasn't as enthralled.

"I got 'cold feet,'" George admitted. "Arkell's talk of visionary millions in that bleak environment of snow-clad desert and wind-swept mountain didn't enthuse me at all. I protested against the proposed trip to Goldfield, and insisted that I should be allowed to telegraph to relatives for money with which to return to the Coast."

Arkell hissed that Macdonald would be picking up all expenses. Their return to San Francisco would only be delayed twenty-four hours.

"I left my grip, umbrella and cane in Tonopah, intending to return the same evening, and boarded the automobile for Goldfield," said Rice, unaware he was embarking upon the trip of a lifetime.

At one hundred miles from any railroad and twenty-five miles from the nearest known water supply, Goldfield made Tonopah seem like a thriving metropolis. Hallucinatory triple-digit heat and blinding summer sandstorms earned the fledgling camp comparisons to "Dante's Inferno with the lid off." The streets were befouled by sewage, and dead pack animals were left to rot where they dropped, stripped to the bone by ever-circling vultures. "Tradition said that men had died of thirst on the very spot where Goldfield was now adding daily to the world's wealth," George remarked, not yet knowing the worst of it: The soul-crushing desolation of winter—when contact with the outside world was cut off, water froze solid at four bucks a barrel, and coal couldn't be had at any price—drove even the most hardened Nevada miners over the brink of desert delirium.

In contrast to Tonopah, where calculated expansion had been anchored by engineering, Goldfield was a rogues' camp. Even so, its evolution was no different from that of any other frontier outpost: The initial wave of miners lived in tents, and the first firetrap structures slapped together to serve them were saloons. Gambling joints, whorehouses, and opium dens soon followed. By the time Bill and George arrived in Goldfield, watering holes had been established on all four corners of Main and Crook Streets, and shootings and stampedes occurred with roughly equal frequency. Things were so out of control that the camp's more levelheaded businessmen were trying to persuade the Earp brothers of O.K. Corral gun-fighting fame to settle in Goldfield and restore order as the town's lawmen (Virgil would eventually accept the job as deputy sheriff; his younger brother Wyatt opted for the more lucrative position of pit boss at the Northern Saloon casino).

Bill and George got the grand tour, but Arkell never had any intention of purchasing one of Macdonald's overpriced Goldfield properties. When Arkell indicated that the Tonopah Home Mining Company, which had been pointed out to him on the ride down by one of Macdonald's associates, was more to his liking, Macdonald motored off in a huff and left Bill and George to find their own way back to Tonopah.

The appeal, Arkell explained, was that Tonopah Home was already incorporated and had stock certificates printed, "thereby eliminating the delay and expense incident to preparing something for the immediate consumption of the San Francisco public." The plan was for Bill to head back to Tonopah, buy five-cent options on a million shares of the stock with his false line of credit, then return to California to jack up the price on the San Francisco exchange. Rice would remain in Goldfield to promote Tonopah Home by sending out made-up news dispatches about bountiful production.

"How am I going to subsist here for a few days until I can begin to make a living?" George asked.

"How am *I* going to get back to Tonopah and from there to San Francisco?" Bill countered.

They were debating in front of the corrugated-tin facade of the Gold-field State Bank and Trust when Arkell got the idea for Rice to go in and introduce himself as a big-time eastern newspaperman and vouch for Arkell's solvency to cash a check drawn against a bank in Canajoharie, New York.

"I was born and brought up there," Arkell reasoned. "They wouldn't let one of my checks go to protest. Besides, I can get back to Frisco and protect it by telegraph, if necessary, before it reaches Canajoharie."

After a few minutes of silver-tongued repartee between Rice and the cashier, Arkell walked out with $50.

"Now, Bill, come across!" George pleaded. "I'm flat broke, on the desert."

Grudgingly, Arkell counted out $15.

If George knew then that he was never going to see Bill again, he might have pushed for more.

Within three days, Arkell would unload a portion of his Tonopah Home shares on the San Francisco exchange at a price far higher than what he had paid for them, raking in a fat profit without ever sending a dime to his stranded "partner." When George later wrote to confront him for his share, Bill refused to acknowledge there had ever been a partnership between them.

Alone in Goldfield, Rice learned the hard way that the old adage about playing crooked poker also applied to mining: If you're invited into a game with strangers and can't immediately figure out who the sucker is, it's you.

When George ran out of cigars, he pegged *The Goldfield News* as his best bet for gainful employment. The banner atop the eight-page weekly proclaimed to print "All That's New and True in the Greatest Gold Camp Ever Known," so Rice figured his flair for fabrication would be recognized as an asset.

He was hired on the spot. The no-nonsense editor underscored that despite its boosterish motto, the paper was heavy on hard news and light on puff pieces.

"He wanted technical mining stuff," Rice wrote, laughing. "I didn't know a winze from a windlass, nor a shaft from a stope."

For his first assignment, GG was sent to profile a sage old mining executive named Thomas Jaggers, described to him as an austere industry authority. But when Rice ventured to his subject's stone cabin way up in the hills, he discovered "Honest Tom" was a liquored-up eccentric who conducted business in the desert wearing a Prince Albert frock coat and tall silk hat. George couldn't resist penning a crackerjack feature about a whiskey-fueled recluse who was set for life thanks to having stumbled upon a jealously guarded gold mine that Jaggers had christened Dark Secret.

"I wrote what I considered a first-class human-interest story, and handed it to the owner and editor, 'Jimmy' O'Brien," Rice said. "He thought it was fair writing, but not the sort of matter the Goldfield *News* wanted."

George was not discouraged. If there was anything he liked as much as a good gamble, it was a palette of colorful characters.

"Some of the weird yarns I handed in about mine developments certainly did make Mr. O'Brien jump sideways at times," Rice recalled. "I was a tenderfoot and knew little or nothing about the mining business. But the visible aspect of shipment upon shipment of high-grade ore leaving the camp by mule team was convincing. What probably impressed me most was the evident sincerity of the trail blazers who had been on the ground since the day the camp was born. These men had suffered all kinds of hardships to hold their ground and make a go of the camp."

George dashed off spirited copy about boomtown mavericks striking it rich in the middle of nowhere. The heady, highly charged atmosphere coursed through him like a jolt of adrenaline. "My environment became an inspiration," Rice enthused.

This gushing effervescence was not shared by his boss.

"Within a week I was discharged for incompetency," GG wrote, with a chuckle, shrugging off the firing. It was hardly his fault the straitlaced editor failed to grasp the selling power of superior storytelling.

"I was not at all appalled at losing my job on the Goldfield *News*," George would later reflect. "There was an indefinable something in the atmosphere of Goldfield—a new, budding mining camp, at an altitude of 5,000 feet and on the frontier—that stirred me. . . . I decided to stay awhile. . . . I had begun to like the life and was convinced there were some real gold mines in the camp."

A t this early stage, Goldfield was small enough that supporting industries had yet to establish themselves. Rice could see the locals knew nothing about promotion, so he decided to pounce on the publicity angle before some outsider beat him to it.

With the earnings from his one week as a reporter, George ordered a rough pine table made by a carpenter, rented desk space in front of the cashier's counter at the Goldfield Bank, and secured the services of an "expert male stenographer" from Cripple Creek. Open for business, the Goldfield-Tonopah Advertising Agency began actively recruiting clients.

George first called upon the Mims-Sutro Company, a securities brokerage, to pitch a campaign based on educating far-flung investors about mining stocks. When the manager balked that he was already spending $100 a month on advertising, Rice reacted with mock shock. "Why, you ought to be spending that much every hour!" he exclaimed before elucidating the logic of full-page propaganda.

"At first they thought me a fanatic on the subject," George recalled. "But within a fortnight I succeeded in inducing them to spend $1,000 in a single day for advertising. It was not, however, until after I had shown them how to follow up their correspondence successfully that they began to believe in me. . . .

"The most remarkable feature of that advertising campaign to me was that I had never been a stock-broker, had never been a mine-promoter, and had never been in a mining camp before. But still, despite my utter lack of knowledge . . . of the technical end of the business, my advertisements pulled in the dollars."

It didn't hurt that Rice also knew how to negotiate discounts on large blocks of ad space, then mark up the price 45 percent for resale to individual clients.

"Within two months the Mims-Sutro Company was spending at the rate of from $5,000 to $10,000 a week for advertising," George bragged. "And inasmuch as I always sent cash with the order, my copy was in great demand. Indeed, my agency was fairly inundated day after day with blank contracts from newspapers all over the country, the managers of which were clamoring for the Goldfield business. In addition to the Mims-Sutro account, I soon had many others.

"In fact," GG gloated, "I had all the others."

George began hanging out at the Northern Saloon, which was reputed to have a bar so long that eighty servers were required to staff it. The Northern also housed the town's most boisterous casino and doubled as Goldfield's stock exchange, with round-the-clock trading erupting as demand dictated. "Here fully seventy-five percent of the camp's male population gathered nightly and played faro, roulette and stud poker; talked mines and mining, sold properties, and shielded themselves from the blasts that came with piercing intensity from the snow-capped peaks of the Sierras," Rice recollected. "The brokers of the camp gathered every night in the Northern and held informal sessions, frequently trading to the extent of 30,000 or 40,000 shares of the more active stocks."

Rice was fascinated by the psychology of stock bidding. He saw that trading securities was like gambling, but the mesmerizing difference was how profit or loss could spike or plummet based solely on the mood of the marketplace. George was intrigued by the juxtaposition of how on one side of the Northern men were willing to risk a life's fortune on the random turn of a playing card, while on the other side decent stocks sometimes changed hands for pennies, attracting little or no bidding.

Couldn't the urge to gamble be fused with fractional investing? What would happen if, on a grand scale, low-budget speculators were able to enjoy the thrill of plunging like big shots?

One night, amid the haze of cigar smoke and auction chatter, it came to Rice: Dirt-cheap mining stocks were *exactly* the product to allow the allure of striking it rich to trickle down to America's lowest common denominator. Dollar-per-share, million-share stocks already existed. But what about a million-share mining company whose shares traded in penny increments? Using the same tactics that had persuaded Maxim & Gay clients to believe they had been granted access to the inside world of horse betting, George aspired to turn small-town yokels all across the nation into vicarious, stay-at-home mining enthusiasts.

"Here was an opportunity for the great American speculating public to take a flyer on something much more tangible and lasting than a horse race," Rice rhapsodized. "Tens of thousands of people who for years had been imbibing the daily financial chronicles of the newspapers, but whose incomes were not sufficient to permit them to indulge in stock market speculation in rails and industrials, found in cheap mining stocks the thing they were looking for—an opportunity for those with limited capital to give full play to their gambling, or speculative, instinct.

"The mining stocks which were advertised through my agency in those early Goldfield days were generally of the ten-, twenty-, and thirty-cent per share variety. . . . My agency advertised twenty-five or fifty companies of the average quality, and [when] one of them made good in a handsome way, he who purchased an equal number of shares in each would at least break even with the profits from the one winner."

In other words, make it easy for working stiffs to get hooked on the action. Slip them the convincer, take off the touch—then put the suckers on the send for more money.

Decades later, historians would dub Rice "the Henry Ford of the speculation game" for giving working-class investors easy access to the

stock market. But in actuality, it was George who was ahead of the automobile pioneer with his vision of affordability for the masses: Ford's
first low-cost Model T cars did not roll off assembly lines until 1908—
four years after Rice first championed cut-rate pricing as a way to ensnare the average Joe.

To complement his ad agency, George created a fully staffed news
bureau, encouraging reporters to stretch the truth while spreading the
good word about Goldfield. Grandiose accounts of the mad rush west
were augmented with tall tales about life-changing fortunes discovered
by accident.

"Human-interest stories . . . were turned out every day by competent newspaper men," Rice explained. "These were forwarded to the
daily newspapers in the big cities of the East and West for publication
in the news columns [and] to obtain publicity for all kinds of sensational
happenings that were common on the desert. Reports of gold discoveries,
high play at gambling tables, shooting affrays, gamblers' feuds, stampedes,
hold-ups, narrow escapes, murders, and so forth were used to rouse the
public's attention to the fact that a mining camp called Goldfield was on
the horizon."

Even newspapers as esteemed as *The New York Times* ran the bureau's
glowing write-ups verbatim as "special correspondence." After all,
the copy was provided for free, and the clout of Rice's gigantic media
buys was usually enough to blur any ethical distinctions between
paid advertising and editorial objectivity.

"I felt confident that the speculating public was going to make a
great big killing in Goldfield," George boasted. "I was head of the news
bureau, and the news bureau was Nevada's publicity agent."

By 1905, Goldfield's mining stocks were gaining in national attention and price. Kewanas, first advertised by Rice at twenty-five cents a
share, climbed to $2.25. Jumbo Extension marched from fifteen cents
to $3.00. Red Top zoomed from eight cents to $5.50. Daisy rocketed from
ten cents to $6.00. Over the course of eighteen months, ten-cent Mo-
hawk would eclipse them all. "Early purchasers of Mohawk gathered 200

to 1 for their money," Rice crowed, "many times more than could usually be won on a long shot at the horse races, and not so very much less than was formerly won by lucky prize winners in the Louisiana Lottery."

Not every stock George advertised ended up being a winner. But the losers were providing him with the opportunity to learn securities promotion with other people's money. "I had passed through the experimental stage and now marshaled a cardinal principle or two that I decided must guide me," Rice wrote in his autobiography, where he outlined the psychological subtleties behind his advertising:

> *I resolved never to allow an advertisement to go out of the office that was unconvincing to a thinker. If my argument convinces the man of affairs, I determined, it will certainly win over the man of no affairs.*
>
> *Dogmatically expressed, the idea was this: Never appeal to the intelligence of fools, no matter how easily they may part with their money. Turn your batteries on the thinking ones and convince them, and the unthinking will follow.*
>
> *That principle was applied to the argument of the advertisement. The headlines were constructed on an entirely different principle, namely, to be positive to an extreme.*
>
> *The Bible was my exemplar. It says, "It is" or "It was," "Thou shalt" or "Thou shalt not." The Bible rarely explains or tells why.*

Six months after he was stranded in the desert, Rice's agency was $65,000 in the black, and George was the most popular man in Goldfield. "I was an enthusiast," he wrote, beaming. "I believed in the merits of the camp, and my enthusiasm undoubtedly carried itself to the readers of my advertisements." GG had even reconciled with his second wife, Frances Drake, and sent for her. He gave her a soda fountain to run and let her dabble in the Goldfield stock exchange to keep her out of his thinning hair.

"Never in my life had I lived in an environment that inspirited me as this one," said George. "I went about my business like a man who sees dazzling before him a golden scepter, and who is imbued with the idea that if he exerts the power, he can grasp the prize."

Even as Goldfield was thriving, its pioneers were aggressively hunting for the next big boom elsewhere. The real money in mining, George was learning, was in dealing claims, not developing them: Flip properties before they got past the paperwork stage. Ride the wave early, and leap off before it crested. If no such wave existed, it was up to a savvy promoter to create one. That was why when high-grade surface ore assayed at $700 per ton was unearthed near the Amargosa underground river seventy-five miles south of Goldfield, Rice was the man Nevada power brokers called upon to put the new camp on the map.

This new district—Bullfrog—took its nickname from the region's green-tinged quartz that was said to be liberally studded with free-floating gold. Despite being even more inaccessible than either Tonopah or Goldfield, Bullfrog stood to benefit from being the third wave in Nevada's twentieth-century mining boom, leveraging the momentum of previous strikes. Within weeks, the sagebrush flats were staked for nine miles in every direction and shortages caused supply prices to spike sharply. Lumber cost $10 per hundred board feet, and hay for animals shot up to $100 a ton. Claims traded hands so fast that entire towns packed up and moved overnight. By the time George was summoned by the mining bigwigs, Bullfrog's center of power had shifted several times, relocating to an encampment called Rhyolite.

Rice and his stenographer were chauffeured to the Rhyolite saloon, which was so new it didn't have a name yet. In a back room, men in suits and string ties were on their hands and knees, where it looked as if they were shooting dice. In actuality, these gentlemen cowboys were divvying up the district on huge maps spread across the floor. The ringleaders of this high-stakes Nevada real estate game were the U.S. senator

George S. Nixon and George Wingfield, millionaire owner of the Tonopah Club casino.

The power brokers paused long enough to acknowledge Rice, but he
knew what was expected of him—to get far-flung investors "to believe
that when all the riches of that great treasure-house were mined, gold
would be demonetized." Rice was handed deeds to seven corner lots of
prime Rhyolite real estate "to help along my enthusiasm." Another mining baron slipped him twenty thousand shares of stock whose price he
wanted inflated. Rice now had a vested interest, but he could plainly see
that the men establishing the new camp were simultaneously planning
exit strategies. He sensed it might be wise to take his profits up front
and unloaded his Bullfrog shares soon after leaving town.

Rice later wrote that the stock "turned out to be a rank mining failure, as [did] practically every other property in the camp." He had also
quickly sold his seven lots "at figures which netted me, in all, in excess
of $20,000 for my one day's trip to Bullfrog." Putting shovels in the
ground was for suckers. Profiteers never went broke trading paper for
cash.

GG had asked for a tour of the Montgomery-Shoshone mine because
he wanted to experience firsthand "the powerful magnet which attracted
everybody to the camp." He was escorted through a seventy-foot tunnel, and the miner guiding George told him you could strike a pickax
anywhere along the talc and come away with chunks of ore that would
assay at $2,000 a ton—triple the initial estimate. Rice didn't quite be-
lieve the miner but did his best to convey the imagery to readers of his
advertisements. Within weeks, he had planted the rumor that the property's owners had turned down $3 million for the mine, and wiseguys
were murmuring that the lode deeper within this "Infant Wonder
of the Desert" was expected to exceed the preposterous valuation of
$15,000 a ton.

"I've seen many gold rushes in my time that were hummers, but nothing like that stampede," said Frank "Shorty" Harris, one of Bullfrog's
discoverers. "It looked like the whole population of Goldfield was

trying to move at once. . . . They all got the fever and milled around wild-eyed, trying to find a way to the new strike. . . . Men even hiked the seventy-five miles pushing wheelbarrows. . . . When [I got back to my] claim a week later, more than a thousand men were camped around it, and more were coming every day. A few had tents, but most of them were in open camps. That was the start of Bullfrog, and from then things moved so fast that it made us old-timers dizzy."

What George didn't publicize was the fact that the power brokers had opened the Montgomery-Shoshone main shaft alongside the main body of ore and not across it. The discoverers were confident this isolated section didn't extend ten feet in any other direction. Because of this, the mining barons wanted to off-load the entire overhyped property on a single wealthy sucker as soon as possible. Could Rice reel in a bigger fish than the penny stock minnows he had a knack for attracting?

Apparently, the answer was yes.

Charles M. Schwab was the planet's largest independent steel producer. Like many captains of industry, Schwab believed his Midas touch extended to investments he knew little about, as if his very involvement were the sole ingredient for success. Rice's glowing write-ups were strong enough to induce Schwab to purchase Montgomery-Shoshone for a price that was undisclosed but said to be the most expensive land deal in Nevada's history. "Mr. Schwab at once reorganized the company, took in two adjoining properties that were undeveloped, and changed the capitalization to 500,000 shares of the par value of $5 each," Rice explained. "He, in turn, permitted his friends and the public to subscribe for the new stock at $15 per share. Later the shares advanced to $22 on the New York Curb."

It was during this run-up that Ricecakes and his Nevada bosses hightailed it out of Bullfrog, collapsing stock prices by cashing out shares as they retreated. It would be a year before Schwab fully realized he had been taken, yet—like a typical sucker who did not want to be the last man holding the bag—he continued to exert market influence to salvage as much of his stock's value as he could. Montgomery-Shoshone shares eventually sank to the two- to five-cent range, and George took delight in hearing that Schwab's mucky-muck friends at his private Pittsburgh club were snubbing him for yanking them into such a stinking failure.

For years, Rice and Schwab would carry on a long-distance feud over which of them had more flagrantly exaggerated the prospects of Bullfrog. Rice smeared the steel magnate as a "welcher who pleads the baby act," commencing a character-assassination pattern GG would refine over the coming decades, accusing big-name insiders of the very same frauds he was perpetrating himself.

"Mr. Schwab, at the time he became a promoter of Nevada mines, was an expert steelmaker," Rice chastised in his autobiography. "He knew little or nothing about silver, gold and copper. . . . Possibly Mr. Schwab relied on newspaper accounts, and promoted the property on the strength of them. . . . Mr. Schwab's lack of caution, however, is instructive to the losing speculator. It furnishes a startling example of the danger in banking alone on an honored name for the success of an enterprise, and it also drives home the truth of the adage 'Every shoemaker should stick to his last.'"

The bubble had burst in Bullfrog, but Goldfield kept cranking out profits. Mine production tripled, with ore values topping $15 million. By late 1905, the town's population had soared past twenty thousand, making it Nevada's largest municipality (by contrast, newly incorporated, often misspelled "Los Vegos" struggled to attract *thirty* residents). Goldfield's five-story downtown boasted a French restaurant, a posh theater, vibrant dance halls, and, on one block alone, a raucous red-light district with twenty-five gambling establishments and high-class brothels. Plans for an exorbitant 150-room hotel were in the works, featuring private baths, a lobby lined with solid mahogany, and chefs who would serve exotic delicacies like lobster and quail. The camp was served by five banks, five newspapers, four schools, three railroads, a steam-powered brewery, and churches of all denominations. Postal volume was so crushing that when the mail train pulled in every afternoon at three, the post office pulled the shades and hung out the "Heavy Mail Today" sign, closing until eight-thirty the next morning to sort it.

"It is acknowledged that [my] news bureau accomplished much for Nevada," Rice told anyone who would listen. "As a matter of fact, it is generally conceded by Goldfield pioneers and by mining-stock brokers throughout the country that the news bureau was directly responsible for bringing into the State of Nevada tens of millions of dollars for investment, and was indirectly responsible for the opening up of the Mohawk and other great gold mines of the Goldfield camp."

Prestige aside, it was a private relief to Rice that not a soul in Nevada knew him as a former jailbird and failed racetrack tipster. "I had a youthful past" was his vague reply whenever anybody asked about his background.

George had a close call when the *San Francisco Chronicle* ran an exposé about Bill Arkell that implicated Rice as a shady eastern accomplice, but GG squelched the story by buying up every edition in Goldfield when that day's paper arrived on the inbound train. A few months later, when *The Daily Mining Record* published a series of articles that raised questions about his ethics, Rice sued the publication for libel, and Goldfielders sympathetic to the town's biggest booster ran the reporter out of town.

While George was coasting to kingpin status, he learned his youngest brother, Charles, had settled out west as a mining engineer. Upon graduating from Columbia University's prestigious School of Mines in 1895, Charles had gone to work for an Australian engineering team led by the future U.S. president Herbert C. Hoover. Now, nearly a dozen years after their last conversation, the estranged siblings were traveling in the same professional circles. Each gave the other a wide berth— Charles because the family had disowned the black-sheep brother; George because he was adamant about not allowing anyone from his former life to poison his new one.

Plus, Ricecakes thought his kid brother lacked the chutzpah and imagination to make it big in mining. Charles, despite years of formal schooling, would never grasp what George knew to be the industry's most fundamental maxim: that there were easier ways to acquire gold than by digging for it.

Outwardly, GG was riding high. People were talking about his publicity prowess all across the district. But by his second year in Goldfield, conversations behind his back began taking on a darker tone. Despite the success of his ad agency, anyone who frequented Goldfield's gambling halls knew Rice was hardly getting rich. He had an insatiable appetite for action, and the most baffling aspect of George's addiction to risk was that his vice of choice was faro—a card game so notorious for being rigged in favor of the house that it would be outlawed by every state in the Union except Nevada by 1906.

Today, you'd be hard-pressed to find anyone in America who knows what faro is. But in Rice's time, it was the national card game, played far more widely than poker. Fast paced and easy to learn, faro enticed gamblers with a flurry of high-odds action to close out each game. In its theoretical on-the-level version, the chances of winning were evenly split between players and the house. In practice, this was rarely the case. "If faro were honestly played, it would be one of the prettiest banking games in the world," *Foster's Encyclopedia of Games* explained in 1897. "But unfortunately the money to be made at this game is so great that the richest prizes in the gambling world are offered to the men who can so handle the cards as to 'protect the money of the house.'"

In faro, the house (bank) deals cards off the deck in twos. The first card is considered a "loser" and the next a "winner," alternating like that until only three cards remain in the deck. Multiple players place bets on a layout of the ranks of cards (suits play no role), trying to predict whether the next four (or nine or jack or whatever) will come up in the "loser" or "winner" pile. The house pays even money every time a player bets correctly, but more advanced gamblers can parlay a series of outcomes to increase their odds. An abacus tracks which specific cards remain in the deck, and to win the "final turn," players must predict the exact order in which the last three cards will emerge. Correctly "calling the turn" nets a four-to-one bonus.

The main edge for the house is that if a pair comes up in any turn, the bank gets half the bets placed on that rank and pays off no winners on that turn. Because pairs are the house's chief advantage—and because card-sharp dealers only have to conjure them slightly more often than they naturally turn up to ensure a winning margin—crooked faro evolved as a game that appeared to hinge on short-term randomness while guaranteeing long-run profits for the house.

To covertly mark pairs, dealers lightly sanded the backs of cards or trimmed them to be minutely convex or concave (originating the phrase "playing both ends against the middle"). When players complained of corrupt dealers, a special box was invented to dispense cards (the forerunner of the modern-day casino shoe). But instead of making the game more fair, these devices were gaffed to deceive, spitting out pairs or putting a fifty-third card into play with the press of a hidden lever. Cheating boxes became faro's worst-kept secret, so ubiquitous that gambling supply houses openly advertised them in the back pages of sporting magazines.

"Faro is a hard-hearted monarch whose constant delight appears to be a slaughter of the innocents," the betting guidebook *Sharps and Flats* warned in 1894. "When a man is idiot enough to lose his money, as some do day after day, in a game where his own common sense ought to tell him that he stands every chance of being cheated, he may be looked upon as a hopeless case. There is nothing that will ever knock intelligence into him, or his gambling propensities out of him."

Rice fit the pattern of a bad gambler sucked into faro's vortex. It wasn't that George was unaware he was being rooked; he knew full well faro was fixed and could probably calculate the exact odds against him. Yet night after night, GG sent good money spiraling after bad, relentlessly trying to prove (to himself as well as others) that his superior intellect gave him an edge against a stacked deck.

A fatal attraction to faro was perplexingly common among con artists. "It is indeed strange that men who know so much about the percentage which operates in favor of the professional gambler will risk their freedom for the highly synthetic thrill of bucking the tiger," Maurer wrote in *The Big Con*. "In a word, most of them are suckers for some other branch of the grift. . . . Con men are well aware of this weakness, yet few of them, it seems, are able to curb their gambling instincts and gear their lives down to the speed at which the ordinary citizen lives." When asked why he couldn't quit playing fixed faro, the noted 1870s swindler William "Canada Bill" Jones—a talented cardsharp himself—deadpanned, "It's the only game in town." A generation later in Rice's Nevada, it still was.

F aro was the pastime of practically everybody in Goldfield in those days, and I played for want of some other means of recreation and lost heavily," George admitted. "I found myself gossiped about with [men who] rolled in money one day and were broke the next."

GG probably had a ringside seat at the Tonopah Club when Abe Brown—the casino's off-duty manager—got taken for $300,000 in a five-hour faro frenzy, a loss so devastating ($7.5 million in today's dollars) that it was reported nationwide. In October 1905, Rice became mired in his own devastating losing skid that cost him tens of thousands of dollars. Ashamed and in debt, he decided to bolt for Nevada's newest mining sensation, Manhattan. Eighty miles north of Goldfield, the fledgling camp consisted of three huts, a dozen tents, and wild rumors of mines aglow with gold.

"I bought blankets, a suit of canvas clothes lined with sheepskin, and a folding iron cot, all on credit," Rice recalled. "I packed the outfit off to Tonopah. There I climbed aboard an old rickety stage-coach of the regulation Far-Western type, and started for Manhattan. We rode over a snow-clad desert, up mountains and down canyons—a perilous journey that I would not care to duplicate. The $10 I had in my pocket, after paying my fare, was borrowed money. When I arrived that night at Manhattan, situated in a canyon at an altitude of 7,000 feet, I set up my cot on the snow, wrapped myself in my blankets and slept in the open."

The next morning George was dazzled by piles of ore with gold visible to the naked eye—or at least that's the story he told back in Goldfield after handpicking a few impressive samples and acquiring some cheap mining rights.

"The Stray Dog, the Jumping Jack and the Dexter were the three principal producers," Rice affirmed. "They honeycombed one another. [The prospectors] informed me that there was one group of claims adjoining that could be bought for $5,000. With $10 in my pocket I proceeded to purchase it. I gave a check for $100, signed a contract to pay the balance of $5,000 in 30 days or forfeit the $100, and immediately started back to Goldfield to induce the president of the bank to honor my check on presentation. He did."

George persuaded a local jeweler to display his specimens in the store's front window. He then had his publicity bureau telegraph news of Manhattan's brilliance to a long chain of newspapers.

"There was great excitement, and before night a stampede from Goldfield to Manhattan ensued which in magnitude surpassed the first Goldfield rush," Rice noted with satisfaction. "A few days later I returned to Manhattan and sold my option for $20,000 cash. . . . I was again in funds as the result of my profits in the Manhattan boom, and it was again my wont, for want of any other pastime, to play faro at night."

At the Palace bar in Goldfield, Rice's frequent need for credit got him acquainted with Lawrence M. Sullivan, the club's bombastic boss. Sullivan, forty-two, was a loud, intimidating former prizefighter from Oregon who had acquired the nickname Shanghai Larry during his days running a boardinghouse on the Portland docks. Sullivan's racket was to befriend arriving sailors, then drug them with liquor laced with knockout drops. A day or two later, the groggy crewmen awoke captive on ships bound for the South China Sea, with Sullivan having pocketed the blood money for selling them into forced labor. When this line of work became too costly (in terms of bribes he had to pay public officials), Sullivan relocated to Goldfield, figuring he could capitalize by cornering the market on girls, booze, and betting. He and George hit it off immediately.

Ricecakes was chummy enough with Sullivan that when he won, he often asked Larry to lock up his winnings in the Palace bar safe so he'd have a stash set aside for the next night. One evening, Sullivan took $2,500 in gold pieces from George, matched it with an equal amount of his own, and implored Rice to let him in on his next mining deal.

"Put that money in a sack," George instructed without hesitation. "Go and get that big coonskin coat of yours, take a night ride by automobile to Tonopah, and in the morning go by stage to Manhattan. When you get there look up the owner of the Jumping Jack mine. I have met him. He is a member of the Ancient Order of Hibernians. An Irishman can buy that property from him much cheaper than anybody else. You go and buy it."

The asking price was $85,000. Sullivan, after lubricating his Emerald Isle compatriot with numerous toasts to their homeland, returned to Goldfield with a contract to purchase Jumping Jack for $45,000 with only $5,000 down.

"At this juncture Sullivan, who knew as much about the mining promotion and mining brokerage business as an ostrich knows about ocean tides, inquired what my next move would be," Rice gloated. "Sullivan seemed to be bewildered, yet full of faith."

George talked the saloonkeeper into opening the L. M. Sullivan Trust Company, with Larry fronting a get-rich-quick clearinghouse for GG's stock shenanigans. In February 1906, the firm started promoting Jumping Jack, Stray Dog, and other dubious Manhattan stocks. Utter ignorance about mining didn't stop Sullivan from spouting balderdash whenever journalists called with serious questions, yet Rice could only cringe because he wanted to remain shielded behind the loudmouthed figurehead. "Right now I've got a whole carload of winzes coming in to rush development work on a half dozen properties," Shanghai Larry once boasted to a group of investors—unaware that a winze is a hole in the ground, a vertical shaft between mine levels, and not some piece of equipment that arrived via train.

Once Rice got a taste of promoting his own mines, he felt less inclined to plant rosy news dispatches about those of his competitors. In turn, Nevada's power brokers began to align against him, and the Goldfield exchange refused to list most Sullivan Trust securities because the underlying properties were so spurious. This was fine by Rice, who was aiming for higher visibility on the San Francisco exchange. GG had dusted off his sucker list from Maxim & Gay and was actively courting his highest rollers. So long as Sullivan Trust raked in more money from speculators than it spent on gaudy advertising, the firm's precarious house of cards remained standing.

Rice insisted on luxurious offices, complete with all the trappings of turn-of-the-twentieth-century technology. He aspired to make Sullivan Trust the Nevada headquarters for visiting eastern brokers and encouraged them to use the firm's lounge and telephone. This allowed George to listen in by lifting the extension in his adjoining office. When it was reported to him that one broker was doing the same to him, Rice became bent on getting revenge and a good laugh at the expense of his adversary.

J. C. Weir was the dean of New York mining-stock brokers. Sullivan Trust had extended to his firm an option to buy 100,000 shares of Stray Dog at forty-five cents. On March 13, 1906, George had Larry use a phone elsewhere in town to relay a private message to their engineer at Manhattan, Jack Campbell, instructing him to call the office with a fake report about a blockbuster development. "We've just struck six feet of $2,000 ore!" Campbell shouted into his phone while a wide-eyed Weir eavesdropped on Rice's extension. "It's a whale! Never saw a mine as big as this one in my life! Don't sell any more Stray Dog at under $5 a share!"

In a stage whisper, George ordered his engineer to pipe down. "Don't tell your mother, and don't let any more miners down the shaft," he instructed. "Close it up until I'm able to buy back some of that stock I sold cheap."

GG hung up and tried to hold back a sly smile. When they heard Weir start to scurry out of the lounge, Rice and Sullivan stepped into the hallway and casually asked the broker for a favor.

"Weir," Rice said nonchalantly, "your option on Stray Dog expires on the fifteenth at noon. So far, your New York office has ordered only 85,000 shares of the 100,000 that were allotted to you. We have decided to close subscriptions on the moment and wish you would wire your New York office not to sell any more."

Weir tried to bluff his way out.

"You are wrong!" he stammered. "Why, when I left New York we had oversold our entire allotment! If the office has not notified you of this, it has been a slip. We will, in fact, need at least 25,000 shares more."

"You can't have them," Rice countered.

"Not in a thousand years!" wailed Sullivan.

George had someone tail Weir while the broker scrambled to send coded messages to New York. Sullivan then spent the entire next day with Weir and grudgingly "allowed" himself to be bribed into letting the broker have all the stock he wanted, vowing to go behind Rice's back to get it if he had to. Just before the options were set to expire, Sullivan Trust shipped twenty-five thousand shares of Stray Dog to Weir Brothers & Company at forty-five cents a share. Weir was convinced he was acquiring stock whose value was ten times what he paid for it. George and Larry knew the stock was barely worth one-tenth its sale price.

GG probably lit up a celebratory Optimo cigar and pondered how he could further exploit Weir's confidence. Rice had parlayed a meager amount of capital into a pyramid of paper profits on the San Francisco exchange, and now he had mining's most prominent market mover strung up like a marionette. If there was a force that could derail such an artful fleecing, he couldn't conceive of it.

In fact, no one could have seen the crushing blow coming: The shock that blindsided Sullivan Trust came from four hundred miles away just before dawn on April 18, 1906.

At 5:12 A.M., the most devastating earthquake in American history leveled San Francisco, killing at least three thousand people. Eighty percent of the city—497 blocks—lay in ruins.

One notable exception was the fifteen-story granite stock exchange, the tallest building in California. Miraculously, not one of its ten prismatic windows—imported from Europe and said to be the largest single panes of glass west of Chicago—had cracked. But the paper contents of the structure, representing billions of dollars in banking records, weren't so lucky.

Once the ground stopped shaking, brokers rushed in to salvage stock certificates. But it soon became difficult to distinguish between legitimate businessmen and looters, and police had orders to shoot anyone suspected of ransacking. Then the danger to paperwork became rapidly spreading fires sparked by severed gas lines, which were raging out of control because water mains had snapped too. The third wave of peril came in the form of untrained firefighters who detonated dynamite in misguided attempts to create firebreaks. The haphazard explosions instead only fanned the flames.

"The San Francisco Stock Exchange, which was the principal market for Manhattan mining shares, was compelled to discontinue business for over two months," Rice lamented. "Brokers and transfer companies lost their records, and the coast's property and money loss was so appalling that no more money was forthcoming from that direction for mining enterprises. Every bank in Nevada closed down, just as every California bank did. . . . Nevada banks, as a rule, had cleared through San Francisco banks, and practically all of Nevada's cash was tied up by the catastrophe. The Sullivan Trust Company faced a crisis."

George and Larry's enterprise had been built not on actual cash but on the illusion of it. The only currency they could put their hands on was $8,000 in gold coins locked in the office vault.

But two days after the quake, when Larry dialed the combination and yanked open the iron door, he found only $1,500.

Ricecakes hadn't yet told his partner of his latest extravagant gamble: Even as San Francisco smoldered, George was betting $6,500 on the purchase of a custom Pope-Toledo touring automobile. He intended to race it across Death Valley as a publicity gimmick.

In the aftermath of the earthquake, a disquieting unease settled over Goldfield. A smattering of production continued at the better-funded mines, but wheeling and dealing in new endeavors ceased entirely, sapping the camp of its entrepreneurial spirit. Rice and Sullivan sweated out the crisis as best they could, but because most folks in town were in a similar bind, their illiquidity did not stand out.

"For two months we eked out a bare subsistence by the direct sale of Manhattan securities at reduced prices to the Eastern brokers," George wrote. "Then the clouds rolled by. No sooner did the San Francisco Stock Exchange open for business than it became possible for the Sullivan Trust Company to borrow some much needed cash on Manhattan securities, of which it had a plethora."

Goldfield was still Nevada's best-producing camp, and its reflected glory was the only reason there was an appetite for Manhattan stocks. In addition to the securities that traded on national markets, Goldfield boasted 175 highly speculative "cat and dog" stocks on the town's several unlisted exchanges, and the whooping, screeching, speaking-in-tongues babble of the Northern Saloon trading sessions could once again be heard through the swinging barroom doors from blocks away.

"Castle-building and fumes of fancy usurped reason," George cracked, scoffing at the commoners he had whipped into an overzealous frenzy. "The camp was rapidly becoming drunk with the joy of fortune-making."

Rice believed it was imperative for mining stocks to be front and center in the national news as the San Francisco exchange reopened.

This is where conquering Death Valley with his gleaming new Pope-Toledo fit in.

The horseless carriage was making over—and taking over—America. GG believed it was critical for mining to adopt the latest technologies to be perceived as a modern, forward-thinking industry, and the subliminal advantage of associating the automobile's mark of social distinction with mining made cooking up a scheme involving a car a no-brainer for Rice.

Sullivan Trust was branching out and had a new camp to promote at Emigrant Springs in Death Valley. But Rice was fearful the public would be put off by the idea of investing in "the earth's inferno." To prove that mining in the hottest place on the planet was not only feasible but bold and courageous, George's solution was to script a 250-mile treasure hunt through the rugged Nevada hills into California, across the searing unknown of the valley floor, then up the steep volcanic ash ridgeline of the Panamint Mountains.

Considering that in 1906 *any* automobile trek into Death Valley was a life-threatening risk, it was preposterous to think that Rice would send a team of motormen careening across the open desert in a gasoline-powered buggy. But the genius of George's plan was not so much the stunt itself as the compelling description of it that he planted in newspapers nationwide. The widely published adventure captivated readers like the best pulp fiction of the day, and for all anyone knows a century later, the Death Valley motor rally might have been entirely made up. The only surviving accounts are derived from "special correspondence" written by George himself. Without independent corroboration, there's a strong chance the Pope-Toledo was nothing more than an expensive prop for an elaborate hoax.

The top-of-the-line Pope-Toledo for 1906 was the Type XII Chrome Nickel Steel model, a seven-passenger powerhouse that did not skimp on luxuries like cushioned seating, brass control knobs, and acetylene-fueled headlamps. George told everybody the car had an eighty-horsepower engine (it was advertised at forty), and he liked to point out the manufacturer's guarantee that buyers got with it "the assurance that your right of way on any road, anywhere, is absolute."

Rice had the car fitted with chains, tools, a shovel, a block and tackle, winter robes, blankets, spare canisters of water, and a professional chauffeur. George claimed the Death Valley trek began spontaneously just before midnight on June 15, when the Pope-Toledo screeched to a halt in front of the Sullivan Trust headquarters and Jack Campbell, the firm's engineer from Manhattan, sprinted out bearing crucial news.

The story went like this: An Emigrant Springs prospector was selling the rights to a spectacular new strike on the far side of Death Valley, and the first claims dealer to make it through with a decent offer would win the most lucrative gold mine in the region. Sullivan, supposedly presiding over a late-night board meeting, decided to dash off immediately when Campbell told him rival developers were already on the way. A Utah newspaper named (ironically) the *Truth* was one of many that ran Rice's exaggerated account verbatim:

> *Seizing a box of cigars and his big automobile leather coat, [Sullivan] stepped into the machine. A short stop was made at the garage to take on extra tires and gasoline, and then the big machine . . . buzzed out into the open country. . . . The two men leaned forward in the tonneau, their teeth crunching upon their cigars. At intervals with short exclamations they urged the chauffeur on. The latter, a long, thin fellow, all humped up, as if eternally cutting his way through a recalcitrant atmosphere, drove like a demon. At times the iron flaps covering the engine raised with the friction of the air, and she seemed to fly on extended wings. Above, the stars blazed. . . . On each side, distorted cacti lurked in the shadow like huge tarantulas.*

They gunned the first eighty miles in three hours (the "vertiginous speed" George described calculates to twenty-six miles per hour). Crossing the Amargosa riverbed, the Pope-Toledo blew a rear tire, but the chauffeur expertly repaired it. The trio roared through Beatty, leaving a cloud of dust and the baying of startled dogs in their wake. At 3:00 A.M., they stopped for breakfast and gas in Rhyolite.

They started off again with the green sky of dawn behind them and whirred down a dry wash through a canyon of red walls. The enfevered breath of the still-invisible valley struck their faces, as if she were hissing a warning to them.

After a while the canyon walls opened, and Death Valley was below them—a huge bowl, its bottom leprous with some loathsome-hued sediment. They whirred on, down a wash of black flint rock; with each lunge of the machine they entered a layer of air hotter than the preceding 'til they panted as at the finish of a mile run.

They rolled on, and the mountains rose on all sides, veiled, painted mysterious mountains. Finally they were at the bottom, one hundred feet below sea level, and stopped at Stove Pipe Spring, a hole in the sand from which a little black water oozed.

Larry and Jack had made arrangements for a mule team to meet them for a supply stock up. Half a mile later, they hit sand dunes, and the Pope-Toledo got hopelessly stuck, its wheels spinning furiously. They shoveled away as much sand as they could and laid down gunnysacks for traction. Campbell and Sullivan shoved from behind, while the chauffeur stomped on the accelerator.

The car leaped forward all of three feet before bogging down again.

The men repeated this dig-and-shove process until they had made two hundred yards of progress. Then Larry remembered the mule team.

They ran back, fetched the mules, and roped them to the front axle. The beasts strained. The car wouldn't budge. The harness broke. Sullivan improvised a new one out of a mining pick and hooked it directly to the frame.

The wheels began to take hold, the machine gave a jump, and rolled forward. For a hundred yards it went. Then the mules stopped, ex-

hausted, and the men rolled over, half dead. The perpendicular sun fell on them like drops of molten lead. . . . The heat waves, rolling like gigantic breakers, caused strange illusions. . . . They were in the land of delusions, and everything was false. . . . Before them, far, mysterious as a veiled woman, the Panamint Range rose with its promise of golden splendor.

According to Rice (who was not present but told the tale from an omniscient viewpoint), they worked the mules in hundred-yard bursts for seven miles until the car reconnected with a rocky path.

The team ditched the mules and made up for the lost afternoon. The Pope-Toledo cornered on two wheels and gained extra speed on downgrades. At the bottom of one dip, the trail ended abruptly, and the driver had to slam on the brakes to keep from pitching into an alkali swamp.

After reconnoitering the bog from atop a knoll, they decided their best shot was to make the car as light as possible and gun it across the crusted ooze like a stone skipping atop water. Sullivan and Campbell picked their way across on a footpath while the chauffeur backed to the top of the grade and revved the engine.

Down she came a-roar, like a meteor from the skies. An involuntary cry came from the men in the marsh as she bore down upon them. She cleared the first hundred feet as if with one spring. She slowed, hesitated, yawed from side to side, then, the wheels catching a bit on harder ground, jumped forward again. . . . And thus, by a series of mad leaps, she went almost across. . . . On the further edge, a few feet from safety, she seemed to mire for good. . . . But the men alongside, frenzied, threw their coats, their hats, their shirts beneath the wheels, and slowly, inch by inch, she at length rose upon the hard ground.

Even though the Pope-Toledo's frame was cracked, "everything afterward was easy in comparison." They braced the frame with a shovel handle. When the radiator blew, the men hiked five miles to a cistern, "and their tongues were almost swollen out of their mouths before they reached the little pool of stagnant water." At midnight, exactly twenty-four hours after the journey began, the car skidded into Emigrant Springs. From there, the team hiked several hours to the claim site, "and just at sun-up they were standing upon a monstrous outcropping of gold-bearing quartz."

According to George, Sullivan and Campbell offered the prospector cash, took samples, and finalized the paperwork back at the camp. But Rice refused to end the tall tale there:

> Hardly had they made a preliminary examination and closed the deal [when] the puff-puff of an auto drew them outside of the tent. Slowly, painfully, a crippled automobile was rolling in from the other side of the mountains. Campbell recognized the man in the auto—a confidential agent of Charles M. Schwab, the great steel magnate . . . too late! The race had been won, and just won.

In GG's world, every enthralling adventure—real or imagined—required a villain to be vanquished.

Shanghai Larry pined for the free-swinging days of his prizefighting prime but was trying to bust fewer skulls at the Palace bar now that he was a semi-respectable mining executive. He found a kindred pugilistic spirit in George Lewis "Tex" Rickard, a plainspoken, dapper boxing aficionado who ran the nearby Northern Saloon, and the two often kibitzed about the top fighters of the day. It was common for disputes in mining towns to be settled with bare-knuckle matches, and in the summer of 1906 Larry and Tex partnered to form the Goldfield Athletic Association, hoping organized bouts would bring a few extra bucks into their watering holes.

Rice liked Rickard. They were the same age, thirty-six, and George thought the country-bumpkin "Tex" act was a good front for the saloon-keeper's incisive shrewdness. GG would not be surprised when, over the course of several decades, Rickard blossomed into the preeminent fight promoter in America. But that July in Goldfield, George thought Tex and Larry were way off in terms of scale. Why not aim higher? Why not put up serious money to lure a championship match? Just think of the publicity of the two best boxers in the world slugging each other senseless in triple-digit heat under the broiling desert sun!

Sportswriters, Rice envisioned, would flock to Goldfield to trumpet the camp's rags-to-riches splendor. They could pose the fighters with pickaxes at the mines for flash photographs and host wine-drenched banquets every night. The value of positive press would far exceed the amount spent to stage the extravaganza, which George promised to bankroll if Tex could find the right fighters.

Rickard first tried to lure a popular featherweight from New York, but the boxer's manager had never heard of Goldfield and thought the exorbitant $15,000 purse was a hoax. Then Tex learned Joe "Old Master" Gans, the lightweight world champion, was in San Francisco and looking to defend his title. His most logical challenger, Oscar "Battling" Nelson, was not too far away in Salt Lake City, where he was pummeling palookas as part of a "will fight all comers" vaudeville sideshow. Both sides were agreeable to making the match happen, but there was one potential deal breaker Tex had to run by GG first: Gans was black, and Nelson was white.

Mixed-race prizefights had occurred before 1906 but never at a high-profile level. Gans, boxing's first black champion, won the title fairly in 1902, but supremacists had been trying to strip him of the honor. When Jimmy Britt, a white California fighter, lost because he fouled Gans in 1904, supporters claimed Britt was the true champion because only a technicality had prevented him from winning. Then, in 1905, Nelson knocked out Britt, and Battling commandeered the moniker "white world champ." For months, newspapers had been clamoring for a Gans-Nelson fight to settle the matter, but no promoter would make the match, and Rickard wasn't sure how Rice would respond to the idea of Goldfield's being portrayed as a proving ground for racial equality.

George did, in fact, have a strong reaction: He nearly swallowed his cigar in excitement.

A black-versus-white title fight was better than anything he could have scripted. GG had no intention of characterizing Gans-Nelson as a unifying event. Instead, he would bill the championship as a battle for racial superiority: a desert fight to the death, if necessary. The race angle would be an easy sell in 1906 America, and it didn't really matter to Rice which boxer won so long as the match turned Goldfield into a household name. He authorized Rickard to double the purse and to schedule the bout for Labor Day.

As different as the two boxers were in skin color, they were just as polarizing in fighting styles. The graceful, Baltimore-born Gans possessed fast hands that unleashed five-punch combinations with precision and power. Even at age thirty-one, his low center of gravity and exceptional reach allowed him to control brawnier opponents from the center of the ring. The essayist H. L. Mencken praised the Old Master as "probably the greatest boxer who ever lived." Even today, more than a century after his reign, Gans still tops many experts' lists as the most artistically gifted lightweight ever.

Nelson, twenty-four, had none of Gans's agility but immeasurably more raw savagery. Born in Denmark but raised in Chicago, he ran away as an adolescent to join the circus, where he fought toughs from the crowd for spare change. He won his first pro bout at fourteen, gaining a reputation as a brawler who fought dirty and fouled often. Weighing barely more than a jockey, Nelson was said to have an unusually thick skull, and after his vicious punch-out of Britt the journalist Jack London described him as an "abysmal brute . . . callous to pain and shock." Battling's strategy was to flail for his opponent's head while barely bothering to defend his own, grinning maniacally through distorted, pulpy features. When a reporter asked him about taking on a black man for the championship, Nelson, true to form, replied crudely, "All coons look alike to me—and this one I really want to clean."

Although Gans was the champion, Nelson was white, so his handlers got to call the shots. Nelson's manager first insisted that the ring be as small as possible, which would take away Gans's maneuverability. Then he pushed for not one weigh-in (the standard) but *three* separate weigh-ins on the afternoon of the fight, with a $5,000 forfeit if either boxer was over 133 pounds (Nelson never had any problem making weight, but Gans routinely struggled; the final weigh-in would be right before opening bell, giving the champ no time to rehydrate). Further to Nelson's advantage, the match was to be a "finish fight" with no set number of rounds, continuing until one man was knocked unconscious or couldn't step up to the mark. But the most outrageous demand was the prize money itself: Of a record $33,500 purse, Nelson was to receive two-thirds, win or lose. Not only did Gans have to defend his championship under tactically detrimental terms, but he had to do so for half as much money as his challenger was guaranteed.

As soon as the deal was inked, Rice instructed Rickard to have a local bank stack up the value of the purse in $20 gold coins, then photograph the dazzling pyramid for distribution to the press. If Goldfield was going to host the richest prizefight in the history of the sport, they had better let the world know about it.

Even though there was no arena in which to stage the fight, hotels sold out within days. A dust bowl next to a graveyard on the outskirts of camp was transformed into a seventy-two-hundred-seat wooden amphitheater. The train yard was expanded with enough siding to park two hundred Pullman cars, and a vast swath of scrubland was cleared for temporary lodging. Society swells who weren't quick enough to make proper reservations would have to rough it in tents the way George did when he first arrived in the mining camps.

Rice was inundated with offers from opportunists who wanted a crack at Goldfield's captive gamblers over the long holiday weekend.

Among the proposals George turned down were a Thoroughbred race meet with horses shipped across the mountains from California, a cock-fighting tourney with champion roosters from Mexico, and (in keeping with the racial angle) "an offer from Neromus, a New York negro who has the reputation of rough-house wrestling . . . to wrestle with some wild bull for the edification of the crowd."

One newfangled technology fascinated George—moving pictures. Rickard recognized that "foto fights" were about to become big business, and he persuaded Rice to contract with the Miles Brothers film company out of San Francisco to record the championship with hand-cranked cameras. As promoters, they would own the rights to distribute the silent panorama to nickelodeons across the country, which, if the match turned out exciting, would bring in thousands of dollars in royalties. When advocates for the boxers suggested that the ring be covered by a shade to protect the fighters from the hellish sun, Tex and George nixed the idea out of concerns that a covering would interfere with the quality of the lighting. Rice and Rickard had no idea they were about to pioneer boxing's pay-per-view model, but after the fight the film company had a hunch it might be in possession of a historical record: Miles Brothers mailed a copy of the Gans-Nelson print to the Library of Congress, where to this day the ghostly, herky-jerky footage exists in the public domain, freely available on the Internet.

GG let Rickard and Sullivan control the boxing while he concentrated on pushing suckers toward Goldfield stocks. Larry's key assignments were to handle Gans and oversee the selection of the referee, and he was in his element. "Prize-fighting suited his tastes better than high finance," Rice remarked. "And he was as busy as a one-armed paper-hanger with the itch."

On August 7, 1906, Gans pulled in to Goldfield on the 9:15 P.M. train. Joe always made it a point to carry himself in a dignified manner everywhere he went, yet the champ knew many whites tolerated him only as a "good nigger." His one crushing vice was gambling, and he routinely squandered his fight winnings, but the Old Master always retained enough to maintain a fine three-piece suit, complete with diamond stickpin, gold pocket watch, and a jaunty derby. Gans peered out at the dust-crusted faces on the platform—all white, with tough, hardened features—and wasn't quite sure what he was getting himself into. The local papers had been running absurd caricatures of him as a wild-eyed darky who had taken some dives, and the thought must have briefly raced through his head that they were there to lynch him, not greet him.

Big, booming Larry was first to embrace the champ as he stepped off the train, and the garrulous crowd broke into hip hip hoorays. Sullivan wanted to set the tone for how Gans should be treated, and hereafter the newspapers only ran sketches of the black boxer as an elegant gentleman. While in training, Gans was welcomed everywhere he went, but only after Shanghai Larry whisked him into the Pope-Toledo and over to Sullivan Trust, where he and GG planned to wise him up in private.

Larry knew that Gans was broke and had recently fired his manager. So after he introduced him to George, the first thing Sullivan did was guarantee that he and Rice would put up the required $5,000 weigh-in bond on his behalf.

Gans was relieved and expressed his gratitude. He had no idea this was the "slipping the convincer" part of turning a man's confidence.

Larry, in the kindliest tone of which he was capable, then let Gans know that because his firm was footing the bill, he would now be in control as the Old Master's new manager.

"If you lose," Sullivan promised Gans, looking him straight in the eye, "you'll never get out of Goldfield alive."

Gans tried to make a joke about being able to beat Nelson one-handed. Shanghai Larry lowered his bulk over the seated lightweight and bent down face-to-face so there would be no misunderstanding.

"My friends are gonna bet a *ton* of money on you," he asserted, drawing out his words emphatically "They will *kill* you if you don't beat Nelson by a *mile*."

"If I had any money," the champ replied, locking Larry's gaze, "I'd bet it on myself."

Sullivan glanced at Rice, who beckoned him for a whispered conference.

The saloonkeeper returned beaming a broad smile.

"Are you willing to prove your good intentions, Joe?" Larry asked.

"How can I do that, boss? Like I told you, I ain't got a quarter."

"If you're on the level, Joe, you can prove it by turning over your end of the purse to me to bet on yourself at the best odds I can get. How about it?"

"Why not?" conceded Gans, who knew he didn't really have a choice.

Nelson arrived in Goldfield a week after Gans but couldn't find a suitable spot to train. He tried to rent a storeroom at the local brewery. Then he switched to the town swimming pool, but the water was rancid because the pool was right next to the slaughterhouse. Realizing he was in a pinch, the Ladies' Aid guild let the challenger use its auditorium. As a gesture of thanks, Nelson said he would open his makeshift gym to guild members so the fairer sex could see what a prizefighter's training looked like.

This seemingly innocuous invitation ignited a morals firestorm, complete with picketing clergymen enraged that the good ladies of Goldfield might get a glimpse of a boxer's bare chest. But the protesters were trampled by the eighty or so women who barged past them into the gym, and Rice seized on the controversy by announcing that Gans-Nelson would, in fact, be the first championship to welcome female spectators.

Sullivan gave Gans some walking-around money that the Old Master parlayed into a few grand shooting dice. Joe wired some of his winnings home to his mother in Baltimore, who replied with a good-luck telegram that included a curious reference to pork. Rice had never heard the phrase before but liked the way it sounded. He shared it with the press, and "Bring home the bacon!" got repeated in newspapers—and rooted in the American lexicon—as a popular rallying cry.

Larry's next priority was to get the referee in the champ's corner.

Oddly enough, Sullivan set about accomplishing this by spreading malicious lies about George Siler, one of the most respected officials in the sport.

At Nelson's suggestion, Gans had agreed to have Siler officiate. The ref was already on his way from Chicago, but Sullivan was overruling Gans. Several days before the fight, Larry summoned the cadre of out-of-town reporters to the Sullivan Trust offices, where he accused Siler of being a vehement bigot who would never give Gans a fair shake.

"I'm four-flushing about that race-prejudice yarn, but it won't do any harm," Larry said, chuckling, to George as the newspapermen scuttled out to report the brouhaha. "He's broke and I'll make him eat out of my hand before I'll agree to let him referee the fight. They've already invited Siler to come here, and I won't be able to get another referee, but I'll beat them at their own game. When Siler gets here I'll thrash matters out with him and agree to his selection. But first I want him to know who's boss."

Upon arrival, the ref was summoned to a closed-door meeting. Siler and Sullivan argued back and forth about the ref's ability to be objective. Then the topic turned to Nelson's flagrant fouling. To prove his fairness—and how much he wanted the job—Siler pledged to give Gans "the benefit of every doubt." Larry feigned reluctance but relented, knowing the seeds of partisanship had been planted.

"But, remember," Sullivan said, glowering, "if you don't keep your word you'll have just as much chance of getting out of this town alive as Gans will have if he lays down! You understand?"

Siler, straw hat in hand, nodded yes.

Goldfield was swarming with fight fans as Labor Day approached. Special trains had been chartered from as far away as Chicago and St. Paul, and Southern Pacific Railroad affixed wooden benches to open flatbeds for no-frills transportation. Miners walked across the desert for days from rival camps, and on Goldfield's main drag they brushed with New York millionaires and professional gamblers. The camp's roulette wheels spun, its faro banks dealt doctored pairs, and counterfeit money passed so freely that no one bothered to police it. Haps, the Chinese opium dealer, couldn't keep up with the insatiable demand for narcotics, and the working gals of Goldfield didn't sleep a wink, even though they spent the entire weekend in bed. For the first time since the camp was founded, talk was dominated by something other than gold. Just like with mining, everyone thought he was an expert on boxing.

The early betting had favored Nelson, but the so-called smart money was swinging the odds in favor of Gans by a two-to-one margin. There were persistent rumors that one fighter or the other would be doped or take a dive, and the gossip was a boon for bet takers because backers of the challenger suddenly wanted to hedge with wagers on the champ and those who at first fancied Gans now made last-minute saver bets on Nelson. Rice and Sullivan bet a total of $45,000 on Gans and booked an additional $32,500 from those wanting to wager against him. Depending on the odds, Sullivan Trust stood to win or lose roughly $80,000 ($2 million in today's dollars) on the outcome.

On the morning of September 3, 1906, Goldfield's twenty-piece fireman's band bleated a cacophony of marching music from the balcony of the Miners' Union Hall as a dust-choked standstill of humans, horses, burros, and automobiles inched toward the amphitheater. In hundred-degree heat, news rippled through the jam that men would not be allowed to bring firearms into the arena, and there was a wave of disbelief when word got out that no saloons would remain open during the fight. To the best of anyone's recollection, the bars had *never* closed in the three-year history of Goldfield. But there wouldn't be any customers to serve, because even those without tickets were planning to hike the steep hillside to watch the fight from afar. Every other business in camp would similarly shut down, the lone exception being the telegraph office. It would remain staffed not only to transmit round-by-round updates to the outside world but because George was insistent that the incoming crush of buy orders for Goldfield stocks be processed immediately. He saw no sense in taking a holiday from bilking suckers, even on Labor Day.

The preliminary matches were interspersed with the championship weigh-ins. Nelson made 133 pounds comfortably, while Gans had to sweat every ounce. The Old Master took no chances, shaving all hair from his head, face, and body. He did not tape his hands, wore no socks, and tied his ring shoes with thin string instead of sturdy laces. At the final weigh-in, Gans tipped the scales four ounces below the limit, barely escaping forfeit.

The semifinal was supposed to go fifteen rounds but ended with a knockout in two. That meant over an hour wait in the shimmering Nevada sun for the 7,491 spectators, plus the uncounted thousands jamming the hillsides. Men at ringside removed their suit coats (but wouldn't dream of removing ties), and the several hundred ladies in attendance took shelter beneath gaily colored parasols, the only slivers of shade save for a sturdy umbrella in each pugilist's corner. Celebrities in the audience included Kermit Roosevelt, son of the U.S. president, Teddy, and the star vaudeville comedian Nat Goodwin. Both were prolific drunkards; GG had extended invitations to each because both were in his confidence-swindling crosshairs for future fleecings.

Spectators began to circulate fevered falsehoods: Gans had dropped dead from fright. Nelson and his manager had been spotted boarding an outbound train. Bets continued to pour in, and when the fighters finally appeared, the crowd's reaction gave away the favorite: Gans, in light blue trunks and clutching something in his fist, was greeted with a lusty ovation. Nelson, wearing pale green and a sneer, entered to catcalls and heckling.

Sullivan called for attention through a megaphone, then promptly became paralyzed by stage fright. Larry intended to warn the crowd that three hundred lawmen would be policing the grounds, but he mispronounced so many officious words that ringside wiseguys were snickering before he got halfway through. Then he botched the reading of telegrams sent by absent dignitaries. Crimson, Sullivan rushed through the remainder of his spiel so fast that he was out of the ring before Nelson's manager could remind him he had forgotten to introduce the boxers for the title fight. After the match, Rice would wisecrack that "announcer Sullivan's attempt to reach lofty flights of eloquence" cost the firm $100,000 in lost stock business.

Within earshot of as many people as could hear him, Gans stepped up to make his own announcement: He would not accept anyone from his corner throwing in the towel on his behalf. To underscore he would be fighting on the level, Gans unwrapped what was in his fist—$2,000 from his dice winnings that he wanted to wager man-to-man with Nelson. The challenger's manager testily swatted away the champ's side bet, and when Gans reached out to shake hands, Nelson refused to touch gloves.

A t 3:23 P.M., the opening bell clanged, and the fight was on.
For several perplexed seconds, Nelson took a stance that suggested he was actually going to try to box with the artful Gans. Then two searing jabs from Gans brought Nelson to his senses, and he reverted to his classic battering ram style, leading with his head while uncorking telegraphed haymakers. The challenger took more punishment, but it was the champ who headed to his corner with a thin stream of blood seeping from his mouth at the end of round 1. Assistants furiously fanned the fighters with towels, and the crowd settled back, relieved to be rewarded with the expected primitive spectacle.

Nelson charged out aggressively for round 2, but Gans darted away at impossible angles. Nelson's manager kept screaming, "Butt him, don't let him get away!" The Old Master drilled three- and five-punch combos, but the body blows Battling managed to land were so jarring that even Gans had to resort to clinching just to get a breather.

The second round concluded with Nelson bleeding from both ears. By the fourth, he was spitting blood. By the seventh, his face was sliced to ribbons, but the trancelike leer affixed to his lips signaled the brute was impervious to pain. Gans peppered him with staccato precision, and Nelson flailed wildly, content to rely on a low-percentage, high-impact barrage he knew would wear down the champ if the fight lasted long enough.

The first knockdown came in round 8 when Gans socked Nelson with a right-cross-left-hook combo. But Battling leveraged his rage to turn the momentum of the fight. Both boxers started throwing a fantastic flurry of punches, but Nelson was now landing them at a four-to-one ratio. Siler warned Nelson repeatedly about butting.

In the twelfth, Battling slipped, and the Old Master could have belted him squarely in the temple. Instead, Gans graciously extended a hand to help him up. Back on his feet, Nelson refused to release Gans's wrist and began bashing away at the champ's solar plexus with his free fist.

"It was a vicious trick and it caught Gans utterly unprepared," the *Los Angeles Examiner* reported. "Gans staggered back with a bewildered look on his face. There were hisses and boos from all over the wooden arena. But at the bell the Battler kicked Gans in the shins and Joe kicked back at him."

The next few rounds were a blur of elbows, arm twists, and low blows, all inflicted by Nelson and protested by Sullivan. When Gans and Nelson locked together and fell between the ropes, the crowd heaved them back into the ring. At round 20, one hour into the fight, Nelson's eyes began to swell shut. Gans, though, was breathing harder and appeared more sapped stamina-wise.

As was the custom of the day, bookies took wagers throughout the match, and the men who represented Sullivan Trust had been instructed to keep supporting Gans by accepting bets on Nelson. "This doesn't look like the cinch for Gans you said it would be," a concerned Rice murmured to Sullivan. Larry visited the champ between rounds to get a firsthand update.

"Gans says he can't win this fight, but he won't lose," Sullivan reported. "Don't bet any more money. I'm going to stay close to the ringside. Watch close."

At the end of round 23, Nelson floored Gans, and the champ would have been counted out had he not been saved by the bell. In round 28, the sun dipped behind the Montezuma Mountains, and Gans ripped a vicious salvo that sent Nelson reeling. As the fight approached the two-hour mark, fans across the country hovered outside telegraph and newspaper offices for updates. By round 30, the moving picture company began to worry that the miles of film it had brought would not be enough to record the finish.

In round 33, Gans was methodically beating Nelson's face to jelly. The champ lined up the dazed challenger and slammed a piston-like right into his forehead.

This was it, the crowd sensed, rising to a crescendo.

Then Gans backed off and stopped fighting.

The Old Master was in distress, hopping around on his right leg as if his left were badly injured. Nelson, too weak to capitalize, could only end the round by clinching. Gans limped to his corner and refused to tell anyone what had happened.

The last good punch Gans had thrown would have been enough to knock out any other mortal. But because of Battling's abnormally thick skull, the force instead shattered the champ's fist. A raw, searing jolt shot up his arm, but Gans camouflaged the agony by pretending the pain was from his opposite leg. This was his way of conning Nelson, who would attack him relentlessly on the right if he knew Gans could barely hold up his glove, let alone throw or deflect a punch with that hand.

The next eight or nine rounds swirled in a miasma of heat, pain, and delirium. The champ vomited over the ropes between rounds. At six o'clock, dusk settled over Goldfield. Nelson was fighting half-blind, Gans one-handed—just as he had joked he could in GG's office. Nelson's weapon of choice was almost exclusively his skull, and Gans, uncomplaining most of the fight, now started to demand that Siler enforce the butting rules. Sullivan, too, was lacing into the ref from the Old Master's corner, and everyone in the arena could hear his full-throated roar as he menaced the ref about keeping his promise.

At the start of round 42, Gans smashed Nelson with a jackhammer left, and the two locked in another exhausted clinch. Nelson let his right hand slip to his side and shot it upward in a half-scissors hook, nailing Gans three times squarely between the legs. "He went down in sections, like an imploding building," is how the Associated Press described the champ's collapse to the canvas. Gans writhed and clutched his groin before briefly losing consciousness.

Siler stood over Gans and began counting to ten.

"Now, Siler, you saw that foul didn't you? It's a foul, isn't it?" Sullivan bellowed, leaping into the ring to confront the ref. "Gans wins, doesn't he?"

The ref recognized Sullivan's animalistic rage as a palpable threat and not a rhetorical question. Pale as a ghost, he whispered something inaudible and nodded his head.

Then Siler helped Gans to his feet and raised the champ's arm in victory.

"Gentlemen, the referee declares Gans the winner on a foul!" Sullivan exulted.

The crowd roared its approval. At two hours forty-eight minutes, the sunburned throng had just witnessed the longest championship fight of the twentieth century. The forty-two-round record still stands, a mark that will never be broken. ("Finish fights" went out of vogue shortly after Gans-Nelson. The championship standard then became fifteen rounds for most of the twentieth century. Since 1987, globally recognized matches have been capped at twelve rounds.)

"It was as clear a foul as I ever saw, and I could do nothing except disqualify Nelson," Siler later insisted, saving face. "It was my only possible course."

In Goldfield, no one outside Nelson's entourage protested. But across the country, the announcement of Gans's win sparked waves of race rioting.

In Nelson's hometown, one thousand blacks and whites clashed through the night with clubs and stones before Chicago cops could restore order. In New York, dozens of accounts of mayhem were reported, including one in which Staten Island police arrived just as a mob had looped a noose around the neck of a black Gans supporter.

Newspapers blamed the violence on Negroes whose "excess of joy at the triumph of a black man had been permitted to bubble over." For months, years, and even decades afterward, conspiracy-minded supremacists would claim the Library of Congress fight film had been doctored to include phantom below-the-belt blows that Nelson never really threw.

To many Americans, this stranger-than-fiction prizefight—like Goldfield itself—was nothing more than an elaborate mirage in a far-off, mystical desert.

The day after the marathon fight, Rice should have been basking in Goldfield's radiant publicity. Instead, he was furious and holed up in his office trying to stanch six-figure stock losses. From GG's perspective, the low blows Gans had suffered were nothing compared with the sucker punch his Nevada enemies had just blindsided him with.

The stock ploy Rice envisioned in concert with the boxing match was supposed to be an old-fashioned "pump and dump." George and Larry had incorporated a round of worthless companies, allotting themselves large blocks of stock at no cost. Rice then bought full-page ads touting the Sullivan Trust stocks alongside the prefight publicity, betting that the Goldfield name recognition would attract speculators. Once the dupes started buying in, prices would rise. Then, over a period of weeks, Rice and Sullivan planned to cash out, earning back many more times their advertising costs while letting the underlying securities free-fall into insolvency.

But George had not foreseen that Nevada insiders would be quietly accumulating large chunks of shares along with the suckers and that Senator Nixon and his cronies were conspiring to collapse the market before Rice could do the same to small-scale investors. The power brokers wasted no time, yanking the bottom out from under Sullivan Trust with a massive stock sell-off barely twelve hours after the championship. The Nixon/Wingfield contingent might even have lost money on this orchestrated gutting, but a modest up-front loss was worth it in the long run if it forced Rice out of business and eventually out of Nevada.

Nixon and Wingfield wanted GG gone because they had committed $6 million to merge the district's top-producing mines into their new Goldfield Consolidated Mining Company, and Rice and Sullivan were keeping the deal from going through by holding out and refusing to sell their properties. Sullivan Trust had also made the political mistake of aligning with the Democratic governor, John Sparks, listing him as president of all the firm's mining companies. In exchange for his cloak of credibility, George and Larry were bankrolling Sparks's reelection, so Nixon saw crushing Rice as a two-birds-with-one-stone strike: Getting rid of GG would both wipe out Sullivan Trust and flush the Democrat out of office, allowing for completion of the mining consolidation and the installation of a Republican puppet governor of Nixon's choosing.

"The securities of the Sullivan Trust Company were under attack in all markets," Rice complained. "Great blocks were being thrown over. Soon it was reported to me that Senator Nixon was advising people at all points who held Sullivan stocks, or knew of anybody who held them, to unload. From San Francisco came word that a clique of brokers was operating for the decline."

In addition to the attacks launched by Nixon, GG had a myriad of other worries in the aftermath of the fight. Muckraking journalists were refocusing on the erratic mining sector, and Rice was coming under fire from both in-depth newspaper exposés and jeering editorial cartoons. In the mines themselves, union trouble was about to boil over. Nixon and Wingfield were slashing everyone's pay as part of their grand consolidation, and miners were increasingly accused of "high grading" (the fancy term for stealing gold nuggets by concealing them in body cavities or clothing). At Sullivan Trust, Rice was toiling eighteen hours a day because Shanghai Larry was off on a bender. Sullivan had started drinking heavily after Gans-Nelson, slighted that Rickard was getting all the credit, and no one had seen him for days. On top of all that, George and Frances were once again separated. It is unclear whether an exasperated

Rice ordered his wife back to New York in a fit of annoyance or if the past-her-prime actress had stormed off in a huff after throwing another one of her theatrical tantrums.

The cumulative strain was evident in Rice's waxy pallor and the circles of gray beneath his eyes. George spent little time outdoors and was starting to resemble a pasty vulture with poor posture. Even his long-dormant skull cyst from Elmira Reformatory was flaring up, throbbing like a metronome in flux with the festering stresses of deception.

"It was a pet belief of mine that obstacles create character," GG cracked sarcastically, cigar clamped tightly between his teeth. "I rather liked the sensation."

With both the stock market and his personal life overheating, Rice seized upon his most combustive con to date—an entirely fake copper camp way out in the Funeral Mountains. Existing only on maps and not in the true sense of a sustainable mining town, the far-flung desert outpost was so dry and lifeless that the fraudsters who cooked it up couldn't resist juxtaposing its parched desolation with the lush and flowing name of Greenwater.

George would later admit that he had been late to the party in Greenwater, which he bitterly categorized as "the monumental mining-stock swindle of the century." Although he pretended to be outraged that the public had been rooked, GG's annoyance stemmed from the fact that he missed out on the bulk of the pillaging. He claimed to have been so busy dealing with his Goldfield woes that he was caught unaware when a new $3 million copper stock based out of Greenwater started trading in New York that autumn, bypassing the traditional route of first going public on a local or regional exchange.

"Greenwater is situated about 150 miles south of Goldfield, across the state line in California," Rice griped. "No one ever went to or fro without passing through Goldfield. If there was a Greenwater boom, how was it that we in Goldfield, who were in touch with all Nevada mining affairs, did not know about it?"

Greenwater had reported sporadic strikes over the years, but no more than a single railcar of high-grade ore had ever shipped out of the camp. When GG learned that officers of the new company included the brother-in-law of Charles M. Schwab, he was quick to deduce that the direct placement of stock in New York was designed to make it difficult for western engineers to weigh in on the veracity of the copper claims—a stunt Rice wished he had thought of himself.

"The fact that Mr. Schwab was interested in the camp was an argument that appealed with great force to Nevada promoters," George groused, "for the fraternity had learned to attach just as much significance to having a market as to having a mine."

In GG's words, New York investors ate up the unproven securities "blood raw," triggering at least fifty copycat Greenwater stock offerings. Promoters weren't bothering with publishing assay reports, because speculators weren't bothering to read them.

Rice, for a time, railed against the insider scheming. But when Greenwater hit high tide, he felt compelled to leap into the surge lest it pass him by. On the halfhearted recommendation of the engineer Jack Campbell, Sullivan Trust paid $125,000 for two ten-foot holes in Greenwater. The chief attribute of this "mine" was that the property abutted Furnace Creek Copper Company, the original overhyped strike in the camp.

"Did I fall for Greenwater? Yes, and at the eleventh hour," Rice admitted. "Greenwater, a rich man's camp, in which the public sank $30,000,000 during three months that marked the zenith of the Goldfield boom, is another case in point where a confiding investing public followed a deceiving light and was led to ruthless slaughter."

At the peak of the 1906 Greenwater craze, a mesmerizing stranger appeared in southern Nevada, introducing himself as an East Coast doctor who had invented a miracle cure for deafness and wanted to parlay his medical riches into a mining investment. Commanding and buoyant, the newcomer carried himself with an air of distinction. His athletic vitality caused women to swoon and made men want to channel his confidence through a firm handshake. The suave stranger frequently dressed all in red, complete with a long velvet riding coat that matched his crimson roadster. Although nearly everyone in the desert who met the doctor was drawn in by his hypnotic allure, few paused to consider whether his aura was more chilling than charming.

After touring available prospects, the stranger thought he spotted a bargain in the Rush mine at Bullfrog for $150,000. It is not known precisely how the doctor learned that Rice was the man to see about getting his property promoted. But George almost certainly had his lackeys try to divert the speculator's interest upon learning the property was in Bullfrog, the district that was already three or four busts behind the boom cycle. If the doctor couldn't be talked into a more current scam—like Greenwater—Rice probably ordered his underlings to shoo him away.

The stranger, though, would have stood his ground. "Tell Mr. Rice I'm an old friend," he might have said, persistently, breaking into a Cheshire grin while handing over his calling card. "From New York."

George was never easily rattled. But when he squinted at the card and read "Dr. J. Grant Lyman," odds are his face blanched and his insides liquefied.

John Grant Lyman, forty-two, was a hustler extraordinaire whose charismatic overdrive masked a maliciously imbalanced personality. By the time Rice first met Lyman on the betting lawn at Saratoga around 1901, the doctor had already been kicked off the New York Stock Exchange for pillaging a zinc-mining company. Back then, Lyman knew all about George—his alias, his stints in Elmira and Sing Sing, and his tipster business—but Rice knew little about the cryptic doctor. There was a swirling mystery about how Lyman had talked his way into a medical degree and patented some sort of "gold eardrum," but rumors were rife he had also been blackballed from practicing medicine in Chicago, Los Angeles, and London.

After Lyman turned his obsession from quack hearing aids to stock swindling, his life became a blur of sham ventures and unpaid debts. Yet even as he scrambled to avoid jail, the doctor made it a point to make sure his name still appeared regularly in the society pages, and he liked to foster the impression he had cash and yachts stashed in ports around the world. Once, Lyman persuaded a judge to let him turn himself in for a prison sentence at a more convenient time; during another incarceration, he conned the warden into letting him out for trips to the barber to maintain his impeccable tonsorial habits. At a subsequent trial, Lyman's own sister would testify he was "crazy" after he tried to cheat her out of the family farm, a portrayal the doctor didn't try to dispel when he later wrote a book from jail titled *Am I Insane?*

Warily, Rice gave Lyman a cordial audience but sensed malevolence beneath the doctor's too-polite veneer. George tried to explain how, like many Bullfrog properties, the Rush parcel Lyman coveted was located on the site of an ancient mountain slide. The top four hundred feet had widely distributed mineral deposits, but beyond that drillers had encountered a solid bed of lime, which signaled that the property was barren beyond its surface ore. When these reports had first become public in 1905, Rice had walked away from promoting the district.

Lyman didn't seem to listen or care. He thought Rice was trying to hoodwink him out of a sure thing. Beaming a poisonous smile, the doctor told George to start working his promotional wizardry. He wanted Bullfrog Rush incorporated into a million shares at par value of $1 each. The shares, Lyman insisted, were to be sold through eastern brokers on a major exchange, and Sullivan Trust's stamp of legitimacy—the trusted signature of Governor John Sparks—was to be plastered prominently on all advertising. The doctor considered himself a gentleman grifter, which meant the "or else" part of his demand went unspoken.

Rice was quite used to sharpies attempting to swindle him. This was his first go-round at being blackmailed.

GG knew that if he used Sparks's name to tout a mine everybody in the industry knew was barren, the governor would be doomed to defeat in the upcoming election and Sullivan Trust would be swept out of Nevada with him. If Rice didn't promote the stock as directed, Lyman would expose his criminal past, providing deadly fodder for Nixon and the muckraking journalists to run him out of Goldfield on a rail.

Sullivan Trust reluctantly incorporated Lyman's company, but George stalled by selling only under-the-table treasury stock to a handful of inconsequential brokers. "Bullfrog Rush had not yet been listed," Rice explained. "We were afraid to give it a market quotation."

Several weeks later, Lyman barged into Rice's private office unannounced, displeased with the slow pace of the profiteering.

"I have formed here in Goldfield the Union Securities Company," Lyman announced with a sinister flourish, leaning uncomfortably close to George. "And I am going into the promotion business myself. I don't believe a word of the reports you have that the Bullfrog Rush is a failure. I am going on with the promotion."

Rice tried to explain his predicament. As a con man proficient at cooling out marks, he knew never to blame the other fellow, but to blame circumstances instead.

"Governor Sparks, who is the best friend the Sullivan Trust Company has, accepted the presidency of the Bullfrog Rush on our assurance the property was a good one," Rice reasoned. "We are in bad enough as the matter already stands. Don't dare go on with the promotion at this time."

Lyman did an about-face and left without uttering a word. George caught a pathological glint in the doctor's eye as Lyman stormed out.

Forty-eight hours later, Rice was in receipt of a searing telegram from Sparks in Reno, who was livid that the *Nevada State Journal* was running a full-page ad featuring his unabashed endorsement for Bullfrog Rush. George found out that the same ad, placed by Lyman without Sullivan Trust's say-so, was scheduled to run the next day in all the big papers back east.

Rice sent one of the bouncers from the Palace bar to fetch Lyman. Half an hour later, the doctor stood in George's office, glowering. George dismissed the bouncer so the two grifters could speak in private.

"If you move a finger to stop me," Lyman seethed, "I'll expose every act of yours since you were born and show up who the boss of this trust company is!"

GG sat back and removed the cigar from his mouth. His cyst was throbbing like nobody's business. Years later, he would describe what raced through his mind as he pondered the risk of losing everything: "Dr. Lyman was tall as a poplar and muscled like a Samson. He was fresh from the East, red-cheeked and groomed like a Chesterfield. I was cadaverous, desert-worn, office-fagged, and undersized by comparison. In a glove fight, Dr. Lyman could probably have finished me in half a round. But the disparity did not occur to me. The sense of injustice made me forget everything except Dr. Lyman's blackmailing threat."

Rice sprang upon Lyman like a feral cat. In all his decades as a swindler—in otherwise strict keeping with the unwritten code of confidence men—this would be the only known instance of George's resorting to fisticuffs to settle a dispute.

Ricecakes would normally have had trouble knocking over a tray of chocolate éclairs. But the element of surprise put him atop Lyman like a whirling dervish, fists flying. More startled than injured, the doctor tottered backward, lurching off balance toward George's ornate office door.

"In a second he had collided with the big plate-glass pane, which fell with a crash," Rice recalled. "In another instant he recovered his feet, turned on his heel and ran."

In his devil-red suit with his face bloodied from glass shards, Lyman must have cut quite a sight as he tore through the Sullivan Trust reception parlor and out into the noonday bustle of Goldfield's main drag.

"Several clerks who followed him, thinking he had committed some violent act, reported that he didn't stop running until he reached the end of a street 600 feet away," Rice claimed. "Conscience had made a coward of the doctor."

L yman sprinted all the way out of Nevada. But not before tipping off the press about George's secret former life as a felon. The story spread like wildfire, accompanied by newspaper cartoons depicting Rice in a striped jailbird suit.

The blackmail triggered waves of malaise. George sued newspapers for libel and Lyman for misrepresentation. He was forced to run apology ads on Sparks's behalf and buy back Bullfrog Rush shares from any investor who wanted a refund (not in cash, of course, but in exchange for something equally worthless in the Sullivan Trust portfolio). Under intense selling pressure from political insiders, the rest of the Sullivan Trust securities hemorrhaged.

Rice tried to salvage his firm's stocks by buying back shares. But on December 26, 1906, Sullivan Trust ran out of cash. When George and Larry could not repay $284,295 in unsecured loans, the default wiped out Goldfield State Bank and Trust, the largest financial institution in town—the very same bank from which Rice and Arkell swindled their initial $50 on the mining frontier.

On January 5, 1907, a dizzying crash on the San Francisco exchange sank the remaining Sullivan Trust stocks. Within seventy-two hours, four Esmeralda County sheriff's deputies took possession of the bankrupt Sullivan Trust suite, mindful of the broken glass door to the back office as they seized furniture to satisfy creditors.

GG's sucker list, rumored to contain 100,000 names, was the firm's most valuable asset. Rival promoters tried in vain but couldn't get their hands on it.

"By this time I was 'all in' physically," Rice conceded. "I had a cyst, of fifteen years' growth, on the back of my head. It had become infected. I was threatened with blood poisoning. I suffered much pain. I had been on the desert for nearly three years without leaving it for a day."

Nevada's publicity agent had to sell his seat on the Goldfield stock exchange to scrape up enough cash for a train ticket to get his head examined in New York.

"I departed from Goldfield as broke as when I arrived," GG rationalized. "I landed back in the big city with $200 in my pocket—the exact sum with which I had left town three years before."

3

BLUE SKIES AND BUCKET SHOPS

Back in New York, George Graham Rice had his cyst surgically depressurized. But as the stress ebbed away, so too did his ego and speculative spirit.

In the winter of 1907, Rice was out of work and still outcast as the black sheep of the Herzig family. He might or might not have reunited with Frances, and it's unclear where he lived upon returning to the city. George was reluctant to call upon connections in the brokerage business out of fear of being laughed at over his role in the implosion of Sullivan Trust. GG had never fared well with idle time on his hands and was well aware that hustlers who lose confidence in themselves are in no position to manipulate that same trait in others.

"My reward for three years of untiring work on the desert was a big fund of Experience," said a deflated Rice. "Had I kept out of politics, been a good market general, and taken cognizance of the fact that the law of supply and demand is as inexorable in mining-stock markets as in every other line of human endeavor, I could have saved myself and associates from financial ruin. . . . It was my first experience, and, like so many beginners, I was overconfident, lacking in judgment, and fatally ignorant of the finer points of the game."

When he did finally rouse himself to visit the offices of mining-stock brokers, George was surprised at the reception he received. A blown $3 million? That was nothing! Big-time New York traders flipped that much profit or loss in a week. What was his next move? When was Ricecakes getting back into the game?

"Wherever I went a hearty handclasp was extended," said George, relieved and emboldened. "Not one of the Eastern stock brokers was involved to the extent of a single dollar in the Sullivan Trust Company failure. The brokers were convinced that [my] embarrassment was honest. The trust company's credit had always been good. Had the failure been meditated, I could have involved Eastern brokers for at least $1 million. Because I didn't, New York brokers were not slow to express their good feeling. A number of them offered to extend a helping hand did I wish to embark on a new enterprise."

Rice's forced departure from stock promotion ended up being timed right. Despite warning signs that markets were about to boil over in early 1907, ultra-confident speculators continued to throw cash at stocks until a severe sell-off in March rocked the nation. George got to witness the financial carnage from a front-row seat, having accepted an invitation from insider acquaintances to immerse himself in the "orgy of market manipulation" in its natural habitat—the glorious underbelly of the New York Curb Exchange.

In the first decade of the twentieth century, the exclusive and stodgy New York Stock Exchange was rivaled by the smaller but livelier curb exchange, a motley open-air securities market a block and a half south of Wall Street. This loosely regulated exchange was where unlisted "over the counter" stocks changed hands, literally on the curbstone outside the prestigious "Big Board" trading floor. The bedlam of the curb in full cry provided one of Manhattan's most vibrant spectacles of city life: a feisty, controlled chaos at once cosmopolitan and visceral. Six days a week when the curb was in session, Broad Street became impassable to horse and vehicle traffic, and the narrow elbow between Exchange Place and Beaver Street was commandeered by a swarm of low financiers who

blocked off the road with ropes and iron stanchions, even though no specific law entitled brokers to monopolize the thoroughfare. Clanging
bells, a barrage of auction jargon, rapid-fire bidding, occasional fistfights,
barking dogs, craps-shooting bookies, off-key organ-grinders, hawking
fruit vendors, headline-yelling newsboys, and a bewildered crush of
gawking, gaping tourists all contributed to the pandemonium of gray-
market capitalism in action: an unscripted circus performed every
day but Sundays in a gritty urban canyon beneath a citadel of towering skyscrapers.

A typical day on the curb began at 9:45 A.M., when brokers and
traders straggled into Broad Street to stake out customary spots in the
pit, killing time by smoking, shooting dice, and cracking wise about
market conditions. This diverse cast of characters—ambitious young men
who viewed the curb as a rough-and-tumble prep school; grizzled
sharpies who had been kicked out of or were unable to meet the more
stringent requirements of the Big Board—resembled a fidgety mob
waiting formation orders for a parade of shylocks. At precisely 10:00 A.M.,
when the signal came in the tympanic form of a large Chinese gong,
hundreds of speculators burst into commotion as if sparked by a
photographer's flash powder.

Highly animated traders began shouting, gesticulating, and elbow-
ing in the roadway while office boys high above scampered onto
window ledges with telephones, dangling precariously while waving
a complex frenzy of buy and sell codes. The coat-and-tie business attire
of the pit brokers was offset by the gaudy array of brightly colored skim-
mers, straw hats, dusters, and bowlers each specialist wore to be identi-
fiable in the crowd, lending a carnival atmosphere to the convulsive
surge of thrusting arms and wagging fingers. Under a broiling summer
sun and in the icy sleet of winter, there was no such thing as a coffee
break, lunch hour, or sick day on the curb. No matter what your racket,
if you stepped away even for an instant before the 3:00 P.M. closing gong,
competing opportunists would clamor to fill your void.

Every few minutes, one random curb denizen would leap onto a discarded fruit box and let out an Indian war whoop. A gang-tackle throng would surround the man in agitated chatter, the turmoil escalating for half a minute until the huckster's long index finger singled out the highest bidder and definitively boomed, "Sold!" The knot of unsuccessful buyers would drift away indifferently, while the two men involved in the transaction lingered only long enough to scribble the trade details on slips of paper before handing them off to messenger boys and blending back into the tumult.

Although securities were the primary goods that changed hands on the curb, by no means were stocks the only vehicle of speculation: You could bet on a horse race. Borrow money from a loan shark. If you were in a jam, it wouldn't take much asking to get in touch with a fixer who knew how to funnel bribes to the proper city official or police captain. Best of all, unlike the NYSE, you didn't need to buy an ultraexpensive membership seat to gain access to the trading floor. The notion that any man could conduct business in the Broad Street pit (and it was truly a boys' club; the curb would strictly exclude women until 1941) gave the outdoor market an everyman, underdog appeal. But this same lack of standards also brought Broad Street a well-deserved reputation for shadiness. With its proliferation of penny stocks and the easy availability of usurious credit, the curb became known as the poor man's exchange. Even though it was widely known to be crooked, the down-and-out played the rigged game anyway; it was their only option.

Exchange-based trading in New York dates to the early eighteenth century, when merchants and auctioneers congregated at the foot of Wall Street to swap commodities like furs, tobacco, and slaves. A market for long-term securities did not exist in America until 1790, when the First Congress of the United States authorized an $80 million bond issue to pay down Revolutionary War debt. In 1792, when stock and bond trading was conducted beneath a well-known buttonwood tree between the present 68 and 70 Wall Street, the leading brokers drew up an agreement establishing a closed organization in which members pledged to trade only with other members. This was the birth of what was then simply called the Stock Exchange. In 1863, the prefix "New York" was added to give America's foremost trading board the official NYSE title it's known by today.

Having an unregulated outdoor stock market alongside a better-established indoor exchange was not unique to New York in 1907. Open-air securities venues dated to the eighteenth century in London, Paris, and Amsterdam. A version of the curb sprang up in Manhattan around 1830 when the need arose for a market to float securities deemed too chancy by Stock Exchange members. Emerging infrastructures and technologies—canal- and turnpike-building shares, railroad bonds, and eventually electricity and the telephone—all got their starts when risk-embracing financiers created artificial markets and issued proclamations over values to encourage trading. As America's market makers, this is precisely how robber barons like Big Jim Fisk, Cornelius Vanderbilt, and Jay Gould amassed grudge-fueled fortunes in the mid-nineteenth century.

Around the time of the Civil War, a group of unaffiliated traders known as the Open Board of Stock Brokers began meeting in various New York locations, including one dingy basement rendezvous known as the Coal Hole. When the NYSE absorbed the Open Board in 1869 (as a means of killing it off as a competitor), its void was filled by the independent Unlisted Securities Market, which within fifteen years switched over to handling listed-only stocks. Loosely formed organizations of over-the-counter stock-trading "guttersnipes" then congregated at the corner of Wall and Hanover, floated a block away to William Street, and eventually shifted to the New Street entrance of the NYSE. By 1900, these quasi-legal brokers had settled on Broad Street, where their burgeoning practice of auctioning stocks up and down the sidewalk gave the informal outdoor market a nickname that stuck—the curb exchange.

In 1907, just as Rice was getting his inside look at rigging the marketplace, the "father" of the curb, E. S. "Pop" Mendels, was forming the New York Curb Market Agency to take the first steps toward legitimizing Broad Street. Mendels had been working diligently since the 1870s to establish a code of standards so that a secondary market would be tolerated alongside the Big Board (and eventually recognized as an official exchange in 1911). But as with any rogue organization, it was a stretch to think the curb could affect serious ethical change from within, and Mendels's laboriously planned framework for regulation went largely ignored and unenforced. Too many Broad Street market makers were openly functioning as manipulators, and even though there was constant pressure from the NYSE to get this den of thieves barred from the financial district, it didn't happen. Wall Street grew to tolerate its seamy Broad Street neighbor as a necessary evil, shrugging off the curb as a "devil you know is better than the devil you don't" type of annoyance. History had shown that every time a secondary market got quashed, some other entity sprang up to take its place. The curb, with its unlisted stocks and nefarious practices, was bad enough. Fear of some unknown rival siphoning even more money away from the Big Board was worse.

"Goldfield had been the mining emporium, the securities factory," Rice explained. "New York was the recognized market center. Market handling had been my weak spot. I now had a chance to witness the performance of some past-masters in the art of market manipulation, and I tried to make the best of the opportunity. I watched intently the daily sessions of the New York Curb. I was in and out of brokerage offices hourly. Nothing that transpired escaped me."

Out west, George's objective had been to acquire shares cheaply, then cash out when he believed the stocks had peaked. In New York, savvy brokers not only sold out but "sold short," locking in additional profits by betting shares would tank after cresting. In addition, curb sharpies rarely paid full price to bet on their market opinions. Instead of buying or selling shares outright, they traded options contracts, which, for a fraction of a stock's face value, guaranteed the right to buy or sell at a designated price at a future date (generally one to eight months later). To tilt futures markets in their favor, rogue brokers engaged in "wash trading," the now-illegal practice of simultaneously buying and selling the same shares to pump up a stock's volume and give a false impression that demand was robust.

"It seemed quite apparent that the Western game, as compared with the Eastern, was one of marbles as against millions," Rice marveled. "In New York's financial mart I felt like a minnow in a sea of bass. . . . My chief thought at that time, with the Goldfield Consolidated swindle fresh in my mind, was simply that the Western multi-millionaire highbinder promoter didn't class with his Eastern prototype. Indeed, the two appeared to be of different species, as different as the humble but noisy coyote from the Abyssinian man-eating tiger."

By mid-spring 1907, George had the itch to get back into the stock racket. He didn't have the clout or the capital to break into the curb as a broker, so he settled for a return west to engage in " 'scientific' press-agenting." GG vowed to return to New York after he had accumulated a sizable kitty. He avoided Goldfield and settled in Reno, which at the time was gaining a morals-shocking reputation as the easiest place on the planet to obtain a divorce.

"I was as full of spirit as the month of May," George beamed. "I had been broke before, and the sensation was not new to me. . . . I was enthused with the idea that there were other Goldfields yet unexplored in the battle-born state and that opportunity was bound to come to me if I pitched my tent."

On April 27, 1907, Rice launched an eight-page weekly called the *Nevada Mining News*, positioning the paper as an instrument of objectivity that threatened to rip the lid off the old-boy mining sector. In reality, the publication made money strictly off kickbacks from brokers who wanted certain stocks talked up (or down) to sway the public. George hired an editor but ghostwrote most of the material. He used the power of an anonymous pen to rail against personal enemies, churning out vindictive stories like "Goldfield in the Grasp of Wall Street Sharks" and "Nixon a Senator with a Blackmailing Mind." Circulation soared to twenty-eight thousand.

Shortly after the *Mining News* became established, Rice crossed paths with Larry Sullivan, who had also ended up in Reno after a circuitous ouster from Goldfield. Shanghai Larry was in much rougher shape than when George had last seen him: He got roaring drunk the day after Gans-Nelson and stayed that way for nine months straight. On New Year's Eve, Sullivan had confronted Tex Rickard at a Tonopah bar and repeatedly tried to pick a fight; when Larry pulled a gun, Tex deftly snatched it out of his hand and flung it into a corner. Sullivan, so inebriated he could barely stand, retrieved his firearm, wobbled outside, and pistol-whipped an innocent bystander. To avoid arrest, Larry fled to New York, where, at the same time GG was studying market making, he showed up drunk at brokerage houses and made a pompous ass of himself. An eastern investor who had been burned in the Bullfrog Rush fiasco found out Larry was in town and bragging about not being charged for stock fraud, so he swore out a warrant against Sullivan for the theft of $102,700. Again forced to flee, Larry believed he would be untouchable in Reno. He still had some money squirreled away and was contemplating, of all things, a run for the U.S. Senate.

The only part about Sullivan's tale that resonated with Rice was the bit about some cash left to play with. GG proposed they go partners flipping stocks as Sullivan & Rice Inc., with Larry fronting the start-up money and George as idea man.

The brokerage started off promisingly but soon sputtered. After multiple embarrassments, Rice was forced to confront Sullivan about his drinking. On August 5, when George was home sick with fever, Larry barged into the office and attempted to take over the brokerage. None of the clerks would obey his orders, and when Sullivan fired everyone in an intoxicated rage, no one left. Rice's secretary drew a revolver to keep from being forcibly ejected, and Irwin M. Herzig, a cousin George

had conned into accompanying him out west, was severely beaten for
refusing to hand over the keys to the safe. Sullivan was arrested for as-
sault with intent to kill.

Larry's attack made newspapers as far away as San Francisco, but because he held the lease on the office, he ended the partnership by kicking Rice out. Fearful of bad publicity, George downplayed the violence
as a "rumpus" between old pals and turned his concentration back to
the *Mining News*.

In the autumn of 1907, insiders schemed to corner the U.S. copper
market. Instead, they triggered a colossal stock slide that paralyzed trading in all sectors. Liquidity vanished, and terrified mobs started bank
runs. The National Bank of America and Knickerbocker Trust, two of
the nation's largest banks, went under. New York City itself was on the
brink of bankruptcy. By October 22, stocks had sunk to 50 percent of
their value from the previous year. For an entire generation, the panic
of 1907 would lodge in the collective conscience as the benchmark for
economic calamity until the Great Depression obliterated the reference
point. There was not yet a federal reserve, so it was up to tycoons like
John Pierpont Morgan—who literally rode to Wall Street's rescue in a
carriage drawn by a prized white horse—to bail out the nation.

Thanks to the country's yet-unexhausted natural resources and still-
intact purchasing power, near-normal banking resumed within weeks.
But when the panic was more closely scrutinized in retrospect, critics
argued that Morgan was more culprit than savior: Months earlier, he
had leaked a lie to *The New York Times* that Knickerbocker Trust was
insolvent, knowing that the rumor would spark bank runs. Morgan and
fellow robber barons were accused of intentionally undermining the
economy to create the illusion that the financial landscape needed re-
structuring into a centralized banking system—the main beneficiaries
of which would be JP and a handful of superrich industrialists. "The
panic of 1907 was brought about by a deliberate conspiracy for enrich-
ment of those who engineered it," the U.S. senator Robert Latham Owen

of Oklahoma later railed (in vain) on the Senate floor. "I regard it as treason against the United States."

The mining sector was hit particularly hard. In Nevada, labor unrest amplified the stock woes. Owners were now forcing miners to change clothes under the watch of armed guards at the end of shifts to prevent gold theft and were paying wages in company store coupons instead of cash. When the unions protested, Nixon and Wingfield shut down Goldfield Consolidated and kicked thousands out of work.

In December 1907, a consortium of owners pressured Governor Sparks to appeal to President Roosevelt to send federal troops on the basis that an attack by agitators was imminent. Although the situation was tense, it was hardly anarchy. Roosevelt dispatched three hundred troops but quickly realized those reinforcements were not needed. Yet he feared a too-soon pullout would make him look foolish, so the soldiers remained for several months while the president ripped Nevada for not having a state militia to fight its own battles. Nixon and Wingfield had blown the discord out of proportion to break the unions, spinning the ruse so Sparks bore the brunt of the blame and ridicule. The stress and shame were enough to kill him.

"The Governor, [an] honest, simple old man, broken in purse, in health and in spirit, grieved over the President's denouncement, took to bed, and died of a broken heart," Rice lamented, more distressed at having lost a political ally than a friend. "Even at the moment when the grave closed over his remains the troops were leaving Goldfield."

After miners were rehired (under worse terms than before), the power barons struggled to get back to raking in profits. Nixon and Wingfield had gotten rid of Sullivan Trust, Governor Sparks, and the unions, but there was a disquieting sense that mining's peak had passed in the Silver State. Observing the panicky free fall from a safe distance, Rice had an epiphany: If you can't make money promoting stocks, why not cash in by intentionally *demoting* them instead?

"Prices of listed Nevada issues were crumpling like seersuckers in the rain," GG complained. "You have to be a rainbow-chaser by nature to be a successful promoter, but even I, despite my chronic optimism, began to feel the influence of what was transpiring. I made a flip-flop and turned bear on the whole market."

But before George could torpedo any securities, he first had to inflate them to the bursting point.

His new swindling paradise, based entirely on delusions of grandeur, would be an emerging camp called Rawhide, and Rice would prime it for puncture by being one of the first marketers in America to harness the irresistible selling power of sex and celebrities.

Because Rawhide, the new Nevada gold camp, was born during the financial crisis of 1907, I couldn't see any future ahead of it . . . not 'through a pair of field-glasses,'" Rice scoffed. "A revulsion of sentiment toward speculation had set in, seemingly for keeps. Only a hair-brained enthusiast of the wild-eyed order could hope at such a time possibly to succeed in the marketing of new mining issues."

Still, booms are born out of gambles taken during busts, and Rawhide was exactly the sort of pie-in-the-sky prospect George was on the lookout for. Its script was familiar enough: Legitimate gold discoveries had been recorded in the mountains about a hundred miles southeast of Reno, and the initial overstated claims lured the desperate and the downtrodden, who hoped to latch onto lucky strikes in the surrounding area. A ludicrous valuation of $300,000 per ton allegedly sampled from Grutt Hill started the stampede (for comparison, this outlandish claim was five hundred times greater than the $600 per ton strike that had established Tonopah), and fanatics were reporting that instead of quartz bearing traces of gold, Rawhide miners were bringing up "gold with a little rock in it." Rice didn't believe a word of these exaggerations but did everything in his power to spread the hyperbole, laying the groundwork for future decimation.

"The scenes enacted in Rawhide when the boom was at its height beggar description," groused an incredulous Rice. "When Rawhide was born I had neither money nor political power. The camp needed publicity. I had nothing to secure publicity with but my wit."

George planted rosy reports claiming that men would never go hungry in Rawhide because the slag heaps contained so much discarded gold that any miner could get breakfast money simply by panning rubble off the top. Laborers who had been out of work for the better part of a year flocked to Rawhide, rendering Goldfield a "graveyard of a million blighted hopes." George distanced himself from both towns, press-agenting from Reno while partnering with Tex Rickard to ensure the new camp had all the believable trappings of an elaborate big-store con. Rickard, too, was skeptical of Rawhide's long-term viability, but because his Goldfield customers had bolted en masse, he felt compelled to open a new saloon and profit off their vices. Caught up in the exodus on his way out of town, Tex stopped at an abandoned wood-frame church on the edge of Goldfield and nailed a sign on the front door that read, CHURCH CLOSED—GOD HAS GONE TO RAWHIDE!

"Why should not the American public, even in these tough financial times, enthuse about a gold camp with possibilities for money-making such as [Rawhide] offered?" George asked sardonically. "Don't drowning men grasp at straws?"

Rawhide quickly became the West's largest encampment, with massive, gallows-like drill rigs fueled by gasoline engines roaring nonstop and winches and cranes clanking and groaning through the night. By early 1908, the downtown had evolved into a two-thousand-foot boulevard of dance halls, brothels, and pleasure palaces. When Rickard opened his soon-to-be-famous Rawhide gambling emporium, a "kaleidoscopic maelstrom of humanity" christened the establishment with a bacchanal desert blowout that lasted a week. Among the invitees were pretentious politicians, obtuse millionaires, gullible East Coast brokers, high-society gossipmongers, and easily duped newspapermen, all whooping it up in a haze of hedonism. "Champagne was the common beverage," GG recalled. "Day was merged into night and night into day.

Rouged courtesans of Stingaree Gulch provided the dash of femininity that was a prerequisite to the success of the grand *bal masque* that concluded the festivities."

Rawhide marked a fundamental change in Rice's public relations approach. Although he was careful to use euphemisms like "dash of femininity" in polite company, he was much more explicit when discussing sex as a marketing ploy with the exclusively male proprietors of the new camp.

In America, sex as an overt selling tool traced to an 1871 ad for Pearl tobacco that featured a near-naked maiden in a come-hither pose. Images of alluring women helped peddle soft drinks, beer, and coffee for decades thereafter, but it would not be until 1911 that Woodbury's facial soap sparked a morals uproar by featuring illustrations of men caressing the skin of ladies who (supposedly) used the product. Yet in between that first Pearl girl ad and Woodbury's shocking "Skin you love to touch" campaign, GG was ahead of everyone else with his strategic use of sexuality as an advertising tactic.

The main reason Rice is not widely recognized today as the pioneer of sex appeal is that he did not plaster print ads with risqué pictures. Rather, he leveraged the subliminal value of lurid news stories to embed the idea that Rawhide stood for power, wealth, and conquest. In terms of mass-market persuasion, Rice insisted on controlling not just the message but its delivery. To illustrate how everyday events could be crafted into sex-tinged sensationalism, he liked to repeat the following tale about "a young woman of dazzling beauty and fine presence" who one day allegedly wandered into Rawhide unchaperoned:

> *She had been attracted to the scene by stories of fortunes made in a night. Under a grilling process of questioning by a few leading citizens she divulged the fact that she had run away from her home in Utah to seek single-handed her fortune on the desert. In roguish manner she expressed the opinion that if allowed to go her own way she would soon succeed in her mission. But she would not divulge*

the manner in which she proposed to operate. She confessed she had no money. There was a serene but settled expression of melancholy in her eyes that captivated everybody who saw her.

. . . There was no law in the camp which would warrant the girl's deportation, yet action appeared warranted. Within a few moments $500 was subscribed as a purse to furnish the girl a passage out of camp and for a fresh start in life. . . . She refused to accept the present. Next day she disappeared.

There was a corking human interest story here. Newspapers far and wide published the tale.

Once GG got a sense that readers had been hooked, he always followed up with at least one "comeback." George later claimed the girl's photograph had been sent "without her knowledge to the judges of a famous beauty contest in a Far Western State. The judges were on the point of voting her the prize without question when investigation of her antecedents revealed her Rawhide escapade."

In other words, Ricecakes knew Americans lusted for the vicarious thrill of living illicitly, so he recycled story lines that associated Rawhide with amoral adventure. Nearly all these types of tales he cooked up involved mesmerizing female strangers or famous lady celebrities.

In the spring of 1908, the controversial British novelist Ellnor Glyn was the world's hottest literary sensation, having pioneered mass-market erotic fiction while coining the racy term "It Girl." Her novels—scandalous at the time but tame by today's standards—were inspired by rollicking affairs she allegedly had with Edwardian-era noblemen. When George found out Glyn was touring America to promote her bestselling book *Three Weeks* (about an exotic Balkan queen who seduces a much younger aristocrat), he extended an invitation under the guise that Rawhide might provide salacious fodder for her next book. "Nothing," GG figured, "would attract more attention to the camp than having

Mrs. Elinor Glyn at Rawhide—particularly if she would conduct herself while there in a manner that might challenge the criticism of church members."

At dusk on May 27, 1908, the tawny-haired, milk-skinned Glyn arrived in the company of two competing suitors (an overbearing French count and a garrulous Utah millionaire) plus several female attendants. Hundreds lined the sidewalks to gawk at her, and George scripted every aspect of the trip so Elinor's startling green eyes would be brimming with wonder the entire time. The risqué Brit had never heard of Rawhide (or Nevada for that matter), but Rice made sure every hardboot in camp knew the off-color rhyme about the fetching novelist, satirized from a steamy lovemaking scene in *Three Weeks*:

> *Would you like to sin*
> *With Elinor Glyn*
> *On a tiger skin?*

> *Or would you prefer*
> *To err with her*
> *On some other fur?*

Rice took the Glyn entourage straight to Rickard's casino and sat the writer down at a faro bank. The cards, of course, were rigged, but this time not in favor of the house. George had gaffed the game so Elinor lost three consecutive $200 bets but won on the final turn, sending her away from the table with $1,000 in profit and a heady rush of confidence. GG discreetly inquired if Glyn wanted to witness a private poker game with much higher stakes going on in a back room, and the guest of honor practically jumped out of her corset in eagerness. In his memoir, Rice recounted what she saw:

> *The men were coatless and grimy. Their unshaven mugs, rough as*
> *nutmeg-graters, were twisted into strange grimaces. All of them ap-*

peared the worse for liquor. Before each man was piled a mound of ivory chips of various hues, and alongside rested a six-shooter. From the rear trousers' pocket of every player another gun protruded. Each man wore a belt filled with cartridges. Although an impromptu sort of game, it was well staged.

A man with bloodshot eyes shuffled and riffled the cards. Then he dealt a hand to each.

"Bet you $10,000," loudly declared the first player.

"Call that and go you $15,000 better," shouted the second as he pushed a stack of yellows toward the center.

"Raise you!" cried two others, almost in unison.

Before the jackpot was played out $300,000 had found its way to the center of the table and four men were standing up in their seats in a frenzy of bravado with the muzzles of their guns viciously pointed at one another. There was enough of the lurking devil in the eyes of the belligerents to give the onlookers a nervous shiver.

Glyn and her suitors were out the door faster than a Pope-Toledo careening across Death Valley. As soon as the door slammed shut behind them, George gave the signal, and the card players fired their revolvers into the canvas ceiling.

This was followed by hollow groans, calculated to freeze the blood of the retreating party, and by a scraping and scuffling sound that conveyed to the imagination a violent struggle between several persons. Fifteen minutes later two stretchers, carrying the "dead," were taken to the undertaker's shop. Mrs. Glyn and [her suitors], with drooped chins, stood by and witnessed the dismal spectacle.

Of course, the "murder" of these two gamblers, during the progress of a card-game for sensationally high stakes and in the presence of the authoress of Three Weeks, made fine front-page newspaper copy. . . . The camp got yards of free publicity that was *calculated to convince the public it was no flash in the pan, which was exactly what was wanted.*

The next night Glyn was feted at a sumptuous banquet that lasted into the wee hours. Numerous toasts were raised in the novelist's honor as Elinor gushed about Rawhide's swashbuckling spirit. GG capped the festivities with an intentional show of firepower that, by accident, almost consumed the camp:

A fire-alarm was rung in. The local fire-department responded in Wild-Western fashion. The conflagration, which was started for Mrs. Glyn's sole benefit, advanced with the rapidity of a tidal wave. It brought to the scene a mixed throng of the riffraff of the camp. The tumult of voices rose loud and clear. The fire embraced all of the deserted shacks and waste lumber at the foothills of one of the mines. The liberal use of kerosene and a favoring wind caused a fierce blaze. It spouted showers of sparks into the darkness and gleamed like a beacon to desert wayfarers. The fierce yells of the firemen rang far and wide. [All] of a sudden a wild-haired individual thrust himself out of the crowd and sprang through the door of a blazing shack. He disappeared within the flames. Three feet past the door was a secret passage leading to shelter in the tunnel of an adjoining mine. Mrs. Glyn, of course, did not know this. She acclaimed the act as one of daring heroism.

Water in the camp was scarce, so there was a resort to barreled beer and dynamite. Soon the flames of the devouring fire were extinguished. Again the newspapers throughout the land contained stories, which were telegraphed from the spot, regarding the remarkable experiences of the much-discussed authoress of Three Weeks *in the new, great gold camp of Rawhide.*

"I have traveled from Budapest to Bombay, from Boston to Bakersfield," a breathless Glyn told *The New York Times* upon departing Rawhide the next day. "There are few experiences I have not had, but I would not give last night's experience for it all."

George was in his glory and once again on his way to parlaying something out of nothing.

In terms of leveraging the selling power of celebrities, Elinor Glyn was a tasty side dish compared with the well-fatted calf GG was plumping for plunder. For two years, he had been coddling the confidence of America's most beloved stage comedian, and as the planned unraveling of Rawhide neared, Rice was scheming to star the funniest man in show business in a farce that would bankroll his breakthrough on the New York Curb.

Nathaniel Carl Goodwin, fifty-one, had earned top billing as a "comic genius" in the 1890s by playing a wealthy oaf in the wildly popular play *A Gilded Fool*. A decade later, the true laugher was how oblivious the thin-haired, furrow-browed humorist was to being cast in the same real-life role for one of GG's elaborate cons.

Goodwin, who prided himself at never turning down a highball, was well-known for his mimicry and exaggerated facial expressions. But his flair for witty, racy dialogue is what kept patrons doubled over in hilarity. Nat had an eccentric fondness for Turkish baths and high-stakes gambling tables, which meant vaudeville managers routinely had to pry a tipsy Goodwin away from one or the other of those establishments for his twenty-seven minutes of mirth twice daily. Nat often appeared onstage silly drunk, and while this caused him to forget his lines, he was a master of improvisation who always seemed to come up with something funnier than the original script.

An impulsive sort who fancied exotic animals, Goodwin sometimes performed with his prized pack of collies, hounds, and bull terriers, believing the romping dogs contributed to his unpredictable zaniness. At the time Rice began siphoning his trust, Nat was on wife No. 3 (of five; he would be engaged to a sixth when he died in 1919 after complications related to popping his right eye out with a champagne cork). But matrimony didn't stop Goodwin from chasing every cocaine-sniffing soubrette he could slap his paws on. He took particular interest in consoling girls who couldn't cut it in theater and had to resort to being filmed for the new moving pictures fad, which serious stage actors deemed frivolous and beneath their craft.

Nat was vacationing at Glenwood Springs, Colorado, in the summer of 1906 when a grifter working the resort hotels there suckered him for a series of mid-level cons. The hustler gained Goodwin's trust by inviting him on a booze-drenched junket to Goldfield for the Gans-Nelson fight, then pretended to "save" Nat from a stock rip-off by steering him into an investment involving a barren mine that had been salted with gold. When the deal fell through, the con artist convinced Nat it had only bombed because of bad luck, putting the funnyman on the send for thousands of dollars more. Rice at this time was not involved in fleecing Goodwin. But he recognized the potential, and during Nat's binge in Goldfield he treated the vaudeville star magnanimously, setting him up with ringside seats and fawning attention from the camp's most comely courtesans.

"Although I made but little money at Goldfield I was very greatly attracted by its life," the comedian reminisced in his 1914 autobiography, *Nat Goodwin's Book*. "The utter abandon, the manhood, the disregard of municipal laws, the semblance of honor which fooled so many."

A year later, in the autumn of 1907, Goodwin happened to be in Reno when George's roper, Dan Edwards, pointed Nat out to Rice and suggested they renew acquaintances by buttering him up with a free stock tip. This was around the time when George first became keen on shorting the mining sector, and because it didn't cost him anything to part with made-up inside information, he sent word that Goodwin should bet against Goldfield Consolidated. Over the course of a month, the stock plunged, and Edwards reported back that a delighted Goodwin wanted to know if Rice would consider letting him in on something bigger.

"How much capital have you got?" Rice asked Edwards.

"Five thousand of Nat's money," the middleman answered.

"Get another man with $5,000," Rice replied, "and I'll talk to you."

A second sucker named Warren A. Miller was recruited, and within a week Nat C. Goodwin & Company was incorporated, with the comedian listed as president and everyone else but Rice on the board of directors. George would get a salary for managing the firm and a cut of any stock or real estate sales. The company would operate not as promoters but as demoters who "turned the tables and made money on the destructive side." This was a sound strategy considering the shaky market conditions, but GG saw no need to share it with his partners. This is how a gullible Goodwin thought the deal was supposed to go down:

> One of my partners was a young man who had gone stranded in Reno and whom I had known slightly in Goldfield as one of the boldest operators in that roaring camp. . . . [Rice] believed in going at the mining game legitimately. By this I mean it is legitimate to buy options on prospects and properties which look good and place them on the market after they have been carefully examined by mining experts. . . . If the properties turn out well we continue to develop them and work them for all they're worth. . . . Stock was worth most in Rawhide itself. All the mining experts there knew the property. . . . So confident were we that we [would be acquiring] a really valuable property that we determined to go to New York and let the public in on the ground floor.

The only part about the scam Nat had straight was that George would be heading to New York—to bet against Goodwin-backed stocks after puffing them up to preposterous levels.

Within four months, GG scooped up eight Rawhide gold claims encompassing 160 acres. Along the southern slope of Hooligan Hill, where the lode was said to be most lucrative, Rice alleged "guards were maintained through the night to prevent loss from theft." Although there was no scientific analysis to support claims of value beyond surface ore, Rice pooled the properties under the name Rawhide Coalition Mines Company and incorporated the business into three million shares valued at $1 each.

This $3 million entity was made up of largely unwanted property Rice purchased for $15,000, arranging creative financing for Goodwin and Miller to cover the amount above their $10,000 buy-in. To accomplish this, George transferred 750,000 shares of the just-incorporated stock into the treasury of Rawhide Coalition. He next delegated Nat C. Goodwin & Company as agent for the sale of this treasury stock, and the firm's first action was to exercise its own option on 250,000 shares at 23 cents per share. This netted the coalition treasury $57,500 for purposes of "administration." The Goodwin company then purchased 1.85 million of the remaining 2.25 million shares of ownership stock at 23.3 cents per share, amounting to $431,050 more (on paper at least) for Rawhide Coalition—minus a commission of $12,500 paid to George. Out of his commission, Rice loaned Goodwin and Miller the $5,000 they lacked in starter capital, almost certainly charging them above-market interest for the privilege.

Confusing? You bet—just as GG intended it to be. Obfuscation and opacity are the hallmarks of confidence swindling, because hustlers know most marks would rather remain silent in ignorance than risk embarrassment by speaking up to admit they don't understand something.

George handled all the paperwork, pointed to where the figureheads needed to sign, and assured Goodwin and Miller they were on the cusp of a monumental killing. After allotting themselves fifteen-cent futures options, they had veiled control over a large block of mysterious stock, and by August 1908 Rice was ready to head east to get Rawhide Coalition noticed on the New York Curb. Like any good sucker, Nat was avariciously optimistic, likening the rush to being invited into a secret society. "It was as exciting as being a member of a suicide club!" he gushed.

The morning of September 4, 1908, was hot and dry with gale-force winds ripping through Rawhide from the southeast. Around 9:00 A.M., a gust blew window curtains into a lit gasoline stove in a doctor's office in the Rawhide Drug Company building, and within minutes an inferno was racing up Balloon Avenue, obliterating everything in its path. Among the first buildings to go was Collins's hardware store, which had recently taken delivery of two tons of dynamite. The explosives detonated with a sonic concussion, scattering debris for miles.

Considering how ineptly volunteer firefighters had performed months earlier when Rice staged the far smaller conflagration for Elinor Glyn, it surprised no one that the blaze raged unchecked for three hours. By noon, thirty-seven buildings lay in ruins, including two banks, ten saloons, every food store, all the town's restaurants, and Tex Rickard's grand gambling hall. Two traveling salesmen trapped in a hotel were feared dead. Scores of people were injured, and three thousand ended up homeless. Property losses were estimated at $750,000 (about $20 million in today's dollars).

For Rice, back in Reno, the loss was personally devastating. He had just spent the better part of a year pumping up Rawhide so he could profit from its demise. Now an unforeseeable disaster had wiped out the camp only weeks before he planned on laying in bets against Rawhide Coalition. Had the fire happened when the stock was at its zenith and George had already shorted it, the blaze would have been a convenient catastrophe. But the stock hadn't even gotten off the ground yet and would surely now plummet without the facade of a thriving camp to lend the mines an air of authenticity.

Because his only other choice was to abandon the enterprise, Rice decided to forge ahead with his return to the New York Curb, committing himself to creating an appetite for Rawhide Coalition. The camp's riches, he preached to anyone who would listen, were still safe underground. Rawhide mining claims were so valuable, he lied, that the rebuilding of the camp had commenced even before its ashes had cooled.

. . .

orking with a valet and a secretary out of the Hotel Patterson at
59 West Forty-sixth Street, George torqued up Rawhide's publicity pressure in New York. Every day for a month in the autumn of
1908, he bought large display ads designed to look like news dispatches,
paying a premium to have them run alongside financial columns in the
nation's highest-circulation newspapers. He spent his afternoons in and
out of brokerage offices pretending to have a hot commodity to peddle.

Rawhide Coalition, at twenty-five cents per share, was touted as "The
Bonanza Mine of the West" that "for five feet was literally studded with
gold." Another ad boasted of "eight feet of real shipping ore," enough to
"keep a 600-ton per day mill busy for years." The campaign preyed on
the public's fear of getting shut out, urging small investors to "buy now
while you can, at the bottom—sell later at the top." One all-caps headline blared of the stock, "THE ONE BEST BUY ON THE ENTIRE
AMERICAN SECURITIES LIST."

A price of $2 per share was predicted by Christmas, and early div-
idends could be expected as soon as a favorable engineering report
triggered $1 million worth of development. Citing "the authority of
far-famed mining engineers," the testimonials promised Rawhide Coalition would blast past $6 within six months. If it didn't, the man who
signed these missives proclaimed, "I shall be the worst-fooled man in
the world."

The signature Rice affixed to every single one of these ads belonged
to Nat C. Goodwin.

Rawhide Coalition clawed its way from twenty-five cents to forty,
then rocketed past $1. By Thanksgiving, the stock was the talk of Broad
Street. At any given time while the curb was in session in November
1908, some twenty brokers surrounded the mining specialists' pole
executing Rawhide Coalition orders. Rice started thinking he might
pull off a successful bear raid after all.

Goodwin basked in the glow of touting a winning stock. In addition

to the nationwide ad blitz that reeled in legions of his fans, Nat had personally persuaded scores of showbiz friends and floozies to buy into
Rawhide Coalition. Even though he was listed as president of his own
corporation, the flamboyant Broadway playboy had no idea how Nat
C. Goodwin & Company functioned on a day-to-day basis. This was
fine by George; as long as everything was humming along swimmingly,
the Gilded Fool was a highly effective front man.

Nat had a habit of wedding, then dumping, his leading ladies. During Rawhide Coalition's big run, Goodwin filed for divorce from wife
No. 3 (the actress Maxine Elliott, later romantically linked with J. P.
Morgan) so he could chase potential bride No. 4 (Edna Goodrich, half
his age and one of Broadway's famously petite "Florodora girls") across
Europe. Nat had hired private detectives to track down the starlet and
convince Goodrich that her current fiancé couldn't afford her. But upon
returning from his conquest of a honeymoon, Nat received urgent word
from GG that they had to move fast to salvage their stock.

There was a problem Rice had not anticipated: His publicity campaign was working too well. In Nevada, Warren Miller had become the
disgruntled third wheel in the Goodwin & Company partnership.
Every day he read glowing reports about Rawhide Coalition, but when
he visited the mines, he could see no such brilliance emanating from the
earth. Miller was jealous that Rice and Goodwin were off gallivanting
together in New York, talking up a storm about the stock, and he leaped
to the incorrect conclusion that they were withholding news from him
about an unannounced new gold vein. GG tried to quell Miller's fears
by explaining that this was how stock promotion worked, that puffery
was part of the sales pitch, but Miller wasn't buying it.

Eventually, Miller became so meddlesome that Rice decided they had
to cut him out. At a Goodwin & Company shareholders' meeting, GG
arranged it so Nat had enough votes to strip Miller of his vice presidency.
Then, after Nat appointed George to the vacant position, they gave
Miller a take-it-or-leave-it offer of $5,000 for his ownership stake. Miller
reluctantly accepted, but now, with the firm's main holding, Rawhide

Coalition, appreciating in value, he was hollering for more money. On December 5, 1908, Miller filed suit in Reno asking for $100,000 in damages and for Nat C. Goodwin & Company to be placed in receivership on the basis that his fraudulent former partners were "wholly insolvent and irresponsible."

In reality, not only did Rawhide Coalition have no recently discovered body of ore being kept secret, but word was getting around that there were no preexisting prospects for gold, either. The editor of the *Mining and Scientific Press* published a caustically honest assessment of Grutt Hill, where "ore, as they call it, is thrown over the dump like waste, and it resembles waste, regardless of the claim being made that it is all mill ore." Miller's lawsuit, coupled with news of the actual barren state of the mines, might have been the death knell for any legitimate company. But for George, dire publicity was exactly what he was after in this instance.

Rice planned to jettison all the Rawhide Coalition shares he had acquired with his fifteen-cent options, and the wave of bad news was going to make it look as if an avalanche of selling were due solely to adverse press. At the same time, George would tell Nat that the prudent thing to do was to "support" the stock with company money, buying up shares as they flooded the market. Unbeknownst to Goodwin, this would guarantee that Rice's personal sell orders were met with the company's buy orders at competitive prices. With these profits, George could then short Rawhide Coalition, knowing it was likely to plunge further. This was sooner than GG would have liked to jump off the stock, but at around $1.40 per share he would have to settle for a 933 percent return on his investment.

By the first week of December 1908, vaudeville's comic genius was a quaking, trembling wreck holed up inside a posh Fifth Avenue apartment, where his yipping and barking pack of pooches had rambunctious run of the house. Newspapers with front-page headlines accusing

Nat of bilking chorus girls out of their life's savings were strewn about the suite, and Goodwin hadn't been this petrified since he fainted in his 1874 stage debut at the Howard Athenaeum. Just weeks earlier, Nat had been enjoying his honeymoon. Now he was under investigation for stock fraud, and articles exposing Rice's crooked past were resurfacing afresh. By the time the weeklong torrent of bad publicity peaked, it was unclear whether Nat had been drinking nonstop for days or if he commenced a fresh bender each morning to brace for the barrage of "Extra!" editions bearing increasingly worsening news.

Goodwin had only partially heeded George's advice about throwing company money into the market to salvage value. Unaware that Rice had triggered the stock slide, a panicked Nat also sold his personal allotment of shares but didn't seem to understand the importance of keeping his mouth shut about it. He had talked numerous Broadway acquaintances onto the Rawhide Coalition bandwagon and didn't want to see them get hurt when the wheels blew off.

When news of Miller's lawsuit hit the papers, the stock at first held steady between $1.37 and $1.42 because the stories detailed how Miller believed he was being defrauded out of secret riches. But within forty-eight hours, the persistent rumors on the curb to unload while you still could became too burdensome for Rawhide Coalition to bear. Around noon on December 10, 1908, shares broke violently to seventy-five cents.

"Price of Rawhide Hit Hard," blared the front page of the New York *Sun*, "Christmas Money for Whoever Had a Lot of Shares to Dump on the Market Yesterday." Rice launched into denial mode, taking out rebuttal ads to detail how the firm had been victimized by double-crossing insiders.

On the curb, George vowed to be doing everything he could to support Rawhide Coalition. But *The New York Times* underscored how the collapse shocked the market "without any evidence of willingness on the part of the promoters to buy in at bargain prices." In fact, *The Times* reported, "Curb brokers said that Mr. Goodwin had within a day or two been advising recent purchasers to take profits." When a reporter called at the Hotel Patterson, GG would only allow his secretary to relay the terse comment that "a word from Mr. Goodwin might explain the slump."

When cornered, Goodwin had that same blank expression of astonishment he mimicked so well in the theater, a flabbergasted face of utter fear you could see all the way from the back row of the balcony. Rice had little tolerance for Nat's intoxicated sniveling but was used to it. Time spent quelling a mark's fears was a cost of doing business as a con artist. His grifter's sixth sense told George another pep talk was in order.

GG knew to slip smoothly into "reassurance" mode whenever Nat morphed into an erratic, frantic cat. He underscored for the umpteenth time that they could still make money even if their firm didn't and—this part intoned more sharply—how if you're stealing suckers blind, you'd better expect to take heat.

Newspapers vilified Rice and Goodwin for netting at least $500,000 in profit taking. But the accusations of insider trading did not differentiate between what Nat managed to eke out in his panic and the lion's share of the splurge George had raked in. Like any credible grifter, GG publicly insisted he took a financial beating on Rawhide Coalition.

Inwardly, it would have been difficult for Rice not to smirk when he thought how easily Goodwin had been conned into taking the brunt of the blame while he walked away with the bulk of the bankroll. By Christmas Eve, the stock slumped to forty cents, but Rice had already moved on. Now that he was established on the New York Curb, it was time to raise the stakes.

Nearing thirty-nine, George cut a well-known figure in the bustle of the financial district. By appearance alone, no one would have recognized him as the scrawny Lower East Side horse hustler who half a lifetime ago did stints in Elmira and Sing Sing for stealing. With a natty derby tilted rakishly over his high-cornered hairline and eyes squinting behind a fat, glowing stogie, GG sliced through the Broad Street throng with a self-assured swagger, nodding and giving little hand waves by way of greeting. His neckwear was a tasteful flourish that always matched his pocket square, and an opera cloak, pinkie ring, ornate cuff links, and hickory walking stick completed his image of bullish gentility. He made a show of commanding a prime parking space on the curb for his canary-yellow roadster, and after hours George was gaining a reputation as a big spender at Broadway's top restaurants. He did not frequent these swank nightspots in the company of his matronly wife, Frances, from whom he was rumored to be separated, but routinely turned heads with the presence of some pert young showgirl on his arm.

Two things had to happen for Rice to advance as a major player on the curb: Nat would have to be demoted to a lesser role within his own company; the blubbering funnyman simply couldn't handle being out in front of swindles measured in millions. More important, George needed the services of a proprietary brokerage. It was too risky and difficult for him to be running around placing market orders that ran contrary to the interests of corporations he controlled. He wanted to be able to underwrite and pawn off new securities without having to cut in a middleman.

A broker named Bernard H. Scheftels of Chicago had represented Nat C. Goodwin & Company in eastern stock offerings, and Rice persuaded Scheftels to transfer his license to New York in a merger of their firms. For this new venture, Goodwin willingly accepted a lesser role as vice president (GG tactfully emphasized that Nat's acting shouldn't have to suffer the strains of being a chief executive). Scheftels, fifty-two, took over as president, while Rice assumed the broad title of promotion manager "in charge of the protection of the company's interests in all markets."

On January 18, 1909, the newly minted B. H. Scheftels & Company opened for business at 42-44 Broad Street, occupying ten thousand prominent square feet on the first floor of the *Wall Street Journal* building. Rice's swindling empire now included mining stocks, propaganda publications to promote/demote them, a direct-mail list bloated with 150,000 suckers, and access to New York's most influential market makers. George brushed aside allegations that an ethical brokerage should not be so closely intertwined with securities promotion, pointing out that (a) Scheftels was hardly the only firm simultaneously touting and transacting stocks on the curb and (b) his Broad Street rivals were simply jealous, because Scheftels was pioneering a more innovative and efficient way of churning securities.

"Before the Scheftels corporation was in business a month it became plain that it was filling a long-felt want," GG argued. "In almost every branch it was performing some function in a manner more satisfactory to mining-stock speculators and investors than were its competitors. . . . Before the Scheftels company was six months old the fifteen men in its accounting department were compelled to work day and night time and again throughout the night until 6:00 a.m. to catch up with their work."

Rice himself was hustling sixteen hours a day, including Sundays. The driving force behind the wave of business was his two-fisted publicity punch of the *Market Letter,* a sixteen-page weekly sent to twenty-five hundred mining-stock holders and brokers, and the *Mining Financial News* that went out to a more general readership of thirty-four thousand as "the Wall Street Authority on Boston and New York Curb Stocks."

The *Market Letter* came out every Monday, crammed with articles ghostwritten by George but signed by "experts" booming Scheftels's pet stocks. The *Mining Financial News* ("This paper does not accept advertisements!") essentially reprinted the same stories three days later. One common Scheftels ploy was to invent a phony stock and send its price soaring before cashing out and walking away. Because the mainstream press didn't cover penny stocks trading at low volumes, it was up to house-organ tipster sheets to promote them. His run-ins with the Feds during the Maxim & Gay era taught George not to solicit money for junk securities through first-class mail, so both publications went out at the less restrictive penny postal rate. But after a while, the sheer volume of the Scheftels daily business made adhering to such precautions impractical.

By the summer of 1909, B. H. Scheftels was raking in $1 million a month in stock sales. The firm employed two hundred workers, includ-

Jacob Simon Herzig circa 1890, a decade before he began bilking a nation of suckers blind as the con artist George Graham Rice. (*New York American*)

Sing Sing prison, Rice's home as a convicted forger between 1895 and 1899. Conditions were so harsh and debasing that the suicide rate was exceeded only by what was then called the "insanity rate." (*Library of Congress*)

Rice made—and lost—millions as a fraudulent horse tipster at tracks such as Saratoga between 1901 and 1904, but the experience honed his confidence-hustling skills for more lucrative scams down the road. (*Library of Congress*)

A 1903 ad for Maxim & Gay, Rice's sham horse-betting service. One of the surest signs of a swindler is when he vehemently accuses others of perpetrating the exact same frauds he commits himself. (*Daily Racing Form*)

A stagecoach crossing the barren Nevada desert to Goldfield in 1906, quite likely the same route that brought Rice to the mining camps two years earlier. (*Library of Congress*)

A panoramic view of Greenwater, the largely fictitious copper camp in the desolate Funeral Mountains of California's Death Valley. Peeved that he did not rake in the lion's share of $30 million in illicit profits at Greenwater, Rice later termed the scam "the monumental mining-stock swindle of the century." (*Library of Congress*)

Rice pioneered sex as a selling tool. In 1908, he conned racy romance novelist Elinor Glyn into visiting his gold camp so he could plant escapades of her debauchery in the press as tawdry publicity for his mining stocks. (*Library of Congress*)

Nathaniel C. Goodwin was vaudeville's funniest stage comedian in 1909. But Rice turned Nat into a nervous alcoholic wreck by casting him as the star scapegoat in an elaborately farcical mining stock con. (*Nat Goodwin's Book*)

Rice's stock shenanigans were vilified by tycoon J. P. Morgan, shown here trying to strike a photographer with his cane in 1910. George did everything he could to rile Wall Street's power brokers, and was convinced Morgan had rescued the nation from the panic of 1907 only after the tycoon had created the crisis. (*Library of Congress*)

Over the course of five decades, Rice made numerous trips across New York's infamous "Bridge of Sighs" that connected the new (in 1902, left) Tombs prison with the Manhattan Criminal Courts building. (*Library of Congress*)

A 1912 newspaper drawing of Rice. Few depictions exist of him. Like most con artists, Rice was constantly on the run from the law. He was reluctant to pose for photographs, lest he be recognized. (*New York World*)

The New York Curb Exchange outdoor stock market, 1918. Messengers, like the one at left, perched on window ledges to flash a complex flurry of buy and sell signals to brokers in Broad Street below. (*Library of Congress*)

A 1912 ad for the tell-all magazine series "My Adventures with Your Money," which Rice later parlayed into a book deal. (*Goodwin's Weekly*)

The bombastic batting skills of home run king Babe Ruth typified the style and swagger of the Roaring Twenties. But the Bambino's off-field reputation for carousing and gluttony were also emblematic of America's "anything goes" era. (*Library of Congress*)

Public Enemy No. 1—Al Capone—bribed his way into a luxurious "suite" when imprisoned for tax evasion at Atlanta federal penitentiary, then invited Rice to move in as his cellmate in 1932. It was an offer Rice couldn't refuse. (*United States Bureau of Prisons*)

The swindling exploits of Rice frequently made for sensational newspaper headlines between 1890 and 1940.

Rice's final resting place at the Herzig family mausoleum, Linden Hill Jewish Cemetery, Ridgewood, New York. Although he had been disowned by his family five decades before his death, Herzig/Rice apparently outlived any relatives who objected to his con artistry.
(*Demetrios N. Papas*)

ing forty typists, twenty brokers, and ten stenographers. Mail room attendants worked with state-of-the-art sorting machinery. The hundred or so girls in the letter-opening department were compensated extremely well, at up to $100 per week (except for brokers, Rice almost exclusively hired attractive young women). There were plans to open a second branch in Boston, and the two offices would be linked by a private wire that allowed for "almost instantaneous" communication. The New York headquarters featured a large glass foyer where customers could lounge on couches and watch hot-off-the-ticker stock quotes get chalked up on wall-to-wall blackboards. Outside, curb tour guides were repeatedly asked by out-of-town gawkers to point out the Corinthian pillars and raised gold letters of the famous Scheftels brokerage they were reading so much about in the papers.

Of course, everything the tourists saw was an illusion. Beneath the glitz and glamour, B. H. Scheftels, in the parlance of the day, was nothing more than a high-class "bucket shop."

If the curb exchange was the mangy dog that hounded the Big Board, bucket shops were the parasitic flea on the dog. As the lowest level of stockbrokers, bucket shops operated across the country but proliferated in New York. The term at first referred to a barroom where you could bring in an empty bucket to carry out beer, and this type of establishment often featured simplistic gambling on stock price movements off a ticker tape (betting whether the next quote off the machine would be up or down). But this sort of bucket shop largely disappeared with the panic of 1907.

Thereafter, the term came to signify a cut-rate brokerage house that dangled low (often zero) commissions to customers as a means of obtaining money that the firm would rarely invest and almost never paid back. Individual stock orders would be entered into the books but not filled on the open market. Instead, orders would be "bucketed," or combined into larger blocks of stock that would be traded only if prices favored the brokerage. When customers requested money out of their accounts, bucket shops hemmed and hawed about arcane rules that gave them the right to settle in thirty (or more) days. If pressed for remittance of stock certificates, bucketeers just dipped into a general fund where all the firm's unsold shares were pooled in a single, swirling mass.

There were several categories of bucket shops in the early twentieth century. The most brazen operators earned the nickname hundred-percenters because they pocketed everything and returned nothing. Hundred-percenters pushed clients to open "margin" accounts that allowed trading on credit, with stocks in the customer's portfolio signed over as collateral. Brokers were liberal about extending credit but rigged the percentages so the client was in a near-continuous state of having to put up money to maintain margin requirements.

The best customers were unsophisticated low rollers who dabbled in penny stocks and didn't follow basic investing sense like knowing when to cut losses. *The Ticker and Investment Digest* explained in a 1910 article how bucketeers profited from this sort of sucker mentality:

> *If you want to learn why people lose money in the stock market, go to some one who has run a bucket shop. There is no better place on earth to study the weaknesses and follies of speculators than in one of those places where small lots are handled on small margins.*
>
> *The average bucket shop owner requires a two-point margin, so that any one who buys will be wiped out on the first decline of 1¾ points, the other ¼ covering "commissions."*
>
> *First glance at this proposition would seem to indicate that the bucket shop keeper was working against his own interest in allowing traders to take such a small loss, and placing no limit upon their profits, but experience proves that the great majority of bucket shop traders do not let their trades "go out" when their first two points are exhausted. They renew the margin and instruct the bucket man to "keep the trade good." When the bucket shop owner can record a long list of trades marked "K.G." (keep good) his face is wreathed*

in smiles, for he knows that these people will keep on margining
their trades as long as they have a dollar left, and be shaken out or
scared out at the bottom.

Shady promoters used bucket shops to unload obscure stocks in specialized sectors like mining. Some securities were so worthless it should have been a crime to peddle them at any price. Others had some marginal value, but their prices were way out of whack due to market manipulation.

Investors should have been able to recognize bucket shops by their advertising come-ons. The most egregious firms went out of their way to stamp themselves as legitimate, even if that meant making promises no legitimate broker would ever make. "No matter should the market decline, you will not be called for margin!" one ad lied. "Stocks are purchased the minute your order is received!" exaggerated another. If they were caught, one popular loophole bucketeers exploited was that in many jurisdictions failure to place an order or deliver stock certificates only constituted a breach of contract, not an actual crime. It was amazing how many orders got "misplaced" by "accident."

In the instances above, bucketeers were trying to ensnare the unsuspecting public by pretending to be on the up-and-up. But some bucket shops operated under an implicit agreement that no trades would ever occur on the open market. Both parties understood that the broker was strictly a bookmaker taking bets on the stock market. The customer got the advantage of being able to make low-commission wagers on the movement of stocks, and the brokerage made money by not purchasing the underlying securities (although it sometimes did as a form of hedging). But clients had zero protection if the bucket shop got swamped by winning bets and abruptly went out of business. In one five-year period in New York, bucket shops that went belly-up in this fashion cost customers an estimated $212 million ($5.6 billion in 2015 dollars).

A New York State statute had gone into effect on September 1, 1908, making the keeping of a bucket shop a felony. But this law had little, if any, effect because it targeted only the type of brokerage that operated as a gambling house. In addition, prosecutors had to show that "*both parties to the trade intended that [the transaction] should be settled by the payment of differences, and not by delivery of property.*" Just like in the goldbrick swindle or green goods game, why would a jilted client implicate himself in a crime by reporting it? The New York law did nothing to address the sale of trumped-up securities.

Rice was one of the few curb denizens willing to go on the record as defending bucket shops—even while insisting he didn't operate one:

> You hear a hue and a cry against bucketshops. There is no Federal embargo against bucketshopping. Yet somehow or other the machinery of the Government's Department of Justice is used to crush out this sort of gambling institution. Now, what is the difference in principle between gambling on margin on fluctuations of stocks in a bucketshop and doing the same through a New York Stock Exchange house?
>
> This is the unimportant difference:
>
> The bucketshop-keeper takes the other end of the play, pays you out of his pocket when the market goes your way and keeps your money when it goes against you. . . .
>
> [On the Big Board] the transaction is the same in principle as the one in the bucketshop, so far as the gambling feature is concerned. The only real difference is that when you gamble on market fluctuations through the bucketshops no contribution is made to the New York Stock Exchange "kitty." . . .
>
> The "kitty," or "rake-off," is enormous. Who pays it? You hear of the stockbroker going to Europe in his yacht every Summer. How many of his trading customers travel that way?
>
> Who pays the freight? Can a game be beaten where so many multimillionaires are created among those who are on the "inside"?

To George, this line of reasoning was just another case of framing the argument as Little Guy versus the Establishment to win over popular support.

By August 1909, GG's propaganda machine had depressed the mining sector to the point where B. H. Scheftels was able to swoop into Nevada to acquire some bargain properties. Rice had been claiming he was saving Americans tons of money by warning them off mining securities. But he realized suckers didn't like to follow bearish strategies, even if they turned a profit. Naïve investors preferred the psychological boost of upward movement. Shorting losers "only carried out the negative end of a grand idea," George reasoned. "The affirmative demanded that the Scheftels corporation must put its followers into a stock or stocks where they could actually make money."

Rice decided copper would be the new gold. He was zeroing in on Ely Central, a dormant mine situated on an irregularly shaped slice of 490 acres in White Pine County in the eastern part of the state's celebrated Copper Flat. The property had been passed over because its top layer was a non-ore-bearing slab that went down four hundred feet, but George believed he could intrigue the public with the tantalizing mystery that the slab might be hiding something better. After all, Ely Central was surrounded by productive copper mines, most notably Nevada Consolidated (which Rice had been bad-mouthing in his newsletters for months). Privately, George coveted Ely Central's aboveground right-of-way, because its roads provided the only path for steam shovels to get into and out of neighboring mines. If he could deny access, Rice could sabotage the stock prices of his competitors.

Two brothers who owned Ely Central had been $89,000 in debt since the panic of 1907. Although GG would not admit to launching a smear campaign, the brothers suddenly became the targets of anonymous personal attacks. "Their credit was assailed in every quarter and they found themselves ambushed and bushwhacked in every move they made," Rice gloated. "They were forced into a position where it was believed they would accept anything that might be offered them for their interest in Ely Central. As fate would have it, the Scheftels company entered the race at this psychological moment."

George scooped up shares of Ely Central, some for as little as three cents each. He bought out the beleaguered brothers and acquired odd lots here and there until he amassed a controlling interest. He kept 880,000 shares for himself and let Scheftels bank the rest. As the stock rose to $1 on the curb, George retained fifty-cent options to buy more within six months.

Rice hired Colonel William A. Farish, an old-school engineer whose good name had somehow remained unsullied despite association with swindlers dating to the 1880s. Without citing scientific analysis, Farish reported Ely Central had thirty-three million tons of hidden commercial ore where previous sampling had found none.

"The prospect fairly took the Scheftels organization off its feet," George wrote, beaming, knowing full well that Farish's exaggeration strained credulity. "We were dazzled. We saw ourselves at the head of a mine worth $25,000,000 to $40,000,000. No time was lost in organizing a campaign to finance the whole deal. Having no syndicated multimillionaires to back it up, the Scheftels corporation went to the public for the money."

Rice's newsletters badgered the masses "to take advantage of an unusually attractive speculative opening," asserting that the nation's shrewdest investors "know that copper is the surest, safest, and most profitable branch of mining." By September, Ely Central commanded $2⅝ on the open market. When the stock zoomed to $3 in October, "all the speculating world was making money in it."

But at least one independent voice wasn't buying the hype: Rice learned through his network of press contacts that *The Engineering and Mining Journal* was gathering evidence for an exposé on Ely Central titled "A New Scheme to Hook Suckers." Not only would the piece lambaste Farish's dubious report, but the publication had done background checks on George and was planning on unmasking him as a dangerous, unprincipled con.

Rice had bet the entire Scheftels business on Ely Central. If the truth rendered the company's pet stock illiquid, the firm would lose everything. George became consumed with obtaining a revised report to counteract the impending tsunami of negative publicity. It had been costly enough to secure the services of Farish. Now GG had to come up with another A-list engineer on short notice to save himself from bankruptcy and, quite possibly, jail. In terms of bribery, the most reputable mining engineers were considered "untouchable." Still, Rice knew, every man had his price.

Then he had a blast from the past.

On impulse, George sent word west that he wanted to meet with an engineer whose say-so had launched highly regarded mining endeavors from Egypt to Australia, South Africa to Central America, and in every European country in between. When the response came back that the man he desired to hire was based no longer in Nevada but in New York, GG's spirit soared.

The world-class mining authority Rice had in mind was Charles S. Herzig, the younger brother George had neither seen nor spoken to in fifteen years.

"I asked Captain W. Murdoch Wiley [a mutual mining acquaintance] whether he could induce my brother to make an examination," Rice explained. "I did not approach Charles myself, because we had been estranged. . . . Captain Wiley arranged for a meeting at the Engineers' Club. I went there, and was formally introduced by Captain Wiley to my brother across a table."

In the same matter-of-fact way he would have addressed a stranger, George asked what it would cost for Charles to conduct a high-priority appraisal of Ely Central.

"What's the purpose of the report?" Charles asked warily.

"The Scheftels company wants confidential, expert information such as you are qualified to give as to the value and prospects of the property," George replied, tiptoeing around the topic of how favorable he expected the report to be.

"I'll take $5,000," Charles said, cutting straight to the chase. "But only on one condition. I am going to the Ely and Ray districts to report for English capitalists, and I can take your property in at the same time. My report is not to be published, and I reserve the right to make a verbal instead of a written one. If you really want to know what I think of the property, I am quite willing to give it a careful examination and let you know. Because of the stock market campaign you are making, I would not accept your offer if, did I report favorably, your idea would be to make use of the report in the market."

Because George's version of this discussion is the only known account of their negotiations, it's difficult to say for certain who was conning whom in this deal. On the one hand, Charles was demanding an exorbitant fee—the equivalent of $130,000 in today's dollars—for a nonbinding appraisal. On the other, George was so desperate to have the backing of a credible engineer that he probably figured he could forge his brother's signature on a glowing write-up, no matter the cost.

George and Charles agreed to terms in late October. Rice—and other curb sharks—felt the first tremors of unfavorable Ely Central news on November 3, 1909, when the ratio of buy orders to sell orders among Scheftels's customers rose to two to one, signaling that specialists were lining up to sell short at $4 per share.

The next day the ratio jumped to three to one. According to Rice, "The professional selling was now accompanied by rumors on the Curb which spread like the smell of fire that trouble of some dire sort was pending for the Scheftels company."

On November 5, the buy-sell ratio for Ely Central spiked to four to one, "pointing conclusively to a great public demand and much shorting by professionals."

November 6 was a Saturday, when the curb traded for an abbreviated two-hour session. George was enjoying his morning cigar in his apartment at the Hotel Marie Antoinette when his valet brought up the newspapers an hour before the market opened. The New York *Sun* had been leaked a copy of *The Engineering and Mining Journal*'s exposé, and the "shameful attempt to inveigle the public into a mining gamble against long odds" was being played up big:

> *The rapidity with which the [Ely Central] price has been boosted does not gibe with the statements and prognostications. . . . We understand that the suckers have been biting freely and that checks by mail have been showering into the office of B. H. Scheftels & Co. like snowflakes in winter. However, under the circumstances we have recited, it does not necessarily follow that these orders have been executed in the Curb market. . . . It is time that a halt be called to these bloodsuckings of the public.*

George leaped for the telephone and commanded his office to have buy orders for twenty-five thousand Ely Central shares waiting in the queue before trading opened on the curb. He then dashed off a telegram to Charles that read, "Savage attack in *Engineering & Mining Journal* on Ely Central. If your report on property is favorable, I beg you to let us have it by wire and allow the use of it to counteract."

With a hyperventilating Goodwin at his side, George worked the phone for the entire two-hour curb session. The firm's large buy order absorbed most of the panic selling, and Ely Central actually closed up one-eighth of a point. But the next day, Sunday papers from coast to coast expanded on the *Sun's* scoop, and GG braced for a fiscal train wreck on Monday.

"All the New York papers featured scathing articles," Rice lamented. "Dispatches indicated, too, that the papers of Boston, Chicago, Los Angeles and San Francisco had played it up on the front page as the most shocking mining-stock scandal of the century. . . . It was plain that we had been marked for the sacrifice. It looked as though we hadn't a chance in a million of weathering the onslaught if we lent the market further support."

George sent another terse telegram to his brother. This one told him not to bother wiring any report.

Rice painted a dire picture of the moments before the opening gong sounded on the curb on Monday, November 8:

> *The air was surcharged with the impending calamity. . . .*
>
> *I could see from my office window a dense crowd of brokers assembled around the Ely Central specialists. Although ominously silent, they were struggling for position and were tensely nervous. . . .*
>
> *The over-Sunday anti-Scheftels newspaper publicity had racked Ely Central stockholders and created a panicky movement to liquidate, which was about to find vent in violent explosion. . . .*
>
> *The market opened. Instantly there was terrific action. Hundreds of hands were waving wildly in the air. Everybody wanted to sell and nobody wanted to buy. The chorus was deafening. Screams rent the air. The tumult was heard blocks away.*
>
> *Every newspaper had a man on the spot. Brokers from the New York Stock Exchange left their posts and came to see the big show; the Stock Exchange was half emptied. . . . The Curb was a struggling, screaming, maddened throng of brokers.*

Without a cent of Scheftels money thrown into the abyss to stop the free fall, Ely Central plummeted from a $4 opening to $1⅝ in less than an hour.

"Curb Lambs Caught by Ely Central; Small Investors Wiped Out," *The New York Times* blared. Pop Mendels, the taciturn curb boss who was trying to impose a code of ethics, told the New York *Sun* he had been besieged with complaints about Scheftels since the day the brokerage opened. He scoffed that ignorant speculators had gotten what they deserved, because "anyone who bought mining stock anyway was a sucker."

Over the next several days, Rice tried to stabilize Ely Central by buying large blocks at $1 per share. At this price point, all the sharpies who had shorted the stock jumped in to cover their positions, transforming

crazed selling into frantic buying. After losing $3 million in market cap-
italization, the price of Ely Central became less volatile, and the Scheftels brokerage settled like an epileptic falling into a deep sleep after a
grand mal seizure.

Only a swindler as audacious as George would attempt to spin his
darkest hour on the curb into a positive, feel-good moment: "It was a
proud moment for me when, at the end of the day's market, I mounted the
platform in the Scheftels customers' trading-room, gave voice to a shrill
cheer of triumph and wrote on the blackboard the following: 'We have not
closed out a single margin account! We are carrying everybody!'"

In 1910, the phrase "No such thing as bad publicity" had yet to creep
into common usage, but George would have been familiar with the
French colloquialism *succès de scandale* that was popular around that
time. He was quick to capitalize on the emotional momentum of Ely
Central by playing the role of wounded martyr and framing the "attack"
against B. H. Scheftels as a classic example of how Wall Street insiders
conspired to crush working-class investors.

"I got busy with the publicity forces at my command," Rice huffed
indignantly. "Through the Scheftels *Market Letter* and the *Mining
Financial News* the story was told of the whole dastardly campaign....
The Scheftels organization now drew its first long breath. Friends and
enemies alike marveled how the corporation had managed to survive.
We had held the fort, but at murderous cost."

Rice sued *The Engineering and Mining Journal* for $750,000 in libel
damages. He marched ahead with commitments to expand the Scheftels empire, opening branches in Chicago, Detroit, Milwaukee, Philadelphia, and Providence. Business rocked into the night, with closing time
extended to 10:00 P.M. to handle the crush of market orders. After a year,
the chain was on its way to selling $15 million in mining stock, which
George touted as a record.

"It was formal notice to the forces arrayed against us that we did not propose to be made victims of an unholy hostility," Rice vowed. "It [also served notice] that we proposed to go through with the Ely Central deal."

In order to make money on Ely Central, George had to execute his fifty-cent options in part by February 1, 1910, and in full sixty days later, so the push was on to boost the stock back to where it was before the implosion. He planted encouraging news dispatches about development at Ely Central, but the only real work going on at the site was the patrolling of sentries to keep enemy steam shovels from trespassing on the property's access roads. If Charles Herzig ever authored a definitive engineering report, it was not made public, but Rice claimed to be in possession of a telegram from his brother that read, "I have formed a very favorable opinion of the property. I feel that it has the making of a big mine." The same wire allegedly contained an urgent request from Charles to have George purchase twenty-five hundred shares of the stock on his behalf.

Rice divided the typists in the Scheftels correspondence pool into round-the-clock shifts to churn out 400,000 "tip letters" that pumped various Scheftels-promoted stocks. The mass mailings hinted at an undisclosed "good thing" whose price would soon skyrocket. To add a flair of intrigue, the letters listed Scheftels's entire inventory of penny stocks, each with a corresponding code word. "Preferred" customers (in actuality, everyone) would be sent a code word just before the secret stock peaked, but George suggested savvy investors buy *all* the stocks on the list right now to avoid missing out. The campaign harked back to the Maxim & Gay practice of tipping every horse in every race, because GG planned to send different code words to different suckers.

Despite Rice's attempts at positive publicity, the brokerage suffered aftershocks for months after the Ely Central debacle. A police inspector barged into the Scheftels headquarters unannounced one afternoon. "He stalked scowlingly through the entire establishment and made vague threats of what was in store for us," Rice recalled. The same cop showed up late one night at Nat's apartment to interrogate the comedian. Postal inspectors went on a "fishing expedition," contacting subscribers of the Scheftels newsletters via form letter to ask if customers thought they had been deceived by the brokerage. "Scores of these letters were forwarded to us by customers with remarks to the effect that evidently somebody was after us," George complained.

Rice was adept at soothing the masses, but dealing one-on-one with aggrieved suckers was a talent he still hadn't mastered. One instance George would come to regret involved D. J. Szymanski, a noted "corn doctor" who had an office adjacent to the curb where he treated the calluses and bunions of brokers who pounded the pavement six days a week. After losing a fortune on Ely Central, Szymanski showed up at the brokerage, at first demanding, then pleading for the return of his investment money. Rice and Bernie Scheftels berated the doctor and kicked him to the curb. The staff had a good laugh at his expense, but the doctor vowed revenge. When a Scheftels tip letter dated January 4, 1910, arrived in his mailbox at 25 Broad Street, Szymanski took the list of coded stocks to the Department of Justice, where his tale of woe fell upon intrigued ears.

In the spring of 1910, every little oddity in America was being blamed on the impending arrival of Halley's comet. Astronomers had announced that the once-every-seventy-six-years celestial sighting would be especially unique this time around because Earth was on target to pass through the comet's twenty-four-million-mile long tail, which was believed to be made up of cyanogen, a colorless toxic gas. Even though scientists assured everyone the planet was completely safe and that any trace amount of gas that made it into the atmosphere would be noticeable only in the form of some spectacular sunsets in mid-May, doomsayers were predicting oblivion.

Conspiracy theorists agitated fears by linking unrelated events like stormy weather, stunted crops, and wacky stock market fluctuations. The panic was a boon for con men who pushed "Anti-Comet Pills" and sold "Comet Protecting Umbrellas." Rice might even have used Halley's comet as an excuse for the bizarre performance of the B. H. Scheftels balance sheet. How else could GG explain his boasts of record business when the firm's chief stocks were struggling to fetch nickels and dimes on the open market?

The key to understanding this conundrum is the phrase "open market," because very few orders from Scheftels's customers ever got executed there. The brokerage was so over-leveraged from bucketing trades that a massive chunk of each branch manager's workday was consumed by having to cool out disgruntled suckers while George and Bernie scrambled to free up cash. The firm's accounting ledgers might as well have been written in an alien language, because Scheftels maintained at least three separate sets of books.

Part of the reason Rice insisted on private telegraph wires was the huge volume of incriminating correspondence that crisscrossed the country between Scheftels's offices. On June 14, 1910, for example, George commanded branch managers not to execute trade orders but to instead "transmit by wire all balances above $500 this morning and repeat the performance at noon." Other times he would wire instructions for an aggressive sales push, like "Stir the lambs up to-morrow on Ely Central. The great move has come." Rice was only half joking when he sent a wire imploring a broker named Crookes to "take a sand-bag with you to-night and look for a live one. If he won't buy Ely Central, hit him a good one."

When customers who bought stock complained about not receiving share certificates, their names went on a "squawk sheet" that noted how likely they were to rat out the company to the police or postal authorities. Managers were ordered to only bother headquarters with the most pressing triage cases, like this one wired to Rice by the Chicago office: "Mr. Thurston was again in to-day, and went after us very roughly for non-delivery of 500 [shares of] Mines America, paid for and due over a month. I regret the necessity of again calling your attention to this matter. Have promised Mr. Thurston his stock Wednesday. So please ship to-night or to-morrow. . . . Will send $1,500 by fast train to-morrow. Also some marketable securities."

If he intended to fill the order, George would mark the telegram "Big kick. Buy for cash. Ship at once." If he couldn't (or didn't want to) locate stock on the curb, the response from headquarters was something like "To all branch managers: Not a damn thing in sight to ship tonight. But some, someday."

Complicating matters, Scheftels routinely sold (on paper at least) more shares of its in-house stocks than had been issued. If the firm was ever compelled to deliver all the outstanding shares at once, it wouldn't be able to produce them, because they didn't exist. Rice often dictated at the start of the day what he wanted the volume and price of Scheftels-backed stocks to look like at the end of the trading session, leaving it to the wire room to report phantom transactions throughout the day that added up to the desired figures. "He held the market in his hand," the telegraph operator in the New York office would later testify. "He made the price what he liked."

George had informants all over the city. One day in June, a reporter on the *New York American* was snooping in the city editor's assignment book and saw a memorandum to watch out for a federal raid on Scheftels. "The information was reliable and it gave us a shock," George said. "The thought that the powers of a great government like the United States could be used to crush us without giving us a hearing seemed unbelievable. To be on the safe side Mr. Scheftels, accompanied by an attorney of high standing, visited Washington."

When confidence swindlers collide with federal bureaucracy, the result can be like the "unstoppable force meets an immovable object" paradox. In this instance, a violent collision was preempted by old-fashioned governmental runaround. The Department of Justice shuttled Bernie and his attorney from office to office until a clerk reported there were no pending charges against the company. The clerk further volunteered that no one in his department even knew the firm existed (this was incorrect; the clerk himself might not have known, but Department of Justice higher-ups certainly did).

Scheftels then hustled over to the U.S. Postal Service. A chief inspector there seemed bemused that the president of a New York brokerage would travel all the way to Washington to inquire if there were any investigations into his company. When the Scheftels lawyer insisted on written confirmation that authorities would give the firm a hearing before taking action on any complaints that might filter in, the inspector consented only under the condition that Scheftels would agree to allow the postal service to inspect his books on demand at any time. Bernie balked, and the Feds would later estimate that by the time he made this trip to Washington, more than $3 million—$75 million in today's dollars—had already evaporated from margin accounts entrusted to the brokerage.

At 2:00 P.M. on August 19, 1910, a rumor ripped through the curb that the National Reserve Bank was refusing to honor checks drawn from the B. H. Scheftels account because of insufficient funds. Within an hour, the lone constable assigned to keep order on the curb had to whistle for backups to hold back a howling mob of brokers and customers threatening to smash the gilded glass entryway of the Scheftels offices. "I want my money!" one enraged check holder kept screaming while pounding on the locked front doors.

Even though the closing gong had already rung out the Friday session, an impromptu auction for Scheftels checks erupted in the trading pit, with speculators buying uncashed drafts for ninety cents on the dollar. After an hour, buyers started growing less sure that Scheftels would make good on its paper, and bidding dropped to fifty cents. *The New York Times* reported that after-hours speculation in suspect checks was "new even to the Curb," and even George himself quipped that "the scene on the Curb was wilder than when there is an active market in stocks."

Rice had spent the missing money freely, and that night he had to make frantic arrangements to keep Scheftels in business. Charles A. Stoneham, a fellow bucketeer (and future owner of the New York Giants baseball club), was the shark who came through with the loan, even though George insisted his brokerage had the funds all along. Rice first claimed the bounced checks were the fault of a courier who failed to make a timely deposit, then later shifted the blame to a "clique" that was hatching another "conspiracy" against B. H. Scheftels. When the National Reserve Bank opened Saturday morning, Rice planted himself at the front door. The *New-York Tribune* described how George fielded questions from reporters who peppered him with inquiries about the solvency of the brokerage:

> *When Mr. Rice was asked if the firm would have any difficulty in accepting deliveries on Monday, he smilingly produced a package of bills six inches thick with a thousand dollar gold certificate on each end and replied:*
>
> *"This is what talks. I have $175,000 here which will more than take care of anything that turns up on Monday. If not, there is plenty more where this came from. Look at it. It's real stuff. Nothing 'phony' about this, is there?"*
>
> *He ran his thumb over the end of the package of bills showing that they were all of large denomination, and, so far as the reporters could see, none of it was "stage money."*

GG had staved off financial implosion. But like a stacked faro deck, the long-term odds were tilted against his bucket shop.

"The strain was great," Rice conceded. "Confidence was again impaired. Many accounts were withdrawn by customers. We were compelled to ease our load by selling accumulated stocks at a loss."

With his firm foundering, George became oddly fixated on winning smaller battles, like his vendetta against Ely Central's rivals over steam shovel access. On September 25, 1910, Rice had his attorney in Nevada secure a restraining order prohibiting the enemy companies from trespassing with their equipment. Before this injunction could be made operative, GG was required to post a bond. The cost of the bond, in all likelihood, was less than $100—pocket change for a swindler who flashed $1,000 bills in the streets. Yet despite numerous telegrams from Rice on September 27 and 28 assuring his lawyer that payment was on the way, the money for the bond never made it to Nevada.

"The sureties never qualified," George lamented. "A catastrophe befell us and brought to an earthquake finish the house of B. H. Scheftels & Company and all its ambitious plans."

The federal raid, when it hit, was spectacular; a sensational display of street theater witnessed by thousands.

One by one, plainclothes detectives slipped into the B. H. Scheftels & Company customer lounge on the morning of September 29, 1910. The fifteen New York cops assigned to assist federal agents had no trouble blending in with the gaggle of penny stock ticker watchers, feigning rapt attention in prices being chalked up on the wall-to-wall blackboards while smoking or jotting quotes alongside newspaper stock tables. Only the eye of a discerning grifter might have sensed something was not quite right: Why were the overcoats of so many men buttoned to the hilt on such a pleasantly warm autumn morning?

Their coats were closed because each officer was packing at least one high-caliber firearm. The special agent George M. Scarborough of the Secret Service had stressed they would be infiltrating the nest of a felon who was the mastermind behind America's most pervasive stock-swindling racket.

Scarborough, thirty-four, was a tall, sinewy Texan with a vise of a handshake. He had been specifically assigned to eradicate bucket shops because he was unknown to Wall Street and thus considered impervious to insider influence. But behind his stoic sense of duty, Scarborough was thrilled for the opportunity to be in New York. He fancied himself an earnest playwright and badly wanted to break into Broadway with real-life dramas based on cases he had worked on. As he positioned his tactical team, Scarborough might even have been taking mental notes on timing and dramatic tension so he could incorporate those elements into some future stage scene.

The Scheftels raid was a challenge to choreograph because the climax was to be played out simultaneously on seven stages. At the same time his men were taking their places in and around the New York headquarters, Scarborough was organizing synchronized deployments in Boston, Chicago, Detroit, Milwaukee, Philadelphia, and Providence. The ambushes needed to be coordinated to the minute to prevent communication between branch offices that would lead to the destruction of evidence and the flight of intended arrestees.

At precisely high noon, Rice was standing on the Scheftels front stoop surveying the curb from behind a thick plume of cigar smoke. There was a perceptible undercurrent of anticipation running through Broad Street, but George couldn't quite sniff out its source. One of his brokers by the mining specialists' pole signaled that the offer for ten thousand shares of Jumbo Extension was sixty-eight cents. GG was trying to unload this stock. But the bid was too low, so he grimaced and shook his head no.

Only because his gaze was drawn in the broker's direction did Rice notice the horse-drawn police transport wagon—a Black Maria—slicing quietly through the throng toward the Scheftels side of the curb.

At that moment, the front door of the brokerage slammed violently shut behind him. George spun and saw through the large front windows that the unfamiliar overcoated men inside the lounge had drawn long pistols and were ordering everyone to stand in place with arms folded.

Scarborough had assigned agents out by the stoop to collar Rice the instant the bucket shop was locked from within. But as fate would have it, a broker from another firm bounded up the front steps of B. H. Scheftels at that very second, his arms laden with stock certificates. The agents, under the mistaken belief this man was a Scheftels employee, tried to wrestle him into custody while the broker protested loudly that he was only a courier.

A phalanx of police officers was advancing toward the building from the street, so there was no way for George to blend into the bustle of the curb. Auctioneers and brokers in the pit, who rarely paused for any reason, were now stopping mid-trade to see what all the commotion was about.

Like a magician taking advantage of a distraction that lured the eyes of his audience elsewhere, Rice turned on his heel and calmly walked into the building's main lobby adjacent to the Scheftels suite. He strode confidently past the agents arguing with the courier but, instead of trying to enter the brokerage, kept going the full length of the block-long corridor and straight out the back exit to New Street.

"That settled it," Rice later recounted. "I concluded that the ax had fallen. The shock of realization that our offices were being raided by the Government did not for a moment throw me off my balance or put fear in my heart, nor did the sense of the outrage affect me at the moment. There was but one sickening thought—the ruin of the edifice I and my associates had labored day and night for so many months to build. . . . In three seconds I was on my way to the place where I thought succor could be found."

George would later tell everyone he went to the offices of the Scheftels attorneys and remained there all evening arranging for the release of his comrades. In actuality, Rice stopped only briefly at his lawyer's before hightailing it to the swank Central Park West apartment he had been renting on the sly for his mistress.

Inside the brokerage, Scarborough flashed his badge and announced with a theatrical flourish that he was in absolute control under the authority of the Department of Justice. Every inch of the establishment was under seizure, and every person within its doors was his prisoner. Scarborough stalked into the telegraph cage, pressed the muzzle of a revolver into the face of the wire operator, and commanded him to cut off the master connection.

The telegraph man was blind in one eye, so at first he didn't see the gun. "When he got his first peep he concluded that a maniac had invaded his sanctum and he almost expired with apoplexy on the spot," Rice was later told.

Scarborough tore into the cashier's cage and demanded the pouch containing that morning's cash and securities. In his thundering Texas drawl, he swore at the cashier when the employee had the audacity to ask for a receipt. According to some witnesses, the special agent slipped fistfuls of bills inside his suit pockets.

The detectives had eight arrest warrants but could only match the documents with seven employees. The eighth was for Rice, but none of the cops wanted to break the news to Scarborough that the ringleader—who only moments before had been surrounded by lawmen—was nowhere to be found.

"I walked across the street to the New Street entrance of a building that extends from Broadway to New Street, ambled across to the Broadway side, jumped on a surface car, rode three blocks to Broadway and Cedar Street, jumped into an elevator, and in a few minutes entered the offices of House, Grossman & Vorhaus," Rice said. "In a moment two members of the law firm were on their way. Within ten minutes after the raiders had entered the offices the lawyers were on the spot. They were denied admittance and had to content themselves with waiting outside the door until the prisoners were taken out."

The attorneys weren't the only spectators hovering around the entrance to the bucket shop's headquarters. When word spread about which firm was being raided, brokers spilled out of offices, and the consensus was that the whole sordid spectacle couldn't be happening to a more deserving den of crooks. The air rang with derisive hoots and catcalls, and for the first time anyone could remember, business on the curb halted in the middle of a trading day. The only men working Broad Street during the raid were opportunistic pickpockets, who enjoyed a bonanza spree pilfering billfolds and pocket watches from the distracted masses.

Inside, Scarborough was briefed about Rice's disappearing act. He took out his anger on the men in custody, namely Bernie Scheftels and his underling managers. Scarborough refused to disclose the charges against the prisoners and ordered them searched for dangerous weapons. He seemed annoyed the frisking yielded only a penknife and a pencil stub.

Bernie could see the swarm gathering outside. He protested that his employees should be allowed to retain their dignity, and he offered to pay for taxicabs to shuttle everyone to the booking station. Scarborough laughed and responded that to the contrary he intended to shackle everyone together in leg irons and handcuffs so the brigade of flash photographers could get good front-page pictures. The special agent with the dramatic flair was orchestrating what was quite likely America's first "perp walk" staged solely for the benefit of mass media.

Bernie was the first captive led out into the mob. His bald head glistened with sweat, yet he grinned defiantly at the crush of photographers. "Glad to see you going," shouted a rival broker. Fruit vendors had their carts looted by hooligans who pelted the detainees with apples. A few supportive friends of the arrested workers approached the Black Maria but were taunted, were knocked down, and had their clothing ripped off their backs by curb vigilantes.

"No prize fight or football game could have produced greater excitement," the *New-York Tribune* gushed. "The frantic crowd which blocked the street and all the entrances to the buildings around about swelled to four thousand, and as the mining 'experts' were helped into the patrol wagon cheer on cheer rose, led by the Curb brokers."

Scheftels branch managers in six other cities were simultaneously whisked off to jail. Most would never be indicted, but their reputations were ruined.

With hand-cranked siren yowling and horse whips lashing, the prisoner transport van lurched through the Broad Street crowd to Wall Street, then ding-donged up Broadway. The vehicle's passage coincided with Rice's trying to make a break from his attorney's office to his girlfriend's suite, and he had to dive into an alley to avoid being spotted.

"My attention was attracted by the clanging of the bell of the police patrol wagon," George said. "As it wheeled past me on the run I could see my associates huddled together in the Black Maria on their way to the bastille. For the moment, I lost full sense of the gravity of what was transpiring and was overcome by a feeling of joy that I had been spared that ignominy."

Even though his primary target was still at large, Scarborough posed for trophy photographs with the impounded loot and announced to reporters that the arrested con men had all been charged with multiple felony violations of section 215 of the U.S. Criminal Code. The special agent said the government was going to prove that B. H. Scheftels & Company abused the U.S. Mail to make fraudulent claims about worthless stocks whose prices were artificially rigged and that the firm collected illicit commissions for trades it never executed. Every violation was punishable by a five-year prison sentence. Out of thousands of complaints, Scarborough said the government had culled fifty strong witnesses, each of whom was willing to testify and could produce documents signed and mailed by Scheftels officials that corroborated their claims of being defrauded.

Chief among the witnesses would be D. J. Szymanski of 25 Broad Street, the bullied corn doctor whose coming forward about a January 4, 1910, tip letter was the first break the Secret Service had in building its case.

Business on the curb resumed within the hour. The value of Scheftels-sponsored stocks evaporated. It took three double-horse wagons to carry away all the firm's ledgers and files. An inventory of the busted company's records would later reveal that part of George's sucker list had been stolen during the raid by a rogue detective and sold to Rice's loan shark and rival bucketeer Charles Stoneham.

As the reporters drifted away, Scarborough reached into his suit pocket and pulled out a wad of GG's money. He peeled off a few bills and tossed them to an errand boy to fetch cigars for his men as a reward for a job well done.

Rice worked late into the night assembling a team of attorneys—eventually there would be six of them—to negotiate his surrender. He knew the Feds would ultimately zero in on his mistress's apartment, but he figured he was safe until morning. Two weeks earlier, George had sensed trouble and moved from the Hotel Marie Antoinette to the Glenmore. Considering how easily he had eluded the agents when they were only an arm's length away on the Scheftels stoop, GG figured a twelve-block dodge would be enough to keep the Secret Service staking out the wrong apartment until he was good and ready to turn himself in.

Early in the afternoon of September 30, 1910, Rice strode into the downtown Federal Building flanked by two lawyers. Reporters were stunned to see that one of them was William Travers Jerome, the man who until the previous year had served as New York County district attorney. Jerome—the same anticorruption zealot who had run Maxim & Gay out of town in 1903—was now at George's elbow insisting his client was an innocent, upstanding businessman.

Rice, impeccably dressed in a blue serge suit, wing collar, and dark red four-in-hand tie, "looked as cool and bland as if he were paying an afternoon call," the *Tribune* marveled. "He preserves perpetually that 'pleasant' look which photographers insist upon, and his drooping eye-glasses hang like crystal tears on the bloom of his cheeks. The delicacy of his expression branded as brutal the thought that he had once had his head shaved and worked in a chain gang."

Jerome had GG out of there in minutes, free on $15,000 bail.

Newspapermen had found Rice's love nest before the Feds did, but no one was able to dig up the true dirt about George's latest "woman of mystery." It was reported that Elizabeth "Bessie" Lafell was a former actress from Kentucky—or a chorus girl, or a circus aerialist whose career had been cut short when she fell twenty feet performing an act called "whirl of death." Lafell was also either a silent, brainy partner in Scheftels or some reckless jezebel with whom Rice was smitten. There was even talk that Bessie was another man's wife. When reporters pressed her, Lafell denied intimate involvement with George yet vowed to pawn her jewelry and expensive French lingerie to help pay for his defense:

I know him well. I am not in love with him, but he is a splendid fellow, one who would go to any length for his friends. They will all stand by him. I cannot believe [the] lie he is a swindler. . . .
I don't think they will get any [money] back from Rice. He has

*little himself. I know that he gave his wife, with whom he was very
unhappy, $300,000, and was paying her $1,000 a month of his own
volition.*

*Rice gave me some money, but I have very little left now. All that
I have now, and all my diamonds, I will give to aid him in his fight.*

If Bessie was the silent Scheftels partner, Nat Goodwin was the sim-
pering partner. The Feds had convened a grand jury to finalize formal
charges against the firm, and Nat, under pressure from his soon-to-be
ex–fourth wife, swore he no longer had anything to do with the company and was willing to testify against it as a voluntary witness. Edna
Goodrich had been a shrill, vocal critic of Rice since the Ely Central
scandal, and for the better part of a year she had been carping to her
comedian husband to break off his business relationship before George
got them all thrown in the hoosegow.

Rice had little respect for men who couldn't put meddlesome wives
in their proper place, and he had tried to impress this upon Goodwin
by setting an emphatic example: When the Feds first came snooping
around Scheftels months earlier and GG sensed his own wife might
make trouble, he had locked Frances away in a sanitarium with explicit
orders not to let her out until he said so.

Through the autumn of 1910, the Feds attacked bucket shops in waves.
With Scarborough at the helm, raids knocked out swindlers in all the
major East Coast cities, plus smaller operations in Cleveland, St. Louis,
Kansas City, and St. Paul. The barrage was reminiscent of what happened
when Maxim & Gay went under and brought the entire tipster sector
down with it. Rice's bust was the headline grabber designed to show the
government was serious about cracking down on mail fraud, while copy
cat scammers were pieces of wreckage caught in the federal riptide.

The moral advocacy magazine *The World's Work* compiled a rundown of every bucket shop kingpin who either had been prosecuted,

had gone on the lam, or was awaiting trial. Rice not only topped the list but commanded his own special section within the article. While the mainstream press generally showered the Secret Service with praise, *The World's Work* was one of the few publications that took the Feds to task for not acting sooner, lashing out at gaping loopholes in the law:

> *First, one may ask, why has the United States Government allowed these swindles to go on, year after year, and only moved, at last, after half a billion dollars has been stolen?*
>
> *The answer is very simple. The Federal Government of this country has no control over business in New York unless, first, it is part of interstate commerce; or, second, it uses the United States mails to defraud. Obviously, if a New York swindler sells a gold brick to a New York laborer, the Federal Government has nothing to do with that.*
>
> *All the recent raids are based on the fact that the swindlers forwarded through the mails circulars, letters, and stocks intended to defraud the public. Therefore the Government prosecutes. It does not prosecute because a fraud has been committed. It prosecutes merely because, in committing that fraud, the swindlers used the United States mails. The Government, then, comes in by the back door, instead of marching boldly up the front steps.*
>
> *Second, the victim wails, "Why does the law of my state allow this crime to go on?"*
>
> *Simply because, Mr. American Citizen, you and all your friends allow it.*

When Capital Investment Company in Chicago and its branches in five other states were raided on December 15, 1910, the division superintendent of the Department of Justice declared, "It is the end of the bucket shop." The Feds were claiming nationwide victory after only a ten-week siege, but everyone on the curb knew bucketeers were still operating in stealth mode. Dishonest brokers were like roaches: If you saw one, there were thousands.

Even the special agent Scarborough grew weary of raiding them. Shortly after the Scheftels case concluded, he took early retirement to fulfill his dream of getting his plays about the seamy side of law enforcement produced. Some of his dramas involved Wall Street corruption and were praised for their realism. One of them, *The Lure,* was censored and later banned because its portrayal of white slave sex trafficking was deemed too graphic.

After the federal muscle flexing, it was up to individual states to keep stock swindlers from accosting citizens. Joseph Norman Dolley, the Kansas banking commissioner, was outraged that con artists like Rice could legally peddle sham securities whose value was backed by nothing more than the "blue sky" of the Great Plains. He railed against fraudsters so vociferously that the Kansas legislature passed the first laws in the nation requiring comprehensive regulation of stocks and the brokers who sold them. The press picked up on Dolley's metaphor and dubbed the statutes "blue-sky laws." Between 1911 and 1933, every state in the union (except Nevada) would enact some form of blue-sky laws.

But the new regulations, while well-intentioned, were difficult to enforce. "Many state blue sky laws were narrowly drawn and haphazardly implemented," the Securities and Exchange Commission Historical Society would note a century later, in 2014. "The increasing complexity of financial regulation . . . meant that state legislatures passed a variety of legal reforms which were often inadequate or detrimental to addressing the problems of reforming securities practices."

Confidence hustlers lay low in the aftermath of the raids. They knew suckers were creatures of habit and would be drawn to whatever new forms of fraud spawned from the eradicated scams.

As the hangover from the raids subsided, 1910 couldn't come to a close fast enough for Big Board and curb traders. Since the panic of 1907, the exchanges had endured four dismal years, and 1910 had been the worst for profits in a decade.

Dating to the nineteenth century, it had always been the custom for brokers to celebrate Christmas Eve with caroling and general gaiety. But for the past several years, there had been no money for decorations or holiday bonuses, and no one in the trading pits felt like raising an egg-nog and belting out "Good King Wenceslas." In 1910, the number of brokers doing business on the curb had dropped 25 percent from the previous year, and the hardest, coldest months of outdoor trading lay ahead. "Very few ventured to wish one another a Merry Christmas," the New York *Sun* reported on December 24, 1910. "It was generally under-stood that such a salutation was a signal for a fight."

Despite ample justification for a gloomy mood, spirits unexpectedly mellowed as the holiday approached. Some brokerage houses surprised workers with modest bonuses, and even curb traders who didn't get a big year-end check felt compelled to pass the hat so messenger boys, ele-vator operators, and switchboard girls all got a little something extra. The duck-for-cover mentality was replaced by a cautious relief that the worst was over. Those who had lived through the panic of 1907 and the raids of 1910 felt destined to survive and thrive and in the mood to let off a little steam.

On the final day of trading before Christmas, the financial district broke out into what the *Tribune* described as an "old-time jollification in which fun ran riot and formality was thrown to the winds." For the first time in the history of the NYSE, a piano was rolled out onto the trading floor, accompanied by a hurdy-gurdy organ-grinder hauled in from off the street. Four dozen footballs rained down from the west gallery, and brokers fueled by clandestine cocktails practiced plays from their gridiron glory days (the market was technically open, but when-ever a broker tried to execute an order, he was good-naturedly booed). Someone had wheeled three barrels of shredded ticker tape up to the top balcony to toss upon the trading pit at the official close of the market, but the high jinks couldn't wait for the final gong. The swirling con-fetti had turned the stodgy stock market into a snow globe of revelry by 2:00 P.M.

A twenty-five piece "Millionaire's Band" consisting of traders in red plumed hats playing kazoos concealed in papier-mâché instruments marched around the perimeter of the pit before two rogue brokers in traffic cop uniforms rode in on stick ponies and "raided" the parade. The exuberance spilled out onto the curb, where traders engaged in an impromptu handstand contest. One curb official shouted to a news-paperman, "The year has been rotten!" as brokers raced him up and down Broad Street in a wheelbarrow. With the kazoo band in full swing, a mischievous Santa Claus appeared with a megaphone and stationed himself underneath the Broad Street gallery to summon reluctant bigwigs to accept gag gifts from his bursting bag of loot.

Most of the presents were harmless, like the toy Noah's ark given to a man who specialized in livestock futures. But one notorious tightwad was embarrassed to receive a tiny coin purse fitted with an enormous padlock, and the crowd roared with laughter when Saint Nick slapped an authentic hunk of bear meat into the hands of a broker known to be especially bearish. One trader with a reputation as an insincere glad-hander got a miniature porcelain hand sculpture, and another was mortified to be presented with a baby doll—presumably because of his proclivity for courting younger women.

If Santa had a bucket with a hole in it stuffed inside his sack of good-ies, everyone would have guffawed over whom it was intended for. But George Graham Rice was nowhere to be found among the merry-makers. The curb was having a grand old time without its most ruthless bucketeer, and if GG's name came up at all during the festivities, it was probably accompanied by a heartfelt toast of good riddance.

4

JACKAL OF WALL STREET

George Graham Rice would have his day—or, as it turned out, weeks and months—in court to answer the federal fraud charges. But before any adjudication of his stock swindling, he first had to appear before a judge (several, in fact) to clear up his womanizing woes.

Humiliated by the scandal stories about George's mistress, Frances Rice presented herself to federal authorities days after the Scheftels bust and offered to testify against her husband. Out of revenge, she planned to spill GG's darkest pathological secrets. "When this man wants anything he will run the chance of prison or any other danger," Frances told reporters. "He is a sublime egotist. He wants to cast me aside for Miss Bessie Lafell. He would be overjoyed if his motorcar ran me down."

Frances filed for divorce. But in 1911, even proof that a husband was an abusive philanderer was no guarantee a court would dissolve a marriage. Three-quarters of states still forbade women to own property, and in a third of states a woman's earnings belonged to her husband. Women were nine years away from the constitutional right to vote. Frances wanted to end the marriage as quickly as possible, so she journeyed cross-country to Reno. The laws for quickie breakups were considered lax in America's "Divorce City"; all a woman had to do was uproot her life and move there for six months to establish residency.

Frances might have been able to get around Reno's six-month stipulation because the Rices had lived there in 1908. Perhaps the second time around, she stayed in one of the city's "divorce colonies" that drew independence-seeking housewives from all over the country. The difficult part was going to be getting alimony out of George, which required filing a lengthy petition in New York. It was common for women initiating a "migratory divorce" in Nevada to first file for alimony where the husband lived, then collect it when (or if) the marriage dissolution was granted.

George didn't plan on contesting the divorce itself. He corroborated the basic facts, acknowledging that they had been separated since 1909 and that Frances had been going by her maiden name while living in Europe and later at an Atlantic City resort. The couple disagreed over Frances's claim that she had bought a house with her own money in 1907 and that only under "duress of mind" had she ceded the home and all her stocks, bonds, bank accounts, and jewelry to George. At one point in 1910, her friends grew alarmed that she had vanished without explanation; Frances testified this was when George had ordered her forcibly committed to the sanitarium. "I am only one of the innumerable dupes of George Graham Rice!" she wailed from the witness box.

A Reno stringer who covered high-profile divorce cases for out-of-town newspapers wasn't moved by the actress's theatrics. "Mrs. Rice sat in court wrapped in a couple thousand dollars' worth of furs and told how she had been made a pauper by her husband," he wrote.

The judge heard enough after an hour of testimony to grant a divorce on grounds of cruelty. This was fine by GG, who was saving his show-stopping encore for the alimony hearing back in New York.

Frances was asking for $1,000 a month—the equivalent of $25,000 in today's dollars. George had delayed the plea as long as he could. When he was finally forced to respond, Rice's answer so flabbergasted Frances's attorney that the barrister had to request a three-day adjournment to prepare a counter-reply: George's nefariously brilliant defense was to admit to bigamy to nullify that he was ever legally married to Frances in the first place.

Even though he had not seen her in fifteen years, Rice tracked down Theramutis Myrtle Ivey, the teenage bride he married on the train to Sing Sing in 1895. Ivey was now thirty-two, impoverished, and disfigured from the loss of her eye. George had abandoned but never divorced Theramutis, and when he subpoenaed her as a surprise witness, each wife was stunned to learn of the other's existence.

George's argument was that he was obliged to support his lawful first wife, not Frances. Rice knew he could openly admit to bigamy in a court of law because the statute of limitations had expired. His bigamy was no longer a crime, he insisted, but a matter of fact.

The case would drag on for eighteen months. A referee assigned by the New York State Supreme Court finally recommended that the alimony suit be dismissed. George was legally free from Frances and never had to pay her a cent.

As for his obligation to take care of long-lost Theramutis, GG forgot all about that trifling detail the moment he strolled out of the courtroom.

More than a year after his arrest, jury selection for George's federal court case began on October 9, 1911. The *New York American* ran a Freudian-slip headline mistakenly stating "Scheftels' Clique Goes to Jail" when the paper really meant "Goes to Trial." The publication ran a correction, but its bigger gaffe might have been printing, "It is expected that the trial will last from three to four weeks." The proceedings would actually languish well into the next year, although no one at the outset imagined *United States v. Rice et al.* would set records for colossal wastes of time and resources.

The clog-and-snarl strategy that plagues the twenty-first-century American legal system traces directly to Rice's intentional bogging down of the process for his 1911 fraud trial. Because chances were slim that Rice, Bernie Scheftels, and three other indicted managers would beat their raps outright, George instructed his team of attorneys to introduce reams of confusing evidence, call hundreds of redundant witnesses, and challenge every snippet of testimony put forth by the prosecutors. His goal was to force a mistrial by making it difficult for jurors to stick with the case.

From the start, the evidence against the Scheftels quintet was damning; the arguments tense and heated. The government fell into Rice's trap by countering with an onslaught of its own repetitive documentation, slowing the pace to a crawl. Judge George Washington Ray contributed to the torpor by allowing a litany of defense objections and then clumsily trying to even things out by letting the prosecution repeat arguments he had previously overruled. Technicalities of admissibility were sometimes debated for an hour while witnesses dozed off on the stand.

At one point, Judge Ray had to order an assistant district attorney to stop snickering at the defense's line of cross-examination, and the prosecutor laughed outright at his demand. On another occasion, the assistant DA took such offense at an insult muttered by a Scheftels lawyer that he sprang from his chair to challenge the defender to step outside and settle the matter with fisticuffs.

"Not a syllable of evidence was admitted without a most vigorous opposition on the part of the defense," *The New York Times* complained. "It is no wonder that the District Attorney's office regards the whole proceedings as a nightmare, tinged with a touch of farce."

By Thanksgiving, the trial had taken six weeks, but the government was another six weeks from presenting the case in its entirety. Witnesses who had been subpoenaed from across the country—there were six hundred of them, ranging from ordinary folks who had been swindled to high-ranking elected officials and mining executives—were forced to live in Manhattan on the unrealistic stipend of $1.50 a day until called to testify. When the witnesses learned they would be compelled to remain in New York over Thanksgiving weekend, they held an "indignation meeting" to protest their paltry allowance and the preferential treatment extended to star witnesses like Nat Goodwin, who was allowed to tour with his vaudeville troupe so long as he checked in by phone once a week.

"I have been played for a sucker certainly in this case," a college professor from the Midwest griped to the *Times*. "First I lost my money on a bucket shop concern that looked to me like a real brokerage house. Then I had to give up my position to answer this subpoena. . . . Now I have to spend about all my life's savings to stick around here on the government's order, and all I hear in the courtroom is story after story as like as another pea in the same pod as mine. Uncle Sam is certainly giving me a rough deal. I'm fairly sick of it."

By the time the trial slogged past the nine-week mark, Rice was not completely confident his stall-and-crawl tactic was going to work. When by chance he happened upon some inside information, GG decided to hedge his bets.

Through his showbiz connections, Rice knew a vaudeville agent named George J. Byrne. When Byrne attended the trial one day, he recognized Juror No. 6 as Frederick S. Dale, a real estate dealer who shared office space in the same building as the agent at 1402 Broadway. Ricecakes gave Byrne a $1,000 bill—plus a little something extra for his time and effort—and asked him to see what he could do to gum up the verdict.

On December 16, 1911, Dale was approached by "a tall man of prosperous appearance" but refused to accept the "gift" Byrne pressed into his palm. Dale agonized for five days over whether to report the attempted bribe. When he finally spoke up, Judge Ray halted the trial, and the Secret Service (which did not customarily handle bribery cases) immediately arrested Byrne. The Feds leaked word to the press that they were investigating similar attempts by the defense to rig the outcome.

The trial remained on hold while Judge Ray took action to stave off the sabotage. When George stepped out of a conference at his attorneys' office shortly after 2:00 P.M. on December 27, he was rearrested by federal agents. Rice was livid that the bench warrant issued by Judge Ray listed no specific charge, and the court kept silent about why it was ordering him locked away in the Tombs for the duration of the trial. It later came out that Judge Ray had yanked his bail to prevent future jury tampering. Indignantly, GG was forced to traverse the same "Bridge of Sighs" he had trudged across seventeen years earlier.

The trial resumed on January 8, 1912, minus the lead defense attorney. Abraham Rose had vowed at the outset to quit if any of the Scheftels crew attempted to bribe the jury. He kept his word and walked away from the case. The remaining defense lawyers unsuccessfully argued for a mistrial, claiming that the alleged bribery attempts were staged by the government to make the defendants look guilty.

Over the next few weeks, the Feds continued to build a strong case while one by one the remaining five defense attorneys either quit or were fired by George. To a man, they were begging him to cave in and negotiate a plea.

"I would consider myself lacking in manhood to submit to any sentence without protest of my innocence while there is a breath of life in me," Rice wrote in a letter to the court. "Given a fair chance to put in my defense, I am convinced that the case of the government will collapse like a haystack in flood."

Judge Ray insisted on assigning counsel to guide the defense, but Rice tersely ordered the new lawyer to keep his mouth shut while he ran the show. After the prosecution rested on January 17, George introduced more than two thousand exhibits, including thick volumes of mining literature he intended as required reading for jurors. If the government was going to try to prove B. H. Scheftels & Company was not a real brokerage, then Rice was going to counter by reading into the record day after day of trade logs dating to 1909 to show the company functioned just like any other stockbroker (while neglecting to mention the far more numerous trades the firm *didn't* execute).

"There isn't a man that can say he ever got a bad deal from me," George fire-and-brimstoned to the jury. "I defy any man in Wall Street, or on any other street, to say that I didn't stand behind my stocks with my last dollar."

George called former employees to the witness box and had them detail the monotonous, day-to-day doings of the business. But the tactic sometimes backfired under cross-examination, like this exchange between a prosecutor and the editor of Rice's *Mining Financial News:*

Q: Didn't you tell Rice he was taking desperate chances in his method of doing business?

A: I did.

Q: Didn't you tell him he was knotting the noose and that he was sure to get into trouble?

A: Yes.

Q: What did Rice say?

A: He said he had played this game before and got away with it.

As the trial approached its fifth month, the press began to wonder if it was setting a record for duration. No one seemed to know for sure, but *The Virginia Law Register* cited a ninety-day case to settle a will in 1851 that it believed was the longest-known jury trial. The Scheftels debacle had nearly tripled that mark, and legal experts were predicting that *United States v. Rice et al.* was likely to extend much further, perhaps even into the summer. Newspapermen grew bored with covering the trial itself, so they wrote stories detailing how 1,650 pounds of paper evidence had been introduced and how 1.39 million words of testimony filled 5,543 pages of transcripts. The government was spending $50,000 to prosecute the case ($1.25 million in today's dollars), but the Scheftels defense was burning through four times that amount. As of March 3, 1912, ninety witnesses were still under subpoena by the defense, and the case was paralyzing the entire federal court docket.

Jurors protested to Judge Ray that the trial was wrecking their lives. At least one man complained of having his business completely wiped out; another had been unable to attend the funeral of a family member.

When the trial schedule was paused so the jury foreman could have surgery on a diseased eye, jurors got a promise from the judge that he would petition Congress for hardship compensation above and beyond the $3 a day they were currently being paid.

Rice didn't exactly want angry jury members deciding his fate, yet he knew the longer the exasperating trial dragged on, the stronger his bargaining power got with the Feds. On March 6, 1912, GG made his move. He abruptly requested a recess so he could meet in private with the U.S. attorney Henry A. Wise, and their three-hour conference fueled rumors that a plea was imminent. "If the negotiations between Rice and the District Attorney arrive at any sort of settlement, it will be received by all with immense relief," *The Times* reported.

The next afternoon, George announced to the court that he was pleading guilty to the charges of using the mails to defraud. Reading from a typewritten statement, he insisted his reversal was not because he was culpable of any wrongdoing but because he had run out of money to defend himself:

> *B. H. Scheftels & Co. did nothing except what is and has been commonly practiced in Wall Street by the most respectable stock exchange houses. I know these methods were fair and honest, as measured by the standards of the Street. We, however, committed the unspeakable and never-forgotten crime of attacking without fear powerful interests in the mining securities markets, and they have broken us on the wheel. I pleaded guilty only when all my resources and those of my friends had been exhausted. I was up against it. The government has more money than it knows what to do with, and I was down to my last cent.*

In exchange for his guilty plea, Rice was sentenced to one year in jail, with time credited for his incarceration in the Tombs for jury tampering. If anticipated credit for good behavior is factored in, he stood to be out of prison in about seven months.

As part of the bargain, Bernie Scheftels pleaded guilty but received a suspended sentence. The three managers had their indictments quashed by the court. The press was shocked that the Scheftels gang got off so leniently after such a considerable expenditure of time and taxpayers' money.

"Many will think the sentence of the court is not adequate to the offense," Judge Ray announced, preempting criticism he knew was coming. "But the court takes the responsibility, remembering that 'Vengeance is mine; I will repay, sayeth the Lord.'"

The *Mining and Scientific Press* scoffed at the government's weak bargain, drawing the analogy that "the mountain labored and brought forth a mouse." The *New-York Tribune* quipped that George's jail cell would merely serve as an incubator for future frauds: "It was said by some of his followers that Rice has already received offers of considerable sums of money to set him up again as soon as he leaves the prison."

As Prisoner K-20973, George was going to spend the next seven months on Blackwell's Island, a foreboding stone lockup in the middle of the East River between Manhattan and Queens. In addition to housing federal prisoners, Blackwell's Island served as New York City's primary asylum for smallpox patients, the mentally ill, the alcoholically addled, and men and women with incurable venereal disease. The dank, medieval fortress was known for its intolerable stench, rancid food, never-ending screaming, and the strict mandate that all able-bodied prisoners toil in daylong shifts at the workhouse, where the primary task was peeling potatoes at gunpoint.

But the gloomy confines of Blackwell's Island didn't deter Rice. Almost immediately, he began penning a brassy, pull-no-punches memoir about bucking the system, a cautionary "champion of the downtrodden" tale that GG envisioned would metamorphose him into one of America's most trusted voices of reason.

Right about the time the *Titanic* sideswiped an iceberg and sank in April 1912, George was huddling with attorneys in his Blackwell's

Island cell in an effort to keep afloat his own foundering affairs. His new lawyers were crafting a petition for bankruptcy protection in U.S. District Court, listing $487,406 in liabilities and no assets outside some obscure penny stock certificates. In their divorce proceedings, Frances had estimated her husband's net worth at $20 million. George now claimed it was zero. At almost forty-two, GG fit the classic grifter's profile of pretending to be well-off when he was penniless and broke when he was flush.

In 1912, laws prohibiting inmates from profiting from the notoriety of their crimes were unheard of. Half a year before his case went to trial, Rice had accepted an offer from *Adventure* magazine to write a series of behind-the-scenes articles based on his personal experience "in various lines of sport, finance, business and travel." With a circulation of 117,000, *Adventure* was one of the widest-read pulp magazines of the day, and George was paid handsomely, from $500 to $1,000 per article. His pieces ran under the general heading "My Adventures with Your Money," and while the focus was ostensibly on exposing how insiders rigged everything from racetrack results to the stock market, Rice treated the series as his opportunity to wield a poison pen against old enemies.

George made it six stories into the series before a rant titled "The Power of the Public Print" elicited a libel suit from a rival Rice had accused of being a blackmailer. The brouhaha sold magazines and kept George's name in the news and sparked interest from a publisher who wanted Rice to expand his stories into book form. "In his articles Rice made himself appear as a paragon of honesty," the watchdog publication *Financial World* noted, "a much misunderstood and much maligned man, more sinned against than sinning."

When a bankruptcy judge discharged all his debts two weeks prior to his release from prison, reporters swarmed GG outside the courthouse as he was being returned to Blackwell's Island, wanting to know his plans for life after jail. "Two societies here want my services as executive head for a movement for reforming the financial district," George lied, triggering headlines like "Rice Is Anxious to War on Wall St." and "Noted Plunger, Temporarily Free, Calls It Centre of All Evil."

On October 26, 1912, George was ferried off Blackwell's Island for good. Having completed his seven-month sentence, he was once again a free man.

Rumor had it Rice borrowed $450 and ran it up to $150,000 playing the races. Impossible to prove or disprove, the story gave him cover in case anyone wondered if he had really stashed away a large chunk of cash before filing for bankruptcy.

Five days after being released, George was involved in a mild scandal at a sold-out rally for the former U.S. president Teddy Roosevelt, who had skipped a third term but was now running for reelection as head of the Bull Moose Party. Two weeks earlier, Roosevelt had been shot in the chest, but the bullet had been deflected by his steel spectacle case and a thick, folded-up copy of a speech. On October 30, some forty-six thousand supporters tried to get into Madison Square Garden to witness Teddy's first public appearance since the assassination attempt, and hustlers scalped counterfeit tickets.

George, thinking he had bought legitimate seats in a private box, was furious and embarrassed to be escorted out of the arena by policemen. On his way out, he could be heard bitterly complaining that a swindler had hoodwinked him out of ten bucks, the equivalent of $250 today.

Rice was keen on Roosevelt because they shared a mutual contempt for corporate America. But George was backing an eventual losing candidate in the 1912 election, a rare four-party showdown among the incumbent Republican, William H. Taft, the Democrat Woodrow Wilson, the Socialist Eugene V. Debs, and the Republican turned Progressive Roosevelt. Although the winner, Wilson, would later be known as the leader who ushered America into the Great War, Rice, like many gray-market entrepreneurs, was more concerned about the president's domestic policies. Within months of taking office, Wilson pushed for the passage of the Federal Reserve Act to establish centralized banking (which, in GG's opinion, only enriched tycoons like J. P. Morgan)

and backed the constitutional ratification of a federal income tax—
giving lawmen a powerful new tool to go after criminals who failed to
report illicit earnings.

During the winter of 1912–13, Rice took a job as the mining investment editor for *The Morning Telegraph* and acquired a weekly financial
sheet he relaunched as *George Graham Rice's Industrial and Mining Age*.
But George spent most of his energy putting the finishing touches on
his forthcoming book, which he had sold to the Gorham Press in Boston. Borrowing the name of his magazine series, *My Adventures with
Your Money* was turning out to be a half memoir, half exposé of Wall
Street, and Rice was betting its sensationalism would spark his new career as a stock market iconoclast.

My Adventures was released on June 14, 1913, with a cloth ornamen-
tal binding, a cover price of $1.50, and an ad campaign that touted it as
"the most illuminating book on modern finance ever written." Hyperbole aside, it was quite unlike anything published until then on the topic
of high-finance high jinks. George tried to disguise that he had done
anything illegal, but anyone astute enough to read between the lines
could piece together that Rice was well acquainted with confidence hustling. In the book's foreword, he sowed seeds of long-term trust with
readers by adopting the role of a credible confidant:

> In boyhood, [I was] a victim of the instinct to speculate. . . . At the
> age of thirty, [I] learned to cater to the insatiable desire in others. . . .
> Ten years of hard work in a field in which I labored day and night
> has disclosed to me that the instinct to gamble is all-conquering. . . .
> Nearly everybody speculates; few win. Where does the money go
> that is lost? Who gets it?
>
> I have a message to communicate to every investor and specu-
> lator. . . . The [most] dangerous malefactors are the men in high
> places who take a good property, overcapitalize it, appraise its value
> at many times what it is worth, use artful publicity and market
> methods to beguile the thinking public into believing the stock is

worth par or more, and foist it on investors at a figure which robs
them of great sums of money. There are more than a million vic-
tims of this practice in the United States. . . .

What are your chances of winning in any speculation where you
play another man's game? HAVE YOU ANY CHANCE AT ALL?

My Adventures sold well despite less-than-stellar reviews. *Life* magazine panned it as "the spicy confessions of a would-be Napoleon of finance." *The Smart Set* gave it a backhanded compliment: "Rice is not
only a good story-teller. He is a racy and amusing character. . . . He com-
bines the guileful enterprise of a middle-aged serpent with the simple
unmorality of a boy of six." The dramatic rights were optioned to a
well-known theater producer. The work never reached the stage, but the
book made it into ten printings, and George succeeded in planting the
subject of swindling at the top of the news cycle. A few months after *My
Adventures* was released, the term "con artist" first appeared in *The New
York Times* to describe a highly specialized grifter.

George basked in the glow of being a literary luminary who wrote
from a wiseguy's perspective. He hobnobbed with Broadway celebrities
and got reacquainted with racetrack pals from his Maxim & Gay days.
Among them was a slim, chalky-cheeked bet runner Rice used to know
from riding the high rollers' train to Saratoga.

Arnold Rothstein—now known as the Brain, the Big Bankroll, or
the Man Uptown—had rocketed to the top of New York's gambling
hierarchy since Rice had seen him last. By 1914, Rothstein was operating as a bookmaker who cleared large bets for other bookmakers, giving volume discounts to the nation's biggest poolrooms. He pioneered
an arbitrage system that ensured he always made a fixed-percentage
profit, which worked because Arnold refused to overextend himself
on any proposition—at least when it came to business.

Although Rothstein was twelve years younger than Rice, they had
plenty in common. Both grew up in the Lower East Side ghetto, sons of
upstanding Jewish fathers who worked in the garment industry. Each

got a rush from defying their families' strict laws of faith and learned to gamble by observing street corner dice games. Both were well mannered, with many acquaintances but no true friends. Rice drank sparingly, Rothstein not at all. George became addicted to faro; Arnold's vice of choice was stuss, a variation known as "Jewish faro" with even worse odds. Although their gambling sensibilities were skewed, both men's business acumen was sound and authoritative. The two equated money with power, honesty with weakness, and found "straight" people dull, even disdainful. Self-preservation was a highly honed instinct, based on the core belief that if someone was less intelligent than you, it was up to you to take advantage of the person. If you didn't, somebody else would.

Where Rice and Rothstein differed was in matters of personality and style. George had the gift of gab, a mellifluous way with words, and could extend hearty handclasps while lying through his teeth. Arnold was an introverted numbers prodigy who spoke in low, clipped diction and loathed shaking hands or personal contact of any kind. Rice wore his wealth in the form of gaudy pinkie rings and flowing opera cloaks; Rothstein preferred understated suits with simple bow ties. George's most prized possession was his gleaming yellow roadster; Arthur's a small black ledger in which he was forever jotting coded notes to himself. While George sucked primo cigars, Arnold crunched apples and sipped milk. When someone Rothstein respected once mentioned figs were imperative to digestive regularity, he began carrying them around in his pockets to snack on during the day. Almost every evening, while George unwound in the boisterous company of hangers-on at some upscale Broadway supper club, Arnold took his usual table for one at the no-frills neighborhood deli, where he sat alone with his back to the corner, eyes glued to the front door.

The Brain believed in diversification of assets and was branching out into real estate and insurance. His day-to-day bet-processing activities made him enough of a "nut" to live comfortably, but Rothstein was always on the hunt for consistent, long-term profit. He was especially intrigued by the concept of bucket shops—could George give him a rundown of the percentages and how the racket worked?

By April 1914, Rice was back in business with a brokerage at 27 William Street, a block south of Wall Street. The endeavor was probably bankrolled by Rothstein, most likely as his first foray into bucketeering (the Brain's involvement with bucket shops over the next decade would be well documented, but the roots are difficult to pinpoint). One of the new stocks George promoted was International Mines Development Company, "the first mining company with any character with which I have permitted myself to become personally interested since 1910."

Former Scheftels loyalists started sniffing around for bargains, and GG dusted off his sucker list while signing on additional stocks to promote. Synchronizing the influential forces of his mining newspaper, best-selling autobiography, and brand-new bucket shop, GG appeared poised to settle back into a profit-churning groove. But just as business got rolling, Rice's comeback was tripped up by a young saboteur concealing a pistol underneath the awning of a delicatessen half a world away.

On the morning of June 28, 1914, Archduke Franz Ferdinand, heir to the throne of Austria-Hungary, was visiting Sarajevo to inspect his imperial forces. Europe was at the boiling point over military superiority, and the parade route was filled with angry Bosnian Serbs wanting to be free from the Austro-Hungarian Empire. One of them threw a bomb intended for Ferdinand that blew up a car behind the archduke by mistake. Despite the maiming of several members of his entourage, Ferdinand insisted on continuing. His royal guards tried to divert the motorcade off the published route, but the chauffeurs didn't speak the same language and took a wrong turn back onto the originally planned thoroughfare. An enraged Austrian officer screamed at the driver of Ferdinand's coupe to turn around, but in the confusion the driver stalled the engine. The car's gears seized directly in front of Schiller's deli—five feet away from Gavrilo Princip, one of seven would-be assassins who had volunteered to take up positions along the parade route.

Never would there be a cleaner, clearer shot. Nineteen-year-old Princip stepped out from underneath the awning and fired twice into the vehicle, killing Ferdinand with a bullet to the jugular and his wife, Sophie, with a shot to the abdomen.

The double murder shocked Europe. Riots were followed by ultimatums from a confusing tangle of alliances. Global trade became paralyzed, and foreign-exchange money markets devolved into chaos. America, officially neutral, wasn't really sure how to react; the conflict marked the first time in history the nation was confident enough in its power to believe it could influence an overseas battle.

Rice, more concerned with his own fiefdom, pushed forward with his attention-getting stock promotions. As the planet teetered on the brink of a "war to end all wars," he hatched the idea to sponsor a tango contest at a Sheepshead Bay lobster palace, cashing in on the latest dance craze by offering five hundred shares of International Mines as the top prize. George instructed the restaurant owner to have his pretty waitresses talk up the penny stock to customers; as soon as the nonsense in Europe blew over, GG assured him, the issue would sell for hundreds of times more than its current market price.

"The resourceful Rice," *Financial World* noted wryly, "is scheming along subtle lines."

For forty-eight hours after the declaration of war on July 28, 1914, the New York Stock Exchange operated as the world's only unrestricted major financial market. International investors cabled brokers with instructions to dump holdings for whatever the securities would bring in America, and the wholesale liquidation of assets triggered a free fall that forced the closure of the Big Board on July 31. For four and a half months, the NYSE would remain shuttered to stave off an avalanche of selling. The curb, though, could only tolerate two dark days of no trading.

On August 3, some curb bucketeers—Rice perhaps among them—banded together to advertise in *The New York Times* that they would

function independently as an "Emergency Stock Market" to handle issues that normally traded on the Big Board. Bowing to outrage from the
neighboring NYSE, the curb chairman immediately put a stop to the un-
sanctioned venture. But an underground "gutter market" for securities
persisted for the duration of the enforced hiatus.

Eager for any form of action, out-of-work curb brokers whiled
away time by making book on how soon the war would end. The odds
were two to one that fighting would be finished in six months, but not
even the most risk-embracing speculators were biting at that price. If
anything, the armies were becoming so deeply entrenched that the
proposition looked like a sucker's bet.

When the NYSE resumed stock trading on December 12, 1914, the
Dow Jones Industrial Average plunged 24 percent, its worst percentage
drop since the index was first published in 1896. But as government
manufacturing contracts rolled in, capitalists figured out the Great
War—no one called it World War I until the 1940s, when a second global
war invited comparison—represented a monumental moneymaking
opportunity. America, on the sidelines, could supply the Allies with
munitions and weapons, and it wouldn't really matter which side won.
Once Europe was completely ravaged, a costly rebuilding would keep
the U.S. economy rollicking for years.

America was rich in iron, steel, copper, wool, cotton, and leather—
all the raw materials that went into rifles, bullets, trucks, flying machines,
uniforms, tents and boots—and the country had a willing workforce to
turn out these products in the millions. Europeans forked over fat prices,
and as corporate profits soared, so did wages. Working-class Americans
began to spend at an unprecedented pace: new homes, automobiles,
washing machines, vacuum cleaners, fur coats, and jewelry. Even
commodities not directly related to the war—like silk—got a boost
when laborers began wearing custom shirts and splurged on fancy
stockings for wives and mistresses.

"The textile industry, the boot and shoe industry, the packing indus-

try, the ship-building industry, the automobile and motor truck industry all found a place at the public trough and waxed fat at the expense
of the government," wrote the financial historian Proctor W. Hansl in
his 1935 book, *Years of Plunder.* "Soon all corporate profits began to swell
and stocks moved up a peg. A peg, did we say? A couple of pegs. Then
five, ten, twenty pegs. It was boom times again! This was not such a bad
war, after all. . . . And here's little Willy playing with his brand new toy
cannon that just came over from Schwartz's!"

America was cocksure. The economy was barreling along while the
country remained politically neutral, yet the nation seemed itching to
storm into Europe and settle the scuffle. A "might makes right" confidence was taking hold, an attitude that was evident even in the country's sporting pastimes.

In U.S. prizefighting, the focus was shifting from artfulness to brute
force. Appreciation for tacticians got replaced by a lust for thunder-fisted
maulers like "Great White Hope" Jess Willard, who slugged his way to
the heavyweight title on April 5, 1915. Baseball, heretofore a pitching-and-
strategy game, was changing too. On May 6, a swarthy twenty-year-old
smacked a baseball high into the second tier of the right field grandstand
at New York's Polo Grounds. The blast marked the first career home run
for a brash rookie crudely nicknamed Nigger Lips by veteran players. But
once George Herman Ruth's bombastic bat and swaggering personality
won over the nation, a generation of Americans began worshiping him
reverently as Babe.

Less than twenty-four hours after Babe Ruth's first home run, the British luxury ocean liner *Lusitania* was torpedoed by a German
submarine off the coast of Ireland, killing more than half its 1,959 passengers, including 128 Americans. In a fervent spasm of patriotism,
flags went up all over New York City, and U.S. entry into the Great War
appeared imminent. But President Wilson exercised restraint, and it

would be another two years before America entered the fray. During this period of prosperous uncertainty, Wall Street strained under the burden of what was dubbed an overheated "peace market."

With easy money from overtime wages, neophyte traders were placing stock bets on companies with hefty war contracts. When Bethlehem Steel, trading at $26 per share just before the war, broke the $400 barrier on October 5, 1915, headlines carried the warning "Nationwide Insanity—Huge Gambling in War Shares." The government began policing farmers who set predatory prices on grain and flour bound for Europe, and citizens were encouraged to report war profiteering. Even Henry Ford, a pacifist at the start, shifted his values on "blood money." The auto tycoon gave in to pressure to build submarines and tanks, but only after vowing to donate all his munitions profits to the country's cause. Over the next three years, Ford's factories rolled out a fortune in weaponry, yet no documentation exists that the richest man in America ever followed through on his pledge to share his spoils of war with the U.S. Treasury.

Americans' eagerness to speculate was out of whack with their investing knowledge. Smooth talkers were able to sell anything to an indiscriminate public, and a nation of unseasoned stock pickers operated under the false confidence that they could make no wrong moves. Misguided but hopeful, people poured money into risky propositions with the unrealistic expectation that outrageous returns would always follow.

Rice capitalized on emerging technology to pair these suckers with his stock offerings. Coast-to-coast long-distance telephone calling had just become possible, and George believed the expense was worth it if salesmen could cover vast swaths of the country without ever leaving the office. The new all-stars of his operation—nicknamed dynamiters—were hired specifically for their confident voices and high-pressure persuasiveness.

Six days a week, several dozen well-compensated dynamiters doggedly worked Rice's candlestick phones, often as late as 10:00 P.M. to cold-call West Coast targets. Dupes on the other end had no idea the enterprising bustle in the background came not from an office full of white-collar finance wizards but from commission-driven hustlers crammed together in a boiler room. The urgency of a long-distance call was a powerful selling point in and of itself in 1916, because even though recipients had no idea who the swell-sounding stranger was on the other end of the line, they figured the offer *must* be important and legitimate. Why else would a name-brand broker like George Graham Rice waste money on phone tolls to single them out for a chance of a lifetime?

The ritual never varied. Call recipients were "papered" in advance with mailings to plant a seed of recognition for some obscure stock. A week or so later, a lower-ranking sales apprentice (an "opener") initiated the first telephone overture to gauge a customer's interest. He pointed out that big stocks had peaked and that little ones were the ones to watch; even the mighty Standard Oil started out small, right? George compelled his stock pushers to use egg timers. If they didn't get a nibble within three minutes, they were instructed not to waste further time.

A satisfactory opening call might conclude with a small sale of stock, but more important was establishing a foundation of trust. If the stock recommended by the brokerage went up in price, a more experienced specialist would call back a few days later to hook the victim for bigger bucks. *Life* magazine later detailed the process:

> The "dynamiter" or veteran "loader" takes over. With a soft but commanding manner he makes the sucker feel as keen as a college girl on the eve of sorority pledge day.
>
> "Now or never is the time to buy. . . . The stock is bound to double within sixty days. . . . Safe? I've bought it myself. Is there any better recommendation?"
>
> Up and up he raises the ante: "A man in your position should buy at least 1,000 shares." No mercy is shown.
>
> "If they find that a man has $20,000," a veteran [law enforcement] man observes, "they'll go not for $18,000 but the full $20,000."

Because phone charges frequently ran into hundreds of thousands of dollars, bucketeers tended to skip out on their bills. The phone company retaliated by reporting suspiciously large call volumes to the Feds, but restrictions against wiretapping kept authorities from listening in on dishonest brokers. Plus, swindling over the telephone wasn't even illegal. Ripping off people by long distance was more expensive, but by transacting scams outside the postal system, con artists could avoid going to prison for mail fraud.

As the combat intensified in Europe, Rice was winning the war on the curb. His latest ploy was to horde Emma Copper and Old Emma Leasing stock, because rival bucket shops had gone short for 1.5 million cumulative shares when George knew only 1 million shares existed. On September 30, 1916, a vicious attack letter began to circulate in the financial district. In bloodred ink, it anonymously vilified Rice and the two Emma stocks. The effect was like adding chum to a shark frenzy, but no one on the curb paused to think that GG might have turned his poison pen on himself in an effort to manipulate the market.

On October 4, George was seen willingly paying cash on Broad Street for the two Emma stocks whose prices were tanking because of the attack letter. The next day, after amassing control over 819,000 of the 1 million outstanding shares, Rice sat back and refused to sell any of them. Bucketeers now panicked to close out short positions, and because demand far exceeded supply, the price shot up to nearly four times what the stock had been shorted for several days earlier.

"Hungry-eyed brokers climbed on one another's backs bidding for Emma Copper and Old Emma Leasing shares in big blocks," *The New York Times* reported. "It was evident to the most casual observer that many people wanted the stocks and found them scarce."

Rice, according to the article, was in a "philosophic" mood as he ordered his lieutenants around the trading pit. "The bucket shop crowd thought they had me," he said with a smirk to a reporter. "But they will have a different idea of this game before it is played out."

On October 6, a fistfight erupted on the curb because of the scarcity of Emma shares. One of Rice's minions mangled his hand smashing it against the skull of a rogue broker known as Butcher Boy, and the headlines blared, "Blood Flows, Price Soars." The next afternoon, the two brokers squared off again, triggering a brawl that required the calling in of the riot squad to quell it.

"The open-air mart exists through the suffrance [sic] of the city authorities," The Times scolded, "inasmuch as the brokers have no more right to the space in Broad Street than any other citizens."

Since the advent of the automobile, the curb had been facing public pressure to move indoors. Financial regulators thought they had been making headway in cleaning up Broad Street's raunchy reputation. But the eruptions of violence—all traced to Rice—were beginning to worry curb officials that GG was going to get America's only outdoor stock market abolished for good.

By the start of 1917, if you owned a bucket shop, business was so booming it became necessary to prioritize clients. What brokers really needed was a Who's Who of America's most gullible high-net-worth individuals. Rice, though, had exactly such a collection of contacts: His well-maintained sucker list was fast approaching 200,000 names.

Other dealers were embracing this nascent form of direct marketing, but George's database towered above all others in both quantity and quality. Soliciting known victims for repeat business was only one aspect of Rice's voluminous customer profiling. An infusion of new blood was critical to any bucket shop, so GG hired clipping services to scour periodicals and out-of-town papers for details that matched wealth to vulnerability. Obituaries often yielded tantalizing clues. Citizens who contributed to charities liked to see their names in print, so society pages were skimmed for details about prideful donors. Poring over legal notices was a way to glean minutiae about estate settlements and alimony decrees, and life insurance companies routinely published long lists of benefactors who had been awarded policy payouts.

When clients bought stock from George, their index cards were updated with purchasing preferences and negotiating weaknesses. All these suckers—contacted over parts of four decades by different dynamiters representing various schemes backed by Rice—were unaware that their names were being plucked from a predatory file that grew fatter with each point of contact. If Rice wanted a specialized list of fifty well-off socialites whose daughters had recently been listed as coming-out debutantes, his staff could likely have filled such a request in short order. Although probably apocryphal, it was rumored that GG's records were so deviously cross-referenced they contained categories like "Millionaire Widows" and "Elderly Philanthropists."

Damaging personal secrets that George learned through his extensive socialization were included in his sucker list. On one occasion around this time, the government made public the contents of hundreds of blackmail-tinged index cards seized from another broker during a raid. The names were redacted, but it is not too difficult to imagine Rice's arsenal containing similarly sordid details:

Prominent philanderer. Age 72. Gave $100,000 to college and another 3,000 acres of land. Supports former mistress, Broadway chorus girl.

Hard-boiled banker. Escorts various young women (not his wife) to the opera. Very difficult to get to, but will bite on elaborate deals.

Most interesting society dame. Has twice thrown out husband. Bridge expert. Drinker. Fearful tantrums. Plaza incident.

Mrs.——and sweetheart at one door. Mr.——and his sweetheart at another. Clever chauffeur!

Although the upper levels of society offered the juiciest pickings, Rice was an equal-opportunity con artist. Believing in volume business, he also went after the impoverished classes, chiefly because poor people believed any fantastic story about getting rich quick. George struck up relationships with clergymen, because men of the cloth were trusted financial advisers to the downtrodden. The most productive periodicals, if swindlers could get their ads in, were religious newspapers.

Once GG set the standard, third-party compilers began to sell copycat sucker lists at prices ranging from pennies to a dollar per name, depending on whether prospects were graded "sold once" or "select." When a subset of his own database was no longer productive, Rice culled the fruitless names and put them on a special list, which he then had a henchman float as "stolen" on the black market.

George's profit cocktail was potent enough with equal parts sucker list blended with a crush of telemarketing dynamite. But when the nation added a dash of war to the mix, the intoxication proved irresistible to speculators who were suddenly being told it was their patriotic duty to throw money at bucketeers like George Graham Rice.

After the interception of a coded telegram in which Germany tried to persuade Mexico and Japan to attack America, Congress voted to enter the Great War on April 6, 1917, detonating a fervent wave of nationalism. Crowds of strangers hugged in Times Square, and orchestras in swank supper clubs played "The Star-Spangled Banner" over and over at the request of tipsy flag-wavers. Sauerkraut got renamed "victory cabbage," and more extreme anti-German zealotry took the form of ripping the Christmas carol "O Tannenbaum" from children's songbooks and stoning dachshunds to death in the streets. This intense jingoism was harnessed by the government, which urged loyal Americans to do their part by buying into a new investment vehicle—Liberty Bonds—to finance the war effort.

On April 24, the government authorized the first $5 billion wave of a $10 billion Liberty Bonds rollout. The 3.5 percent return, although tax-free, was still far less than what a dollar could earn in the sizzling stock market. But fifty million Americans oversubscribed every issue, even though these bonds frequently traded below par value. To entice investors, the Feds would later raise the rate to 4.5 percent. But the sold-out allotments had less to do with the extra percentage point than the systematic coercion of citizens. As the historian Frederick Lewis Allen wrote in his 1931 book, *Only Yesterday,* "The man who kept a tight grip on his pocketbook felt the uncomfortable pressure of mass opinion."

Although anyone could volunteer to sell Liberty Bonds (Charlie Chaplin, Douglas Fairbanks and Mary Pickford were among movie stars recruited to boost sales), the public was encouraged to buy them through brokers. The government had come up with the idea that it could induce the lower classes to participate by letting them buy war bonds under installment plans or through margin accounts, and bucketeers took this as their cue to separate a nation of suckers from their Liberty Bonds. With Rice leading the vanguard, curb sharpies competed heatedly for the right to pocket these government-sanctioned gifts that con artists snidely started calling "war babies."

Seven years after arresting him for running a bucket shop, the Feds were now actively steering war bond sales to Rice and other swindlers. Brokers lured speculators by convincing them they would be allowed in on "special deals" to parlay the collateral of their bonds into other forms of investment—like junk stocks. "Do not waste the power of your Liberty Bond," read one typical come-on. "If idle in a safe-deposit vault, it is non-creative." Purchasers were urged, "Give your bond the constructive element to which it is entitled—it will do its duty to 'Uncle Sam' twice and to you twice." Some brokers actually waited for permission before depositing Liberty Bonds into margin accounts. GG certainly did not.

Many buyers wanted to frame their Liberty Bonds in their homes as a display of patriotism. This was problematic for customers who bought bonds through Rice, because their checks would be cashed but no bonds would ever be sent in return. An Indiana man was typical of many who wrote to George (twice) in early 1918 before receiving a form-letter reply that Rice's staff sent out by the thousands:

I note your further instructions to send you the Liberty Bonds recently bought for your account. . . . Let me recommend, however, that you revise your instructions as to this detail. Many of my valued customers are buying Liberty Bonds to the extent of their resources and then depositing them with me as collateral against which purchases can be made of desirable stocks in which profit will be greater both from enhancement and from a dividend point of view. . . . My recommendation at the moment for your attention would include Okmulgee Oil, Lampazos Silver, Aetna Explosive, and Rice Oil.

It took the Indiana gent several rounds of correspondence to get some of his bonds and a partial return of money, but not before Rice repeatedly tried to impress upon him that he was "making a real mistake not to take advantage of immediate market conditions" and that "with this immediate cash resource and any other funds you may have available, you might instead purchase of a good-sized block of Rice Oil."

The names of GG's sham securities were more or less interchangeable. Petroleum stocks had become the curb's swindle du jour, and when the price on Rice Oil got driven up, George cashed out and walked away from it. After the stock crashed, the same business template was renamed Appalachian Oil. GG was getting audacious with his predictions, insisting that a 100 percent return on investment was nowhere near the top of the market, urging speculators to hold out until profits skyrocketed to the 1,000 percent range. As *The World's Work* put it, "Rice's game is to paint such an entrancing picture of the future that people will not think of the facts of the present." The magazine explained how George got away with it:

Any one who has lost money in Rice's promotions would have a hard time to find in his literature any place where he had actually

misrepresented the stock. He is too shrewd for that. For one thing,
he never issues a comprehensive financial statement of any of his
companies. He indulges freely in opinions, promises, and exagger-
ations. These are the tools with which he ensnares his victims. And
they are the common tools of all get-rich-quick promoters.

. . . The man who sends in his money for stock cannot tell
whether it goes into Rice's pocket or to the company.

George's predatory swindling was earning him a new nickname
among the financial press—the Jackal of Wall Street. One year after
America's entry into the war, the New York County district attorney's
office was alleging that Rice had stolen $5 million in Liberty Bonds,
either directly or in equivalent value as collateral for bucketed stock.
But federal prosecutors lacked the irrefutable proof needed to avoid a
costly repeat of the bungled Scheftels trial.

Considering the astronomical amount of money that flowed through
his brokerage, it was mind-boggling how much GG micromanaged the
operation. The 125 employees on his staff had standing orders not to
bother Rice with questions about transactions less than $40,000, yet
the boss insisted on bickering with individual customers over far more
trivial amounts.

On January 28, 1918, for example, Rudolph W. Hartman of Mans-
field, Ohio, sent Rice's brokerage a $100 Liberty Bond as collateral for
the purchase of ten shares of American Car and Foundry Company
stock. George (untruthfully) wrote back that the trade had been executed, so Hartman sent a check for $721.25 to cover the cost of the
stock and its commission, asking for his Liberty Bond and American
Car share certificates back in return.

The check was cashed, and Rice went through his usual rigmarole
of why the share certificates couldn't be sent (needed a signature on file,
clerical errors, request got lost in the mail, and so on). He underscored
with each reply why Hartman should let the brokerage hold on to his
securities instead so they could be used as margin against future pur-

chases. This ridiculous series of mail exchanges went on for five frustrating months before Hartman got so fed up he brought his complaint to the postal authorities.

In this particular case, George had crossed the wrong man over a piddling sum. Hartman was an attorney and had saved every scrap of correspondence. The chronology of how he had been defrauded by Rice was clear, concise, and definitive.

Two postal officials and a New York County marshal wanted to avoid making a big show of raiding Rice, so they waited until the evening of July 29, 1918, when they knew George was working late in his William Street office. The authorities smashed in the locked front door and took their target by surprise at a back room conference table, where GG was conducting an after-hours strategy session with a select group of underlings.

"What do you mean by breaking in here in this manner?" Rice demanded.

When the lawmen informed George that the purpose of their visit was to arrest him, Rice seemed more annoyed than alarmed. He testily asked if it would be possible for them to instead contact his attorneys, who would arrange for bail so Rice could continue the important conference they had just interrupted. When that idea failed to intrigue his captors, GG said he had $100,000 worth of stocks in a safe and would furnish any reasonable amount to get them to go away.

"You come with us and come now," ordered the marshal. "If the stocks you are talking about are any of your own, they are not worth as much as waste paper."

Rice's attorneys had no difficulty securing his $15,000 bail. They even got a judge out of bed so George wouldn't have to spend the night in the Greenwich Street lockup. The raiders seized what they thought was the entirety of the firm's sucker list but only got 102,000 names, about half. Over the next two days, forty of Rice's employees were summoned to testify before a grand jury, and prosecutors tacked on five counts of grand larceny in the first degree. Over the next several months, other theft charges trickled in from different jurisdictions, all for relatively minor amounts.

At one arraignment, a prosecutor laced into Rice, calling him "the worst crook on Wall Street." George smiled mischievously and asked the judge, "Your Honor, if I'm the worst crook on Wall Street as the district attorney charges, why am I not in State's prison?"

On October 25, 1918, Rice again filed for federal bankruptcy protection. Instead of the colossal six-figure discharge he sought in 1912, this time George was arguing he couldn't even make good on $3,395 in debts.

Within days, creditors seized and sold everything inside the closed brokerage. By the first week of November, prosecutors began to grow concerned over George's whereabouts. His lawyers had been conducting his court appearances on his behalf, and there where whispers that Rice had fled.

Marshals spent several days scouring Manhattan trying to locate him. If they were snooping around GG's customary haunts at lunchtime on an otherwise quiet, overcast Thursday, they probably dove for cover and instinctively grabbed for their revolvers when the concussive, staccato report of an anti-aircraft gun reverberated from forty stories above, where it was stationed high atop the roof of the Equitable Building at 120 Broadway to defend the city from enemy flying machines.

The blasts—most folks at the time did not know they were blank shells fired into the sky—sparked a celebratory tumult. From Harlem to Wall Street, church bells pealed, trolley horns blew, and whistles and horns pierced the air. Office buildings emptied, courts were adjourned, and the stock exchanges closed. Men spilled into the streets to smash one another's hats, climb lampposts, and grab girls to kiss. Whooping, shouting, and weeping, people broke out into song as a joyous mob surged up Fifth Avenue for an impromptu parade. The giddy thoroughfare became impassable to traffic, and gridlocked drivers intentionally backfired their autos to contribute to the raucous din. Within an hour, the NYSE supplied 155 tons of ticker tape, and confetti fluttered down from skyscrapers into a sea of spontaneous jubilation. "Germany's surrendered! Germany's surrendered!" was the repeated cry from the de-lirious crowd.

The Great War was over. It was Armistice Day—November 7, 1918.

On the morning after what came to be known as the "false Armistice," a hungover America felt cheated and deceived. There had been no surrender; the Germans had only agreed to negotiate with Allied com-manders. A United Press reporter had blown the scoop out of proportion, and the surrender story got repeated in error all across the country.

The nation's headlines read like a swindle perpetrated by G. G. Rice: "Public Is Victim of Greatest Hoax in Recent Years"; "Millions Fooled Throughout Country"; "Erroneous Reports Sweep like Wildfire." Three days later, when newsboys shouted earnestly on the eleventh hour of the eleventh day of the eleventh month that the war had *truly* ended, Americans received the news skeptically and were more subdued in their celebrations.

In the weeks after the real armistice on November 11, 1918, the New York skyline finally blazed brightly at night, and housewives were al-lowed to buy sugar with a clear conscience. Yet even as restrictions ended, in many ways the country throttled forward as if still at war. The United States now possessed more than half the world's gold supply, and a newly confident America had learned to lash out first and ask questions later.

Returning servicemen were none too happy to find their former workplaces embroiled in strikes and lockouts caused by Reds and Bolsheviks, so they stomped suspected radicals in the streets. When munitions contracts got canceled, factories cut loose men by the thousands. *Life* magazine ran a cartoon of a grateful Uncle Sam saying to a returning soldier, "Nothing is too good for you, my boy! What would you like?" The soldier morosely answered, "A job."

In addition to the scarcity of work, the nation was mired in the dead-liest influenza pandemic in recorded history. City dwellers went about their daily lives wearing surgical masks, shivering in homes and offices where windows stayed open even in snowstorms to air out deadly germs. For Americans, the first winter after world peace meant burying 675,000 Spanish flu victims, more than ten times the number of U.S. soldiers killed in the Great War.

Rice was rumored to be hiding out at an off-season resort in Atlantic City, where his pal Rothstein had connections. Leaving New York violated a condition of his bail, but GG's lawyers probably produced their client at least once to allay prosecutors' fears that he had bolted for good. Rothstein's motivation to help Rice stemmed from his growing interest in bucket shops. Gangsters of all stripes were getting into stock scamming. But only Arnold could claim George as an ally. Rothstein respected and looked up to Rice as a mentor whose advice gave him an edge in breaking new ground within the racket.

The way the Brain figured it, bucketeering required less up-front financing but more "cost of doing business" bribery to stay operational. Rothstein pooled money from brokers and funneled kickbacks to police to buy protection. If a bucketeer he represented did manage to get pinched, Arnold posted bail and provided legal services. Rothstein became the man you sought out if you were new to Broad Street and wanted a ticker wire illegally run into your cubbyhole office; he was also the go-between if you were an established fraudster and wanted to buy an otherwise unobtainable six-figure seat on the Big Board. Rothstein was able to envision the wild stock market of the Roaring Twenties long before it became a reality, and he acted proactively to get the bull market rolling by paying off politicians to support lax trading legislation. In short, Rothstein "organized" stock swindling in a way that made the entire enterprise run cohesively and efficiently. The Brain's twin compulsions for orderliness and control would be cited by historians as the same traits that enabled him to be one of the first men to "organize" other forms of crime in America.

By the spring of 1919, job prospects were looking up. International trade and the rebuilding of Europe strengthened the U.S. economy, and shipyards were running full tilt. In America's big cities, the cost of living rose sharply. "Curiously, advancing prices were accompanied by a veritable orgy of spending, which extended down into the lowest strata of the population," Hansl wrote in *Years of Plunder*. "It was as if lifting the tension of war had sent the whole country off on a buying spree that knew no bounds."

Shopgirls and workingmen flaunted extra spending money by splurging on jewel-encrusted feather fans and platinum wristwatches. Every household *had* to have a piano, and if you couldn't pay cash, that was what installment plans were for. "More is better" became the American mantra, and while Babe Ruth was swatting a record twenty-nine home runs in a single season, the stock market rode a dizzying wave of days when a record 1.5 million shares traded on the NYSE. The irrational zeal was enough for the Federal Reserve to consider a formal warning against the perils of overspeculation, but just on the rumor that the Fed *might* act to put the brakes on the market, trading spiked to 2 million shares.

Rice spent most of 1919 obstructing the start of his grand larceny trial. The county had whittled its litany of charges down to only the strongest case, the stock and Liberty Bond theft from the attorney Hartman. George sent a henchman to Ohio to try to dissuade the aggrieved lawyer from appearing as a government witness, but Hartman was intent on following through with his charges. When the trial opened on January 7, 1920, Judge James T. Malone made it clear he would not tolerate stalling tactics, even going so far as to schedule night hours in the Court of General Sessions so the case could proceed as swiftly as possible.

Rice's defense hinged on proving that the misplacement of Hartman's single $721.25 order was an unfortunate, unintentional oversight in a place of business that routinely handled $35 million in stock transactions. At one point, George argued that Hartman's paperwork got lost when a brokerage employee passed away and unopened mail piled up on the deceased worker's desk. But under cross-examination on January 15, GG couldn't hold back from launching into a long harangue that accused his prosecutor, Assistant District Attorney John T. Dooling, of being in the pocket of crooked stock market insiders.

"I believe that you are absolutely controlled and swayed by the interests that are friendly to the bucket shops of Wall Street and that [you] are getting hundreds of thousands of dollars from them," Rice railed at Dooling, who let him vent at length. "[Insiders] are on the destructive side of the market and I am on the constructive side. The result is we have clashed and they have ruined me—and they use you; they are just down there stealing money, plucking the public to a fair-you-well."

When calmly asked by the assistant DA to provide names, dates, and witnesses to back up his allegations, Rice claimed he was saving those specifics for his own presentation before a grand jury. Pressed further, GG hemmed and hawed, diverging from his rant only to ridicule Dooling for wearing a purple necktie in court.

Judge Malone ordered large parts of George's "senseless tirade" struck from the record and instructed the jury to ignore the sideshow.

A week later the trial wrapped up. The verdict came back guilty. On January 29, 1920, Malone sentenced Rice to three years at Sing Sing.

GG reached out to Rothstein for help. The Brain got him freed on $25,000 bail pending appeal and assured Ricecakes he'd never serve a day behind bars.

Arnold had a thing for keeping a string of highly skilled attorneys under retainer. "Rothstein held lawyers in peculiar esteem," one of his biographers later noted. "Over the years he collected them as J. P. Morgan collected porcelains and paintings."

Rothstein was going to set Rice up with the most talented—and most mercurial—star of his legal stable: William J. Fallon, a hard-drinking egotist who referred to himself in the third person in the courtroom. Fallon had such a flawless reputation for keeping clients out of prison that his nickname was the Jail Robber.

Fallon's specialty involved persuading judges to look the other way when it came to technicalities of the law. Considering the high degree of difficulty involved in pulling off this risky trick, his services tended to be expensive.

Rothstein, however, made it clear that Fallon worked for *him*. Arnold would pay Fallon out of his own pocket and keep score in his coded black ledger. He and GG could settle up once the decision was successfully appealed and Rice was back in business.

George had little choice but to trust Arnold. His confidence got a boost by reasoning that when compared with more intricate, higher-stakes gambles the Brain had rigged, manipulating the outcome of a New York State Supreme Court appeal should be child's play. After all, everybody on the curb was buzzing about how Rothstein had just won a fortune by fixing an institution the nation had deemed untouchable: baseball's 1919 World Series.

5

VORTEX OF DECADENCE

George Graham Rice's conviction didn't dominate the news like his earlier legal escapades. That's because his 1920 trial coincided with the seismic societal shift known as Prohibition, and the prospect of America's "going dry" was all the nation could talk about. While prosecutors were attempting to punish Rice for his wrongdoings, a constitutional amendment was about to turn millions of law-abiding gin sippers into criminals.

When the Volstead Act went into effect on January 16, 1920, the government handed gangsters America's entire industry of manufacturing and distributing alcoholic beverages. Bootleggers became overnight folk heroes, and society swells—now guests of the underworld—embraced speakeasy culture. Secret passwords, covert cocktail clubs, and silver hip flasks lent flair and intrigue to everyday drinking, and it wasn't just men who were stepping up to the bar.

On the verge of gaining the right to vote, women now stood shoulder to shoulder with men at brass rails, defiantly knocking back Bronxes and sidecars. Even so-called nice girls were bold enough to drag deeply on cigarettes in public, and the fashion critic for *The New York Times* admonished ladies for "lifting skirts far beyond any modest limitation."

The wilder young things would even "roll their stockings below the knees, revealing to the shocked eyes of virtue a fleeting glance of shin-bones and knee-cap." Flappers painted their faces gaudy shades of red and wore sleeveless evening dresses, liberating themselves from the literal and figurative constraints of whalebone corsets.

The idea for Prohibition had gained momentum during the Great War, when idealists insisted abstinence was the surest path to betterment. But as the nation's soldiers departed for battle, an entire generation took up the mind-set of "eat drink and be merry, for tomorrow we die." By the time the war ended, postwar America had grown tired of fighting for noble causes, and people just wanted to kick back and be themselves. Picking up on this sentiment, the presidential candidate Warren G. Harding embarked on a "Return to Normalcy" campaign in the spring of 1920, striking a popular chord with voters who preferred to be left alone by the government.

In its yearning for normalcy, America got caught up in a whirlwind of "crazes" in 1920. When a doctor in East Pittsburgh began sending phonograph music from his barn via wireless transmission, so many amateur enthusiasts picked up the broadcasts that Westinghouse Corporation hatched the idea of selling "radio sets," and the gizmo became the hot, must-have consumer technology. Crowds jammed ballparks just to watch Babe Ruth, newly traded to the New York Yankees, swing his massive bat. In early summer, a fan in the Polo Grounds bleachers was reported to have died from over-excitement while witnessing the Bambino swat one of his record-breaking fifty-four homers. But the most captivating phenomenon of the year had mundane roots: An Italian translator in Boston devised the idea of buying overseas international reply coupons with the intention of cashing them in at a slightly higher amount in America. He thought he could make money off the exchange rate and promised friends he'd double their cash in ninety days if they invested.

The entrepreneur—his name was Charles Ponzi—found out it was too complicated to actually redeem the postage coupons. But so many

speculators wanted in after Ponzi rewarded his initial backers that he took
their money anyway just to pay off people who had invested before them.
Continuing in this fashion, the scheme was soon paying out millions a
month, and average Joes across the country drained savings accounts and
mortgaged homes to get in on this sure thing before it was too late.
Ponzi's pyramid collapsed in August under a $20 million burden, wreck-
ing lives and wiping out fortunes that had existed on paper only.

A few weeks after Ponzi's scheme blew up, a driver abandoned a
ramshackle horse-drawn cart on Wall Street's busiest corner, directly
across from J. P. Morgan's headquarters. At one minute past noon on
September 16, 1920, as the financial district filled with lunch crowds, a
hundred pounds of dynamite nestled in five hundred pounds of cast-
iron sash weights detonated via timer, obliterating everything for half a
block. With thirty-nine dead and hundreds wounded, the attack was the
most lethal act of terrorism on U.S. soil up to that point. But anticapi-
talist anarchists missed their intended target; instead of taking the life
of J. P. Morgan, the bomb mostly killed middle-class twentysomethings:
stenographers, secretaries, and office boys who had stepped out for a
sandwich or a bowl of soup at the wrong time and place.

On November 2, Harding won the 1920 presidential election—the
first announced live on radio—in a landslide. It didn't take the country
long to figure out his "Return to Normalcy" meant cronyism, backroom
poker, illicit whiskey parties, and scandalous rumors of sex with a mistress in White House coat closets. The administration's flouting of order and regulation mirrored the private sector's disregard for laws like
Prohibition, and a collective mentality settled in that as long as everyone was fat and happy, there was little reason to mess with the system.

One aspect of old-school normalcy was about to vanish, though. On
December 5, 1920, New York officials broke ground for an indoor curb
exchange. The colorful tradition of buying and selling stocks on city
streets would cease with the construction of a new building at 86 Trinity Place, and a court ruling was about to make it illegal to deal securities anywhere outside the lawful exchange. Rice himself was absent from

the ribbon-cutting ceremonies, but his misdeeds were cited by the press as an impetus for kicking the curb indoors.

So where was GG during this eventful year? Not in the public spotlight, but not exactly hiding, either.

In April 1920, George ventured to Reno for the first time in a decade. His arrival was newsworthy enough for the *Nevada State Journal* to send a reporter to ask his impressions on how the town had changed since the implementation of Prohibition. Rice admitted the conspicuous absence of gambling houses and saloons on the main drag was jarring. Those lively establishments had vanished upon ratification of the Eighteenth Amendment and were being replaced by bland office buildings and business blocks.

"The drastic Volstead Act carries the confession that we are a race of weaklings and that the people cannot be trusted with liberty, lest they plunge into dissipation," Rice pontificated, glad to be talking about something other than his legal woes. "To be a thirsty soul and to imbibe temporarily is a different proposition from being an alcoholic pervert, and the rank and file of Americans should not be held up to the scorn of the whole world as a race of tipplers."

Some within the mining community welcomed Rice's return to Reno, even if only for selfish reasons. Stocks in general had taken a downturn as postwar deflation triggered a nationwide recession, and the mining sector had fallen far behind. The *Journal* pointed out how George was a throwback to Nevada's booster-driven glory days and that he had been responsible for attracting millions of investment dollars. Was Rice about to try again?

Around the time Rice arrived in Reno, a small-time hustler named Frank Capra also hit town, working his way through the West selling sham penny stocks. Capra saw an older gentleman with a cane sitting by himself in a hotel lobby and went after him because he thought the mark looked like a sucker.

Capra made small talk, then launched into his pitch. The gent listened with interest while puffing thoughtfully on a cigar. Capra thought he had the geezer hooked.

"My son," said GG, introducing himself to Capra, "stocks were made to sell, not buy."

Capra soon quit grifting and got a job in the motion picture industry. Today we know him as the director of one of America's most iconic feel-good films, the 1946 Christmas classic *It's a Wonderful Life*.

It only took a couple of weeks for GG to whip up a new venture that attracted financial backers. By early summer, he was renting a mansion on South Virginia Street and a downtown office where he established a stock-promoting company called Broken Hills Silver Corporation. Editorial reaction to his reentry was mixed.

"It is fair to ask why [the Broken Hills engineer] allowed his name to be used by such a man as Rice, whose career as a fake promoter is notorious," chided the *New-York Tribune* in a column titled "At It Again." Arizona's *Mohave County Miner* shrugged off GG's dubious past, implying that everybody cheated when it came to peddling stocks: "Rice may have done many questionable things, but the only bad feature of his promotions was that he was found out and paid the penalty." *The Engineering and Mining Journal* wrote that Rice's latest venture had the makings of an unsavory mess about to boil over, but "the pot is so actively boiling that it is difficult to disentangle the relation between the good and bad ingredients."

Business wasn't the only thing heating up in George's life in 1920. Sometime during his return to Reno, he began courting a young lady others would later describe as charming, incisively intelligent, and fiercely loyal. She had a soft smile on a delicate face that always seemed on the verge of a blush, and "it would not take much of a stretch to call her beautiful," one observer later wrote. It's quite likely that Katherine (or Kathryn or Catherine, as she alternately spelled it) was at first hired by George to work in his new office. Exactly how they hit it off remains a mystery—just like Katherine's maiden name and how the couple arrived at the agreement to get married only weeks after their first date.

But this much is known about the start of their relationship: George, at the time of his marriage proposal, was fifty years old. Katherine was only seventeen or barely eighteen.

During his 1920 trial in New York, GG had tried to cultivate the image of a reputable banker, a well-organized decision maker of high intelligence. Now, out west, he was either coming unraveled or caught up in the throes of his fling with a much younger flame. Trying to piece together what Rice's life was like in the winter of 1920–21 is one of the more difficult tasks of reconstructing his fragmented narrative. Was he a paunchy, graying grifter on the run out in the desert with a gullible girl one-third his age? Or, because of the strong possibility he might be heading back to prison, was George's involvement with Katherine another calculated deception designed to win over an outside accomplice?

On December 11, 1920, Rice filed a petition for divorce from Theramutis Ivey in Reno, citing desertion (hers, not his) as the reason. This was probably a legal prelude to clear the way for his elopement with Katherine, although it is not clear if the divorce was ever granted or when, where, or if George and Katherine were legally wed. Either way, by the end of the year, the two were calling each other husband and wife, and Rice had abandoned both his Reno office and the rented mansion.

The newlyweds briefly spent time in Weepah, a short-lived Nevada mining camp that quickly went from boomtown to ghost town. George was later sighted in San Francisco and Salt Lake City. In February 1921, GG had the audacity to mail brochures touting his latest scam, Broken Shaft Mine, to the New York district attorney's office. "Officials are wondering whether George Graham Rice is trying to taunt them," one newspaper columnist mused.

In underworld parlance, George "came down with smallpox" in the summer of 1921. "Smallpox" was the term con men used to describe

having a warrant out for one's arrest. Other grifters avoided the af-
flicted, because like the actual disease being wanted by the police was
considered highly contagious.

The California Corporation Commission, acting on a tip, alleged that
on June 22, 1921, Rice, while visiting Oakland, sold shares of Bingham
Galena copper stock to a resident of that city. Because GG was not a li-
censed California broker, the transaction was a felony violation of the
state's blue-sky laws.

But the Corporation Commission had been given the wrong date in
its tip, and George had proof he was in Salt Lake City on the day specified in the warrant. Rice claimed the inaccuracy invalidated the charges
and even went so far as to admit to the commission that yes, he routinely did sell stock to California residents. But, he added, because he
transacted the sales over the phone from his office in Utah, his dealings
constituted interstate commerce and were none of California's business.

When the head of the commission refused to drop the charges, Rice
dashed off a long-winded telegram daring him to issue a new warrant
that specified the stock sale was between two men in different states. He
sent copies to a number of newspapers, and at least one ran the entire
screed verbatim. Aside from the wrongful charge, GG was peeved that
the commission insinuated he was hiding behind an alias:

> I challenge you to swear out a warrant for my arrest . . . and I prom-
> ise you that if you do, I will give the U.S. courts an opportunity
> to act and I will also proceed against you for commensurate
> damages. . . . The complaint sets forth no less than three times that
> my name is "Jacob Simon Herzig alias George Graham Rice." You
> and your deputy know that whereas I was born Jacob Simon Herzig
> I have continually and unintermittently for the past twenty-one
> years used the name of George Graham Rice, and instead of George
> Graham Rice being an alias that I won the name honorably as a
> newspaper and magazine writer and a writer of books. . . . The
> use of the word "alias" in the Oakland warrant was propaganda

*for the sole purpose of prepossessing and prejudicing the public
mind against me.*

While the telegram might have afforded George a satisfying measure of
revenge (it took seven months, but the charges were dropped), the rant
torpedoed the stock he had been trying to promote. When it came to
light that Rice was the man behind Bingham Galena, shares plummeted
overnight from thirty-eight cents to ten.

Back in New York, Rothstein was also making headlines: The Brain
was quitting gambling—or at least publicly claiming to be doing so.
"From now on, I shall devote most of my attention to my racing stables
and my real estate business," Rothstein told the New York *Mail*, granting a rare exclusive interview that ran on September 7, 1921. "It is not
pleasant to be, what some call, a 'social outcast.' For the sake of my
family and my friends, I am glad that chapter of my life is over."

Rothstein had lost his coveted privacy when he was called before a
grand jury to explain his role in the fixed 1919 World Series. He denied
involvement, but prosecutors claimed to have signed confessions from
Chicago White Sox players admitting that a nest of gamblers had paid
them to intentionally lose to the Cincinnati Reds. Then inexplicably, just
as the case was going to trial in the summer of 1921, the confessions and
entire body of prosecutorial evidence vanished from the Cook County
courthouse. Ten days later, everyone was acquitted, although the eight
"Black Sox" players were banned from baseball for life.

Rothstein was never convicted of buying off players (in fact, he was
never convicted of *any* crime in his life). But it was widely speculated
that he won almost $1 million on the series by knowing the fix was in.
True to form, Rothstein probably profited by sending an army of "beards"
(covert betting agents) to make many small wagers with curb bookies
rather than plunging for a single, showy score.

Two years after the scandal, baseball didn't seem to be suffering in
the least. America's "So what?" attitude toward cheating was indicative
of a larger societal shift that prized prosperity over morals. In 1921, Babe

Ruth jacked his home-run record to fifty-nine, and that year's World Series broke records for gate receipts and attendance.

Rice returned to New York to work on his appeal, which for two years
had been bottlenecked deep within the court system thanks to the stalling tactics of Rothstein's attorneys. But there would still be a long way
to go before George's appeal came up before the New York Supreme
Court—two more years, in fact. So GG got busy planning a long-term
con that would come together once he was officially cleared and freed.

Rice recalled an old flooded copper mine in Idaho that had not been
worked in decades. Its neglected shaft was overgrown with brush, but
the most intriguing aspect of the property had nothing to do with its
underlying potential: The mine's chief asset was that it was already listed
on the Boston Curb Exchange, a corruption-infested stock slaughterhouse that was nowhere near as regulated as the newly sanitized indoors version of the curb in New York.

In 1923, America's financial roller coaster was in its initial delicious
ascent, and the big bull market was revving up to put the "roar" in the
Roaring Twenties. Who could blame Wall Street if it was too enam-
ored with the lofty view to contemplate how terrifying the ride down
might be?

The stock market's balance of power was shifting from old-guard investors who sought steady returns to whiz-kid speculators who made
wild bets in hopes of outlandish scores. Giving in to the shoot-the-works
sentiment, conservatives who previously considered 5 percent an inher-
ently risky expectation now jostled alongside gamblers demanding far
more obscene percentage returns. Bankers and brokers won no matter
what the market did, because the sheer volume of buying and selling
generated record commissions. From October 1923 through the end of
1924, the Dow would advance 25 percent. A fast-moving wave of prosperity loomed over America like a tsunami.

One of the driving forces behind the huge run-up was propaganda. After the Great War, practitioners of this trade—based on methods Rice had pioneered through trial and error earlier in the century—began to refer to themselves as professionals. By 1924, when anything deemed scientific gained instant credibility, the art of persuasion was rebranded a "science." A decade later, propaganda would be known negatively as a "racket," but that label was incomprehensible in the years preceding the crash.

"Propaganda . . . permeated the whole structure of the Street," Hansl explained in *Years of Plunder*. "It dealt in misinformation and its instruments extended all the way from customers' men to tipster sheets and paid publicity promoters." Market letters, radio investing shows, newspaper features, statistical services, financial magazines, bank bulletins, and hot whispers attributed to Wall Street prophets all melded into one sonorous chord that vibrated the nation. Advertising copywriters took a cue from con artists and paid less attention to pitching actual products. Instead, they emphasized how whatever it was they were selling would deliver intangibles that consumers weren't even aware they craved—namely, to be desired and envied.

Women's skirts climbed a few scandalous inches higher and men's neckties widened and bloomed in vibrant hues. At no other point in U.S. history were citizens so flush with easy money and free time. Lawn mowers, dishwashing machines, and hired servants freed up countless hours to go to the movies, listen to the radio, or play the piano. But in this age of automation, who could be bothered to practice an actual instrument? By 1924, half the pianos sold in America were of the "player" variety, with rolls of automatic music providing continuous entertainment with zero work.

The crazes that defined the decade grew increasingly bizarre. Marathon kissing contests, long-distance cigar smoking, rocking chair endurance competitions, and watching daredevils dive off bridges were all fads that occupied America's ever-widening window of leisure. When a two-bit boxer named Alvin "Sailor" Kelly got re-nicknamed Shipwreck after losing eleven straight fights, he quit the ring and became a steeplejack. Fearless at great heights, he took a stunt job to promote a new movie. By climbing atop a theater flagpole and sitting there for thirteen hours and thirteen minutes, Shipwreck Kelly became an overnight sensation, launching a pole-sitting obsession that sent copycat record seekers teetering to dizzying heights all across the country.

As the prosperity bandwagon careened onward, Rice laid the groundwork for his next big mining bet. A group of Idaho men owned the abandoned South Peacock mine he wanted in the rugged Hells Canyon territory. GG knew the owners didn't want to waste their own money to develop the property, so he offered them $10,000 in exchange for an option to buy 1.4 million shares of their company at a dime apiece. Together they would capitalize a reorganized corporation, but the catch was that George got to name four of the board's seven directors. After appointing shills that kept his name off the books, George hatched the Idaho Copper Corporation on January 1, 1924, and got to work repurposing a grossly exaggerated, two-decade-old geological report.

That summer George had good reason to celebrate Independence Day. On July 2, 1924, the appellate division of the New York Supreme Court voted 3–2 to overturn Rice's grand larceny conviction. The reason cited was a "reversible error" caused when the lower court allowed George's rambling accusations of corruption to distract jurors. It took four years, but in effect GG's strategy of goading prosecutors into defending themselves had worked to sabotage the case. In fact, the New York district attorney's office had even come under investigation for accepting bribes as a result of George's complaints. A new trial for Rice was ordered, but Rothstein's powerful band of barristers made sure the case never came up.

Six days after winning his freedom, Rice unveiled his latest journalistic venture, the *Wall Street Iconoclast*. Whereas George had previously hidden behind a nom de plume, he now put his name out front, because the supreme court victory had vindicated his credibility as a courageous attacker of the establishment.

"The Truth, No Matter Whom It Helps or Hurts," was the newspaper's slogan. Although the thinly veiled purpose of the publication was to conceal Rice's own sins with merciless denunciations of others, the *Iconoclast* lured readers from Maine to Mexico. George spread alarmist reports on old-line stocks, threatened to expose insiders, and put himself on a pedestal as a defender of the unwary investor. He mixed in some legitimate news but saw no need to be subtle about promoting his pet oil and mining stocks, specifically Idaho Copper. Within a year, the *Iconoclast*'s subscriber base would balloon to 300,000, making it the largest-circulation financial paper in America.

Rice next set his sights on commandeering the Boston Curb. If the New York Curb, in its outdoor incarnation, had been an "honor among thieves" swindling emporium, the Boston version, by contrast, flipped stocks like some back-alley shyster peddling fake watches pinned inside his trench coat. The "exchange" was housed in a third-floor walk-up above a shoe repair shop, and its membership consisted of thirty or forty sketchy brokers who were all in cahoots with one another. "There is not a thread of an excuse for the existence of the Boston Curb," warned *Time* magazine. "It is but the tool of financial swindlers who have made it a national gambling place where the markers are all counterfeits and those who enter its portals come out stripped of their belongings."

GG rented an office in Boston and hired a blacklisted New York broker named William (a.k.a. Walter) Jarvis to run his affairs there. Through the years Jarvis had worked for Rice in various capacities before blossoming on his own as the publisher of a scam stock newsletter. But when the New York attorney general secured an injunction barring him from engaging in tipster activities, Jarvis relocated to Massachusetts, where he served as chairman of the Boston Curb in 1922.

In the heyday of his prosperity, Jarvis had owned a steam yacht and was considered a pillar of his church for his ability to make $25,000 donations to his parish. But now, having been overthrown in a Boston Curb coup, he resented having to do Rice's bidding as a glorified "floor man." Jarvis especially detested taking orders from George, which was problematic because that's all he was paid to do during the winter of 1924–25. Six days a week between 10:00 A.M. and 3:00 P.M., Rice would phone with Idaho Copper trades he wanted executed in specific amounts and at fixed prices on the Boston Curb. Compelled to broker the orders in his own name, Jarvis put between two thousand and seventy thousand shares a day through the wash for GG. On Saturdays, he sent a special messenger on the midnight train to New York to pay off or collect a weekly settlement with Rice.

Rice sang the praises of Idaho Copper in the pages of the *Iconoclast* without disclosing that he controlled it, urging investors to hoard as many shares of the penny stock as they could. On March 17, 1925, the paper published the first of two glowing reports on Idaho Copper's principal mine at South Peacock. The first piece of propaganda was the twenty-year-old geological study GG had unearthed. Not only did Rice fail to disclose how outdated it was, but he claimed the report was being "published in full," even though he had knowingly omitted a key paragraph that said "returns could not be expected from the grass roots down."

The second published appraisal was signed by Walter K. Yorston, Idaho Copper's shill president. It pegged the value of ore at $22 million all the way to the two-hundred-foot level. But Yorston had never been inside South Peacock, nor could he have conducted any such tests; the rotted shaft went only twenty feet in. Beyond that, the mine was flooded.

Idaho Copper rocketed to fifty cents and was on its way to ninety within a month. Boston Curb brokers were swamped with buy orders. The only one selling was Ricecakes.

Unfortunately for George, Idaho was one of the few states that checked the advertisements of stock companies against the actual conditions of their mines. On March 24, 1925, the state mining inspector

wired the following telegram to the Boston Curb, requesting a delisting
of the stock on the basis of fraud:

> *Idaho Copper . . . has never complied with the corporation laws,*
> *mining laws or blue sky laws of Idaho. The mine it professes to own*
> *has been involved in two failures and excepting one lease during*
> *one year has been idle for twenty-four years. The underground*
> *workings are practically inaccessible. Advertising matter being cir-*
> *culated in sale of stock is grossly misleading and in conflict with*
> *Idaho laws. . . . Will gladly furnish all information possible and will*
> *appreciate advice on the attitude [of] your exchange.*

Somewhat surprisingly, the corrupt Boston Curb agreed to suspend
trading of Idaho Copper at ninety-three cents on April 25, 1925, pending investigation of the complaint. The three company directors who had
not been appointed by Rice all resigned and vilified George as a scoun-
drel. Using the corporation's money, Rice sued the Idaho mining inspector for libel and funneled cash to Jarvis to smooth things over on the
Boston Curb.

On July 11, 1925, Idaho Copper regained market privileges at forty-
four cents per share.

In August, Rice orchestrated another rise in price by sending three
dynamiters to Boston, where Jarvis was ordered to record all their sales
under his own name. The Idaho mining inspector, unintimidated by the
libel suit, revisited South Peacock in September and reported that despite a stock capitalization of $10 million, "the entrances to the mine
were still all caved in and the site lacked the necessary surface facilities
and mining equipment."

Rice needed an authority whose opinion would trump the inspector's. Springing into damage control, he hired Walter Harvey Weed, the
nation's foremost copper expert, to vouch for the riches buried beneath
the property.

With forty years of distinguished experience, Weed was a founding member of the Geological Society of Washington, D.C., and served as the editor of several prominent mining journals. He was best known for groundbreaking studies in Yellowstone National Park that proved colors in geysers were caused by algae and that the mysterious deaths of bears and elk could be explained by oxidized sulfur vapors from extinct springs. Weed had a low opinion of Rice specifically and a loathing of swindlers in general because he had recently been impersonated by the con artist Yellow Kid Weil. But the annual salary of $100,000 that GG dangled—$1.3 million in 2015 dollars—was enough to get Weed to swallow his distaste.

That autumn, the *Iconoclast* repeatedly teased readers that America's most prominent mining engineer was about to announce the blockbuster discovery of the continent's richest copper vein.

Weed went and inspected South Peacock. It didn't take him more than a cursory walk around the property to sum up his findings, which he fired off in a November 10, 1925, telegram that read, "There is nothing here and never will be. The mine is a lemon." Walter was afraid authorities would connect him to Rice's scam, so he signed his wires with what he believed to be an ingenious, unbreakable code name: RETLAW.

George received RETLAW's telegram the same day the NYSE broke the three-million-share barrier in daily trading volume. Rice wasn't about to let Idaho Copper miss the market's latest upswell, so he took poetic license and tweaked the tone and spirit of Weed's message.

"The ore is spectacular!" the *Iconoclast* bellowed, citing the renowned geologist as the source of the glorious news.

When Rice saw electric lights burning high up in Manhattan skyscrapers late in the evening, he liked to remark, "Behind every one of those lights is a man staying up thinking how to get the better of the fellow across the way."

Most of the time, the after-hours illumination signified nothing more than janitors emptying wastepaper baskets and charwomen scrubbing floors. Then again, perhaps the workers were cleaning up in the securities racket too. By 1925, it seemed as if all classes of laborers could afford to place bets on the stock market.

Housemaids and trolley motormen were scoring big, trading on overheard snippets of conversation. Plumbers, seamstresses, and speakeasy bartenders all claimed to have inside scoops, and if they were like hundreds of thousands of other Americans who speculated blindly in stocks without any idea of what the underlying companies did, they probably managed to win anyway.

Everyone wanted in on offerings having to do with hot new technologies, so issues like Seaboard Air Line spiked dramatically, even though most plungers had no clue the company was a railroad, not an aviation stock. Ranchers in Wyoming hustled in off the prairie so they wouldn't miss mid-morning market reports on the radio; Ohio housewives whipped open the afternoon paper to peer intently at flash quotes, and dinner-table talk in Connecticut was peppered with debate over how much longer it would take for the family to be set for life. As Allen wrote in *Only Yesterday*, the big bull market had become a national mania:

> *The rich man's chauffeur drove with his ear laid back to catch the news of an impending move in Bethlehem Steel; he held fifty shares himself on a twenty-point margin. The window-cleaner at the broker's office paused to watch the ticker, for he was thinking of converting his laboriously accumulated savings into a few shares of Simmons. . . . An ex-actress in New York fitted up her Park Avenue apartment as an office and surrounded herself with charts, graphs, and financial reports, playing the market by telephone on an increasing scale and with increasing abandon. . . . Even the revolting intellectuals were there: Loudly as they might lament the depressing effects of standardization and mass production upon American life, they found themselves quite ready to reap the fruits thereof.*

By the end of 1925, bullish momentum was so strong that *any* stock could ride the rising wave, making it no longer necessary to invent outright frauds. Yet the torrent of sham securities kept coming. Suckers essentially conned themselves, throwing money into anything that sounded remotely feasible. Extracting gold from seawater, forcing light from pomegranates, and devising a "spirit laboratory" to consult dead inventors were all ideas that attracted actual investment capital in the Roaring Twenties. It was a common ploy for con men to misappropriate the names of well-known captains of industry, to the point where Henry Ford had at least forty gyps using his name to promote products he knew nothing about. Schemes were conceived one day, rushed off share-certificate printing presses the next, and tossed like birdseed to the indiscriminate masses.

For the first time since the 1890s, con artists had to recalibrate the hierarchy of marks. Executors in charge of estates, guardians of trust funds, and even keepers of church funds were now considered prime pickings because there were suddenly so many of them. Real estate developers were coveted because they knew how to quickly raise capital. Retired businessmen were easy because they responded well to magnetic personalities, and bagging a businessman turned bootlegger was the holy grail of grifting because the sucker had already demonstrated a willingness to tiptoe outside the law. Doctors and dentists possessed enormous self-confidence, which meant you didn't have to sell them on the notion their smarts could be applied to moneymaking. Bankers were tricky; you had to really know your financials, but the payoff was access to deep tills. Lawyers were to be avoided, college professors weren't worth the time, and if you wanted to play ranchers and farmers, you had to avoid fast talk and adopt plainspoken country mannerisms. One would think that cops were taboo, but the best of them had minds that worked like a criminal's, which is how one detective who headed a big-city bunco division got taken for $38,000.

Amateur stock swappers yearning to apply their genius more broadly began to dabble in tropical real estate, overpaying for Everglades swampland guaranteed to be the next Miami Beach. "At that time," one con artist would later wisecrack, "marks were so thick in Florida that you had to kick them out of your way." Ropers who had previously worked Pullman cars "retired" to sunny Havana, where they spent their days meeting docking cruise ships and blending in with going-ashore parties to separate suckers from their bankrolls. One con man told of taking a break and minding his own business at a hotel bar when a well-off tourist came up to him and asked for a light. "That match cost him $100,000," the hustler said, laughing.

It was in this atmosphere of exaggerated extravagance that Rice rolled out his most fantastic stock concoction yet—the Colombia Emerald Development Corporation.

Legend had it that for thousands of years, the Inca Empire had plumbed the otherworldly depths of a colossal emerald mine deep within the Colombian jungle. When the explorer Francisco Pizarro ventured from Spain to slaughter the Incas in the 1530s, the last efforts of the dying warriors reportedly centered on keeping the source of their kingdom's most precious riches secret from conquistadors. When their demise was imminent, the Incas closed up the mine shaft and constructed a modest stone church atop its entrance. When the last survivors of the Inca civilization died out, so too did knowledge of the camouflaged entrance to the world's richest emerald mine.

For four centuries, the lore of the unharvested gems stymied treasure seekers. But in 1925, a South American priest stumbled upon an ancient deed pinpointing the location of the mine. In order to raise money for its development, the priest sought out—who else?—George Graham Rice, praying that the world's top stock promoter would help the poor people of his village by incorporating and resurrecting the emerald mine.

The above version is the way George pitched the investment in the *Iconoclast*. In actuality, he had bought an existing corporation at a bankruptcy sale for $7,800, and its holdings happened to include a South American mine no one knew anything about.

Rice got Colombia Emerald listed on the Boston Curb and, to pump it up, circulated doctored photographs that showed vast quantities of emeralds spilling out of the mine's entrance. But the truest wealth was buried deeper, GG promised readers, with a value in emeralds that might exceed the combined worth of all the diamonds beneath Africa. The proceeds from the sale of Colombia Emerald stock, Rice claimed, would fund the purchase of state-of-the-art hydraulic mining equipment to gently float the precious gems up to the surface with forced water, allowing stockholders to corner the global emerald market.

Colombia Emerald began trading at nine cents. By the time Rice pocketed his first few million in profits, the quote on the Boston Curb stood at $17 per share.

As 1926 approached, GG was living sumptuously in a luxurious suite at an exclusive Manhattan hotel, attended to by his devoted young wife, an army of servants, and several trusted bodyguards. Estimates pegged his net worth at $100 million. The true amount Rice had squirreled away would never be known, but considering his top salesmen would later testify to million-dollar commissions, a nine-figure kitty was not out of the question, assuming George had not gambled most of it away.

It's difficult to imagine that the fifty-five-year-old Rice permitted twenty-three-year-old Katherine to explore New York on her own (and certainly not with friends her own age). Yet GG got good mileage out of his wife's name: By their fifth wedding anniversary, "Kathryn Rice" and "Catherine Herzig" had appeared on numerous corporate boards and directorships where George wanted control without candor.

It would be wrong to think that while con artist kingpins like George wallowed in excess, there weren't at least *some* citizens advocating for ethics in America. In fact, long before other economies, the United States was unique in its establishment of antifraud organizations. At the turn of the twentieth century, groups like the Business Men's Anti-Stock

Swindling League and the National Vigilance Committee had been among the first entities to argue for truth in advertising. After the Great War, several of these organizations joined forces to create the Better Business Bureau, a nationwide alliance that attacked fraud by taking advantage of the same propaganda tactics con artists used to fleece suckers.

Spearheaded by the mantra "Before You Invest, Investigate!" the BBB's public relations engine was humming along full throttle by 1926. Posters on street corners, subways, and buses drew attention to the evils of speculation. Tips on how to safeguard finances were prominently displayed near punch clocks in factories. When not speaking in front of women's club luncheons, fraternal gatherings, and civic associations, BBB publicity agents fed stats to newspaper columnists and filled radio airwaves with outreach speeches, often buying competing time slots against flimflam investment shows. Some messages alerted the public to specific scams, while general advice cautioned against any deal that seemed too good to be true. As one business ethics scholar put it, "During the 1920s, the anti-fraud publicity blitz was all but impossible to avoid in urban America."

Still, it wasn't working. In internal reports, dismayed BBB officials expressed amazement at "the gullibility of the public." Guesses of annual losses from stock swindling were measured in billions.

"By the admission of the Better Business Bureaus themselves, all the public warnings, all the rejected advertisements and negotiated adjustments of marketing policies, and all the arrests and convictions did not put that much of a dent in their overall estimates of fraud incidence," wrote Edward J. Balleisen in "Private Cops on the Fraud Beat," a 2009 *Business History Review* article. "At no point in the 1920s did either law-enforcement officials or representatives of the nongovernmental antifraud organizations estimate actual declines in the annual losses resulting from fraud."

In an effort to get tough against rogue brokers, New York had passed article 23-A of the General Business Law in 1921. Known as the Martin

Act, it empowered the attorney general to slap permanent injunctions on fraudulent firms and individuals, a broad form of clout that superseded the powers of blue-sky laws in any other state. But the Martin Act was essentially a dead law until January 1, 1926, when an aggressive assistant attorney general named Keyes Winter was assigned to run the state's new Martin Anti-Stock Fraud Bureau. A rising star with national political aspirations, Winter made no secret about wanting to nail New York's most egregious con artist.

On his seventh day on the job, Winter paid a visit to GG at the *Iconoclast*'s 44 West Fifty-Seventh Street office. Accompanied by state troopers and a briefcase full of subpoenas, Winter indicted Rice and ordered him to explain fraudulent statements published about Idaho Copper, Colombia Emerald, and Fortuna Consolidated (under the Martin Act, the state could compel defendants to testify under oath at an injunction hearing before they were tried on criminal charges). "I have been informed and believe that the stock of these three corporations is substantially worthless," Winter wrote in court documents. "I am also informed that the capital stock of these three corporations is largely owned by George Graham Rice and his associates, which fact is entirely concealed from the public."

Rice and Rothstein reacted quickly to rein in Winter. They hired nine lawyers to gut the Martin Act, and on February 11, 1926, a lower court judge declared the Martin Act unconstitutional, comparing it to the "third degree" because the attorney general acted as complainant, prosecutor, and arbiter. The *Iconoclast* gleefully heralded the ruling as a win for the common folk, and within weeks Idaho Copper spiked to $2.60. George leased a larger loft from Rothstein on East Seventeenth Street in anticipation of a surge in business.

"Sell any stock you own and buy IDAHO COPPER," boomed the *Iconoclast* in April, its circulation having doubled past 600,000. "We know what this language means AND WE MEAN IT." When shares soared to $6.25, the paper urged investors to lock share certificates in a strongbox and not to cash in Idaho Copper until it climbed to the pre-posterously high prediction of $62 per share.

Despite the success of the firm's pet stock, William Jarvis, GG's right-hand man in Boston, was none too keen at having been sucked into the Martin Act indictments. Rice was prepared to testify that he wasn't re-sponsible for any price rigging on the Boston Curb, and technically he wasn't; Jarvis was on the hook for the wash trades and all the sales drummed up by George's dynamiters.

Rice and Jarvis were arguing bitterly in the spring of 1926, a years-long culmination of petty disagreements escalated by a tremendous clash of egos. With Idaho Copper peaking, Jarvis plotted his revenge: He drew on his experience publishing tip sheets, and with access to Rice's sucker list Jarvis let fly with a mass-mailing sabotage that detailed how Idaho Copper was nothing more than a worthless stock floated by a deplorable crook.

George was furious but quite used to counterattacking. The *Icono-clast* fired off a malicious rebuttal asserting that Idaho Copper was the victim of a smear attack by a single greedy predator. But Jarvis's damage had been done, and the stock plummeted to the point where the Boston Curb demanded it be withdrawn from trading.

Rice cooked up an ingenious Plan B, based on his knowledge that suckers were eternal optimists: He spread word that with the help of the ace geologist Weed, the firm was about to acquire several new block-buster mines. Instead of folding the new properties into the existing holdings, George was going to create—on paper at least—an entirely new stock issue.

Like a snake sloughing off dead skin, Idaho Copper *Corporation* be-came Idaho Copper *Company*. This semantic side step was Rice's way of opting for a fresh start with a repackaged (but still worthless) prod-uct, and he pretended to be magnanimous by offering a limited-time op portunity for the public to "salvage" old certificates by swapping them for new ones. GG was so bullish on the deal that he recommended not only trading in existing issues but increasing ownership in Idaho Copper by buying even more of the new shares.

While the backstabbing between Rice and Jarvis was playing out on the Boston Curb, a farmer in South Dakota was having a difficult year. His wife was sick, his milk cow had died, and the mortgage was long overdue. With shaking hands, the man took out his gilt-edged Idaho Copper Corporation certificates, carefully checked their value in the latest edition of the *Iconoclast,* and came to the reluctant conclusion to trade them in for the $2,000 Rice's articles promised him they were worth.

The farmer wrote to GG with his request to cash out. Rice flamboyantly replied to hold on—Idaho Copper was about to skyrocket! The investor wrote back, pleading for his money. He got no reply.

Panicking, the farmer went to his village bank to see if he could trade in his shares there. Had Rice honored the man's request at first asking, there wouldn't have been a problem. But now it was around June 1, 1926, the date when Idaho Copper began trading under its new legal name. There was a slight overlap between the delisting of the old stock and its relisting as a new one. In this brief window of time, Idaho Copper vanished from published stock tables. When the banker couldn't find a quote, he informed the farmer his shares weren't worth the paper they were printed on.

Terrified he had lost everything, the farmer gathered his letters from Rice and spilled his tale of woe to the Feds, who had been salivating for another crack at putting George Graham Rice behind bars for the rest of his life.

Maintaining a high-wire lifestyle placed Rice under so much stress that it left him with little time to enjoy the Gatsbyesque pleasures his opulence afforded him. Rice rarely ventured out anymore; that's where his enemies lurked. He was sleeping only in short bursts, his twenty-hour workdays fueled by cigars and strong coffee. Because he was increasingly on guard, GG's sense of humor had frayed, and his cantankerous temper was taking a turn toward volatile explosivity. The throbbing cyst on the back of his skull waxed and waned, and persistent foot trouble meant the ram's head walking stick George had long prized as a style accessory was now a necessity to maintain his balance in an increasingly unsteady world.

A rising America was ascending fast in 1927. Women's skirts reached above the knee for the first time, and analysts delighted in drawing up risqué charts that linked the trend of showing more leg to the rollicking economy. That spring Charles Lindbergh and the *Spirit of St. Louis* would soar into history with the first nonstop, solo transatlantic flight, igniting "the wildest frenzy of hero worship ever accorded a single human being." That summer Babe Ruth would establish another jaw-dropping record by swatting sixty home runs—a feat all the more impressive considering the portly slugger's legendary exploits as a hard-drinking womanizer who often played hungover. "I swing big, with everything I've got," he boasted to reporters. "I hit big or I miss big. I like to live as big as I can."

In Newark, Shipwreck Kelly ascended a fifty-foot flagpole and looked down upon a sea of rain-soaked spectators. He smoked four packs of cigarettes a day, and his wife hoisted up to him bottles of milk, broth, and coffee (but no solid foods). Shipwreck napped by thrusting his thumbs into strategic holes bored beneath his special wooden seat, having conditioned himself to snap awake in an instant if he leaned too far over and felt a pinching sensation. "Hundreds of passersby, stopping to crane their necks backward at Mr. Kelly, loitered a moment longer to argue with one another whether or not he is a hero," *Time* magazine reported. When the world-record holder spryly shimmied down after twelve days aloft, Shipwreck boasted that he would continue to perch for absurd lengths of time, just to prove how America "overdoes everything."

There had been a sharp correction in stocks toward the end of 1926. But instead of scaring sense into speculators, the shake-up drove high rollers to bet even bigger to recoup losses, which most of them managed to do, reinforcing the idea that it was impossible to lose money in the market. Government officials—from bean-counting economists all the way up to President Calvin Coolidge—began to espouse a philosophy that the nation was embarking upon an era of prosperity that would never end.

Since the start of the big bull market, stock averages had advanced 100 percent, and volume was running over three million shares a day. "To many it seemed that the millennium was at hand," wrote Hansl in *Years of Plunder*. "If three-million-share days were possible, why not five-million-share days, or even ten-million-share days? All that was needed was to pump a little oxygen into the structure."

In New York, Winter continued his relentless rousting of con artists. His office had won an appeal of Rice's overturning of the Martin Act, but like a badminton shuttlecock being batted back and forth at a lawn party, GG was now re-appealing the decision before the state supreme court. The state couldn't move forward with a criminal trial against Rice until the Martin Act matter was settled, so Winter went after other swindlers. He shut down numerous bucket shops and achieved a degree of notoriety as a ruthless interrogator when a stock promoter he was grilling at a hearing dropped dead of a heart attack.

The grudge match between Winter and Rice began to devolve into something like the Whac-a-Mole carnival game. At one point, George marched into the assistant AG's office and had one of Rothstein's top attorneys read verbatim the statute that said so long as a corporation's mine existed somewhere, the owner was free under First Amendment rights to state his opinion about its prospects. Lacking resources to combat GG's stalling, Winter complained about how Rice could afford to pay one high-powered lawyer $15,000 just for a single half-hour case to favorably resolve a procedural technicality.

Still, George was worried enough about his pending case to risk being further charged with extortion. On Saint Patrick's Day 1927, a former county judge hired by Rothstein telephoned the assistant AG to make him aware he had $9,000—roughly the equivalent of Winter's annual salary—in his vest pocket ready to hand over as soon as Rice's main indictment was dropped. When Winter refused, Rice leaked to the press the lie that the prosecutor had contacted *him* soliciting a bribe.

The very next day, Rothstein himself paid a personal visit to Winter. Over a two-hour chat, Arnold made it clear he possessed evidence to ruin Winter professionally. Covertly, Winter had once ordered agents to buy stolen stock certificates from gangsters as a ploy to get inside their swindling ring. Amazingly, the Brain's influence extended into the Fraud Prevention Bureau's own office, because he had acquired the original copy of Winter's memo that authorized the illegal purchase. Rothstein threatened to give the document to Rice to publish in the *Iconoclast* unless Winter backed off and left all of Rothstein's rent payers alone.

Instead of giving in, Winter reported the blackmail attempt. But even as he continued to crack down on bucketeers, rumors of his resignation rippled through Wall Street.

At a higher level, federal authorities were methodically building the mail fraud case against Rice. In addition to the South Dakota farmer, they had scores of complainants now and were whittling the list down to the strongest ten. Postal inspectors visited Idaho and had a difficult time even finding the mine that was making George millions. Prosecutors sent a government scout to report on the South American emeralds. Upon reaching the site in Colombia, the agent found no priest and no ancient church. All that could be salvaged to send back to the United States as evidence was a box of worthless rocks.

Rice claimed harassment by the government and ratcheted up the antiestablishment blather. There were enough conspiracy theorists devouring the *Iconoclast* to rally behind him. As a celebrity martyr, George painted himself as the last line of defense between the public and nefarious Wall Street insiders who hid behind paid-off politicians and prosecutors.

On September 20, 1927, Rice experienced a bad news/good news/bad news day at the expense of his nemesis Winter.

That morning in western New York, a judge unsealed a supreme court indictment—brought about by Winter—charging Rice with grand larceny for bilking an Olean doctor out of $11,000 in the Colombia Emerald swindle.

Later, at a press conference in Albany, the attorney general announced that Winter would be stepping down as the Street's top anti-fraud crusader.

But there was a catch: Even though Winter was switching to private practice, the AG made it a point to announce "he will be designated as a special deputy to prosecute all proceedings instituted against corporations [that] have been sponsored or promoted by George Graham Rice."

Later that evening, in a speech before the national Better Business Bureau convention in Manhattan, a high-spirited Winter capped the biggest day in his career by roasting GG in sarcastic fashion, drawing peals of laughter with jokes about the luxuries his agents walked off with when they raided Rice's offices.

Unbeknownst to Winter, George had planted a stenographer in the audience.

Seething for the last laugh but omitting any context of humor, GG printed Winter's salacious remarks verbatim in the *Iconoclast* as further proof of his unjust persecution by vengeful enemies.

While the nation partied on, Rice hunkered down in his fortress under constant legal siege. By late 1927, his daily grind had become one of desperation masked by affluence as he attempted to appear in control while remaining on high alert for the next incoming salvo. At fifty-seven, George was physically hobbled, soured by paranoia, and pacing a gilded cage of his own elaborate construction.

GG had lost his supreme court appeal, and New York was moving ahead with a trial for his two-year-old fraud case. In November, Idaho

Copper (trading at thirty cents) was ordered into receivership over $40,000 in unaccounted-for funds. Colombia Emerald had all but evaporated from the Boston Curb. When Rice had been indicted on the larceny charge in September, the only assets found in his *Iconoclast* office were a $100 Liberty Bond, a copper penny, and thousands of unredeemable stock certificates from failed ventures. A subsequent audit of George's books revealed $262,800 in "loans"—undoubtedly protection money—due to Rothstein.

The Feds had been ready to charge Rice with mail fraud for nearly a year. But the indictment required a summons be formally handed over in person. Because George knew that under common law a man's home is his castle, he barricaded himself in his Hotel Chatham suite behind layers of security. He now rented the entire top floor, and the main door to his apartment opened only via secret knock, and even then only on a sturdy chain until the caller could be ascertained to be within GG's ever-shrinking inner circle.

For months, process servers lounged in the lobby and guarded the hotel's side exits. But on Sundays—and only on Sundays—Rice ventured outside for fresh air. In 1927, it was against the law to serve court documents on the Lord's Day.

In the first week of December, more shares traded on Wall Street than at any previous time in the history of the exchange. Brokers were floating $3.5 billion in margin accounts, and $2 of every $5 loaned by banks nationwide was for the purpose of buying stocks. When market confidence showed hints of wavering, President Coolidge underscored how fluidly the longest bull market in U.S. history was operating, even though his statements conflicted with statistics on rising unemployment and evidence that a sharp corrective downturn was likely. More sober prognosticators begin cautioning investors not to overstay the speculation party, but these concerns were ignored and even denigrated   much like the mining boom out west decades earlier, when GG branded anybody who uttered a discouraging word a "knocker."

By 1928, Rice was a microcosm of America's decadent vortex: He appeared obscenely wealthy, but his fortune was built on a paper foundation with little core integrity. Impressive from a distance, the illusion up close showed hairline cracks of stress.

By the middle of January, George's foot pain was so severe he had stopped going out on Sundays. It's a good guess he had either gout or a severely infected toe, and at some point he had Katherine or one of his lackeys summon the city's best chiropodist to his hotel suite. In an era when doctors routinely made house calls, the foot specialist enraged Rice by replying that he didn't make such visits. Ordered to make an exception, the doctor testily snapped into the telephone he didn't care who George Graham Rice was; if the discomfort was that bad, the patient knew where to find his office.

George waited it out a few more days in a haze of agony. On January 17, 1928, he could stand it no longer. Rice put on his hat and heavy cloak, tottered down a back stairway, and ducked out a service door. Limping around the corner to Vanderbilt Avenue, he listed in the direction of the chiropodist's, fueled forward as much by anger as by pain.

An alert process server—amazed at spotting his quarry attempting a doddering daylight break—easily caught up to Rice before he blended into the crowd.

In an instant, the server slapped a sheaf of legal papers against the shuffling con artist's chest.

The U.S. government was charging Rice with ten breaches of section 215 of the U.S. Criminal Code. Each count of mail fraud carried a five-year prison sentence.

An infected toe—not the proverbial Achilles' heel—brought down the Jackal of Wall Street.

Rice made $5,000 bail, and Rothstein secured him a hideout at the Ritz-Carlton in Atlantic City. George reengaged his twelve best attorneys, culling the top heavyweights from Rothstein's stable plus

Henry A. Wise, the former federal prosecutor who had sent him to jail on the exact same mail fraud charges in 1912.

GG hunkered down while his defense team went into stall-and-delay mode. But there was something different about being in the clutches of the Feds this time around: Motions to quash were all swiftly denied, and the trial got put on a fast track. Prosecutors had a sense the stock market was in danger of imploding and wanted to bag a trophy swindler as proof they had reined in at least some vice while securities fraud was at its zenith.

Despite Rice's continued rants against insiders in the *Iconoclast,* the big bull operators had seized control of the public's psyche. In the winter of 1928, it was an open secret that a market reckoning was imminent. Nevertheless, stocks continued to trade at zany prices. No matter how sternly forecasters warned the public, the one thing Americans feared more than a crash was getting left behind.

Almost no economist in the country could have envisioned what happened on March 3, 1928: The stock market launched into a sensational three-month blast that made all the gains of the past five years look tame in comparison.

"What on earth was happening? Wasn't business bad, and credit inflated, and the stock-price level dangerously high? Was the market going crazy?" Allen wrote in *Only Yesterday.* "Anybody who had chosen this moment to predict that the bull market was on the verge of a wild advance which would make all that had gone before seem trifling would have been quite mad—or else inspired with a genius for mass psychology."

On March 13, the bull rush was so staggering that tickers nationwide ran twelve minutes behind rising quotes. Four days later, they lagged by thirty-three minutes. Records were smashed on March 27, when NYSE share volume closed at an unprecedented 4.8 million. Stories of average Joes striking it filthy rich—on a scale we would equate today with hitting the lottery—were ho-hum occurrences.

"Suppose all these madmen who insisted on buying stocks at advancing prices tried to sell at the same moment!" one economist warned.

"It was as if the foundations of reason had been swept away and delusion reigned instead," insisted another. "The world was a madhouse."

America had turned the corner from wealthy to greedy. The nation's gluttony was now tinged with a dark, palpable sense of predation.

People quit their jobs and installed stock tickers in their parlors to concentrate solely on making a killing in the market. The newly rich relocated to Paris or bought summer villas on the French Riviera, demanding berths aboard passenger ships that had "speculating decks" so they wouldn't be stuck at sea without being able to trade. Once obnoxious expats reached the other side of the Atlantic, they didn't have to try too hard to live up to the emerging "ugly Americans" stereotype.

Back home, the New York Yankees were emblematic of the nation's unchecked swagger. The team was on its way to a second straight World Series sweep, even as their manager griped about stock-obsessed ballplayers who "turn to the financial pages first and the sports pages later." Babe Ruth was closing in on five hundred career homers but was now so fat that fans snickered over how the Yankees added pinstripes to their uniforms just to make the Bambino look slimmer.

Americans spent a good portion of 1928 craning their necks heavenward. The flagpole-sitting craze had spawned hundreds of imitators, including scores of kids who broke arms and legs and at least one mother with a baby attempting the "infant record." Shipwreck Kelly had at least seventeen known impostors as he prepared for a forty-nine-day perch to put his record beyond the reach of anyone. Shipwreck told the press that sitting hundreds of feet high for weeks at a time was not as bad as having to endure the catcalls from hecklers who tried to scare him into falling. Americans were cultivating an expectation that if you paid the price of admission, you damn well better be entertained, even if amusement meant rooting for horrifying carnage.

The wave of selling that rocked stocks on June 12, 1928, sparked the first five-million-share day, with tickers slipping two hours behind staggering price drops. Was this the big meltdown naysayers had been predicting? Apparently, President Coolidge thought so. On the eve of the

Republican National Convention, he announced he would not be running for another term. But the markets quickly regained steam over the next two trading days, and the party's replacement nominee, Secretary of Commerce Herbert C. Hoover, bolstered the nation with the rallying cry "Four more years of prosperity!" Americans badly wanted to believe Hoover when he predicted, "We shall soon, with the help of God, be in sight of the day when poverty will be banished from this land."

Perhaps the truest barometer that things were off-kilter in the summer of 1928 was the behavior of Arnold Rothstein. Usually steady and methodical, the Brain was running himself ragged over his latest long-term venture: narcotics trafficking.

The return on investment for bootlegging liquor was decent. But Rothstein had envisioned that long after the inevitable repeal of Prohibition, the addictive properties of heroin, morphine, and cocaine would keep drugs wildly profitable. Around 1925, he sent a team of importers to Europe, where pharmaceutical companies were more than willing to sell vast quantities of surgical-grade dope, no questions asked. With assembly-line precision, Rothstein got opiates onto the streets of America's biggest cities. He even realized an unexpected form of revenue when his bail bonds business started to spike in line with drug arrests. In three years, the racket had grown tenfold, and Rothstein was in complete control of the nation's illegal narcotics trade. But Arnold was strapped for cash because he was plowing all his profits back into the endeavor.

On Memorial Day 1928, Rothstein went to Belmont Park, his first appearance at a horse track in years. He lost heavily and left a marker for $130,000. The Brain routinely left six-figure IOUs and always made good on them. This one he let slide for months.

Simultaneously, Rothstein began laying bets on Hoover to win the November presidential election. By the end of the summer, he had discreetly wagered $400,000 on the outcome.

Around this time, Arnold's wife found out he was having an affair with a showgirl. She demanded a divorce and stormed off to Europe.

Rothstein started acting twitchy and short-tempered. He was paler than usual and sweating a lot. Whispers started circulating in the underworld that America's first organized crime boss was shooting his own dope.

On September 8, 1928, Rothstein got suckered into a marathon thirty-hour poker game and lost $320,000, all in IOU markers initialed with his scrawl. When word got around about the magnitude of the loss, Arnold started carping to associates that the game had been rigged and he had no intention to pay.

The gamblers started harassing Rothstein to make good. When verbal threats didn't work, the creditors hired kidnappers who botched the job by grabbing the wrong man.

On the sleety evening of November 4, 1928, Rothstein settled in to do some paperwork at his regular table in Lindy's restaurant. At 10:12 P.M., he got a call on the pay phone—the jilted gamblers again. That was it. Arnold was going to march down to the Park Central Hotel and set the cheaters straight. He had already changed his mind and decided he was going to honor the bet to avoid being branded a welcher. But strictly on principle, the Brain was going to hold off on paying until he was good and ready.

Rothstein took a pistol out of his pocket and handed it to an associate at the restaurant for safekeeping. He didn't want the gamblers to think he had lethal motives in mind.

The discussion in room 349 quickly grew heated. Confronted by the bookie who was responsible for paying off the three gamblers seated around the table, Rothstein barked, "Tell them to keep their shirts on until Election Day." That was when Arnold planned to be rolling in dough after cashing his bets on Hoover.

The four men pulled revolvers. Rothstein, unarmed, stood up abruptly with the intention of walking out. A single blast of gunfire reverberated through the hotel.

A tourist at the third-floor elevator recoiled when a man wearing a gray suit staggered past her clutching his groin. A cabbie taking a break on a side street was startled when a gun bounced off the hood of his car, apparently thrown from an upper window. Detectives followed a trail of crimson on the sidewalk and found Rothstein bleeding profusely outside a service entrance. "I'll take care of it myself," he rasped when they pressed him to name the shooter.

The newspapers called it the "Crime of the Century." It would never be solved. No prosecutor could prove for certain who fired the bullet that blew a gaping hole through Rothstein's bladder and spleen.

Two days later, as twenty-one million Americans enthusiastically voted Hoover and his promise of continued prosperity into the White House, Rothstein died at Polyclinic Hospital. He would have won half a million dollars on the outcome of the election.

Twenty years earlier in Goldfield, George had staged a poker game shoot-out as a publicity prank. The circumstances were eerily similar to Rothstein's murder—four card cheats with guns arguing over $300,000. When New York's master fixer expired, so too did his influence on behalf of Rice.

For the past decade, Rothstein had extended an open line of credit to Rice for his legal bills. When millions in protection money stopped flowing to Rothstein's get-out-of-jail specialists after Arnold's death, George was on his own. Rothstein's lawyers undoubtedly knew that their boss had died with Rice owing him hundreds of thousands of dollars. Without the Brain's backing, they wanted nothing to do with a con man.

A week before his federal trial, Rice was suddenly without the best judicial buy-off artists in the business.

A sleek Rolls-Royce glided to the curb outside the Woolworth Building, the tallest building on the planet and home to the Southern District of New York's federal courthouse. GG had just finished a sumptuous lunch during a break from jury selection and was resplendent in a sable-lined Russian fur coat while smoking a long black cigar.

A hobo accosted Rice as he exited the vehicle. "Gimme a dime?"

It was not so much a question as a demand.

Rice slipped his gloved hand into a deep pocket, produced a crisp dollar bill, and smilingly handed it over.

"Jesus!" the bum exclaimed, peering at the bill in his grimy fingers. "God almighty!"

George, grinning, shot back, "Wait a minute fellow—you're promoting me too fast. Better call me Abraham."

Then Rice doddered inside the courthouse and continued where he had left off before the lunch break, insisting on his right to ask 159 typewritten questions of each prospective juror.

When the trial began on November 14, 1928, Ricecakes selected the most prominent seat at the defense table. He had already informed Judge John C. Knox that he dismissed his entire team of lawyers and would be acting as his own attorney. His next request was for the court to strike all references to his birth name, Jacob Simon Herzig. GG was emphatic about wanting the jury—and those who read the front-page news—to be fully aware they were dealing with the one and only George Graham Rice.

Along with Idaho Copper's president, Yorston, the geologist Weed, and a Colombia Emerald executive named Frank Silva (who might have been Katherine's brother), Rice was facing the ten counts of mail fraud, plus a new eleventh count charging conspiracy. Knowing he had to orchestrate the con of his life to stay out of prison, George embraced the role of "persecuted everyman" with persuasive aplomb.

William Jarvis, the two-timing broker whose vengeful Idaho Copper exposé had brought about the initial fraud complaint, was one of the first witnesses called by the prosecution. Rice laced into an excoriating cross-examination that attacked his former underling's credibility.

When the Feds tried to establish decades-old patterns of swindling, George parried by portraying himself as an avuncular friend of the poor, entrusted with $200 million of their hard-earned capital. When geology experts testified that Idaho Copper properties were barren, Rice wove a highly believable tale as to why the 1905 report he used in his promotion was more reliable than the government's current findings. Injecting passion into the proceedings to ensure the trial stayed atop the news cycle, GG occasionally erupted in court, accusing his federal prosecutor of being bought off by Wall Street insiders. "This man, the tool of the bucket shops," George roared, "is putting on the record lies!"

When the defense opened, Rice and the attorneys for the other defendants were able to get four counts of the indictment thrown out, and all charges against Silva were dismissed entirely. By the time both sides presented closing arguments on December 14, 1928, GG and his cohorts had reason to believe they might skate free. For good measure, Rice filed eight preposterous last-minute motions—to set aside the pending verdict, to arrest the forthcoming judgment, to nullify the entire trial based on obscure technicalities, and the like—but all were denied. Judge Knox sent the jury to deliberate at 6:48 P.M., instructing them that if they did not reach a verdict by 11:00 P.M., he would sequester them for the night.

The jurors filed back into Courtroom No. 2 precisely four hours and twelve minutes later.

The verdicts on Rice and Yorston were guilty on all seven counts. Weed was acquitted.

A week later, Judge Knox sentenced GG to four years in the Atlanta federal penitentiary and a $5,000 fine.

Creditors swarmed the court with petitions to seize whatever assets they could before Rice was sent to prison. Among the ignominies was a demand from a local furrier who wanted back the $14,737 Russian sable coat and mink-lined gloves George had ordered custom made so he would look confident and persuasive during the trial.

"Rice formerly was a spectacular figure in Wall Street" is how *The New York Times* began the story of his downfall. George would have bristled upon reading that America's paper of record was already relegating his notoriety to the past tense.

. . .

Right after Rice's conviction, antifraud organizations floated self-congratulatory press releases linking the outcome of the trial to a nationwide drop in stock swindling. But within a few months, the papers were reporting how copycat con artists were swarming to fill the void created by GG's absence. The general manager of the Better Business Bureau of New York City at first characterized George's conviction as "the outstanding incident in a series of successful battles with the battalions of fraud." Then he lamented that "the apparent sensational success of Rice has given rise to a horde of imitators."

The delineation between legitimate business and lawlessness was blurrier than ever in 1929. Abuse of the European-styled word "banc" was grifting's hot new trend as the public blindly bought into swindles that used terms like "bancshares" and "bancorporation." Following the late Rothstein's lead, crime bosses started to organize their regimes in a corporate hierarchy. When America's top racketeers powwowed at an Atlantic City summit, instead of squabbling over territory as they usually did, the vice lords agreed to abide by the Federal Reserve zone grid to determine boundaries between syndicates.

Prohibition had led to the romanticizing of criminals. Mobsters represented terror and bloodshed yet also independence and cunning. At the same time, America's lust for vicarious violence was dominating popular culture. On February 14, 1929, the gang leader Al Capone ordered henchmen to dress like cops and machine-gun a rival gang of whiskey runners on a Chicago street in broad daylight. Instead of calling for arrests and convictions, the press sensationalized the "Valentine's Day Massacre" to sell papers. When gory news wasn't enough, Americans flocked to movie theaters, where talking pictures like *The Racketeer* and *Alibi* glorified the gangland lifestyle, complete with screams and gunshots.

George was free pending the appeal of his conviction, but his finances remained a mystery. Rice still had rooms at the Hotel Chatham, but he rented two dingy offices, one in Jersey City and another on East Fourth Street in Manhattan, so he could clandestinely tout sham stocks in violation of his bail conditions. To pay $750,000 in legal bills, Rice apparently needed to scrape up cash from his scattering of faithful who still believed they were one savvy whisper away from striking it rich.

The hits kept coming: In March, Rice was indicted by a federal grand jury for not paying income tax on $1.8 million in illicit income in 1925, and the government was only just beginning to investigate what he might have failed to report in other years. A few weeks later, George lost his appeal for a new fraud trial. Rice did manage to score a minor victory when hauled before Judge Knox for continuing to operate as a stock promoter, though. Due to a stenographic oversight, GG knew there had been no official record of the judge's order to cease, so Knox couldn't revoke his bail.

GG knew his only hope of avoiding prison rested on obscure points of law, so he hired new attorneys to blitz the court with technical appeals. It would take three federal judges the better part of 1929 to sift through the catalog of trivialities Rice's defense team proposed as grounds for his conviction to be overturned.

While George's appeal dragged on, the stock market soared. Pricing benchmarks that had been standard for a century were obliterated, and nobody seemed to know what the new ones were. The myopic belief was that stocks would always roar back after brief downturns simply because, for the past decade, they always had

No one knew it at the time, but September 3, 1929, represented the absolute peak of the Roaring Twenties' financial and social orgy. The Dow closed at 381.17—a whopping 27 percent gain for the year and a stupendous fivefold increase since 1923. But the outrageous stock returns weren't even front-page news: That honor belonged to a group of uninhibited New Yorkers who had celebrated a long, hot Labor Day weekend completely in the buff at the nation's first organized nudist gathering in the Hudson Highlands.

A wave of September selling rocked the market, a precursor to the larger, looming typhoon. Commodity prices dipped sharply. Overextended banks began to slide off the grid. By early October, brokers were advising clients to pursue "ultra-conservative" strategies, and investment newsletters sounded alarms over "the great common-stock delusion." But not everybody was buying the gloom and doom: Charles E. Mitchell, the most dominant figure in American banking, not only guaranteed stocks were sound but cited a premature tightening of credit as the cause of all the volatility. "The public," he wisecracked, "is suffering from 'broker's loanitis.'"

Once the dizzying drop commenced, it did not take long for panic to accelerate.

On October 23, Wall Street was swamped with "a perfect Niagara of liquidation" that made all previous losses that year seem puny. Battered investors thought the market had finally hit bottom. But the next trading session would go down as one of the darkest days in U.S. history—Black Thursday.

On October 24, 1929, even brokers who had been bracing for a torrent of selling were astonished when tickers slipped behind free-falling prices soon after the opening bell rang. Forced selling—millions of shares automatically dumped on the market when debtors couldn't meet margin calls—triggered price breaks of horrific magnitude. Within one hour, the Dow had lost 11 percent of its value. With stocks sliding as much as five or ten points between transactions, the market was a blur of panic. An unfounded rumor that armed troops were being sent to seize control of Wall Street only contributed to the nationwide hysteria.

A new record for volume—12.8 million shares—kept tickers chattering four hours after the closing bell. President Hoover commandeered the radio airwaves to reassure a shaken America that "the fundamental business of the country . . . is on a sound and prosperous basis."

A mild stabilization occurred in Friday and Saturday trading. But when Monday dawned, the barrage of chaos began anew.

On October 28, the Dow plunged 13 percent, with the slaughter devastating previously unassailable stalwarts like U.S. Steel and General Electric. On October 29, New York phone lines went dead, and the volume of Western Union telegrams tripled under the burden of a further 12 percent decline. The next morning, the British dignitary Winston Churchill, visiting Manhattan on a speaking tour, was awakened by screams outside the Savoy-Plaza Hotel. "Under my very window a gentleman cast himself down fifteen storeys and was dashed to pieces, causing a wild commotion and the arrival of the fire brigade," he later wrote. It was hardly the only suicide attributed to the crash.

A collective $25 billion—$340 billion in today's dollars—had vanished in five days. Brokers couldn't even begin to calculate exact losses. Stock tickers got so far behind that traders gave up and allowed the machines to run out of tape. Floor men recording individual transactions on slips of paper were so overwhelmed they just stuffed the orders into trash cans.

While the nation reeled, November 4, 1929, was George's personal day of reckoning. Rice and Yorston stood before the U.S. Circuit Court of Appeals to learn how the three judges had ruled on their litany of technicalities.

"We have examined them all, but it would unduly lengthen this opinion to write as to all," read the judgment. "It is sufficient to say that we find no error in the many assigned. The convictions are affirmed."

After decades of keeping cool under pressure, GG blew his dignified con artist's composure and exploded in a spasmodic rage. He shouted curses at the judges and prosecuting attorneys. It required two burly deputies to wrestle the fifty-nine-year-old out of the courtroom.

George applied to the U.S. Supreme Court for a writ of certiorari—a last-gasp legal pleading used after all other appeals have been exhausted to determine whether a lower court was beyond the bounds of its authority. Rice knew that in criminal cases, writs of certiorari only got granted one time out of thousands. He decided his next-best option was to skip town.

There had been confusion over whether the application for the writ meant Rice would be granted a stay of his imprisonment. Initially, George was released from custody. But within forty-eight hours, the court decided it wanted him behind bars while the paperwork went through. When marshals went to apprehend Rice at the Hotel Chatham, the manager told them GG had not been seen for several days.

Newspaper headlines screamed, "Manhunt!" and the Feds were mortified that Rice had once again eluded them. An arrest warrant was issued, and it was rumored that George had fled to Washington to confer in secret with a former U.S. senator and a retired Supreme Court justice.

When that powwow failed to gain Rice his freedom, he stealthily returned to New York. Nearly two years after trying to unsuccessfully sneak out of his apartment past process servers, he now had to slip back in undetected. George made it past the marshals around midnight on November 9 and spent the next day barricaded inside his rooms telephoning contacts at various city newspapers to ridicule the federal officials who had branded him a fugitive. Rice insisted he had been in his hotel suite the entire time, a claim prosecutors called "absurd."

On November 11, Rice consented to being taken into custody from Hotel Chatham, where a reporter described him as "faultlessly attired and retaining a dignified bearing." At police headquarters, George was photographed and fingerprinted before being placed in a lineup. It was then common practice for detectives (wearing masks to conceal their own identities) to get up close and peer intently at departing criminals, committing their facial features to memory in case they ever needed to track them down again.

The police escorted George downtown to the Federal House of Detention. Two days later, he was shackled in a line with dope fiends, forgers, and other common criminals bound for the Atlanta federal penitentiary. After shuffling onto the train, Rice was separated and placed in the last, locked car in the custody of his own U.S. marshal. George began serving his prison sentence on November 13, 1929—the same day the Dow sank to its lowest level of the year, the very bottom of the crash.

Despite how docile and pensive Rice appeared, anyone who witnessed his outburst at the sentencing would have had a difficult time juxtaposing the solemn image of a fallen con man boarding his train to prison with the Jackal of Wall Street's enraged parting vow in the courtroom.

"I'll show all of you!" GG had roared in defiance, thrashing and flailing against the deputies. "I'll come back!"

[6]

VANISHING ACT

In the aftermath of the big bull market's stunning collapse, a dazed America had no way of recognizing the fiscal trauma as a tipping point into a long, lingering era of hardship. Incredulous speculators at first insisted stocks *had* to rebound, even though those optimists were too wiped out to buy back into the dream.

Instead of planning for an altered economic universe, leaders attempted to soothe the masses. The Department of Commerce downplayed the crash, insisting only 4 percent of the population would be affected. The Federal Reserve claimed the shock would "not prove disastrous to business and the prosperity of the country." Bankers postulated "the readjustment in stock prices will be helpful to the business situation." As America hovered on the brink of the Great Depression, President Hoover repeatedly reassured the nation in the closing weeks of 1929 that "within sixty days, conditions will return to normal."

For some, clinging to fanciful myths was better than facing grim reality. For others, discerning illusion from truth was the difficult part.

That's why when a *New York Times* reporter got an incredible tip on January 21, 1930, he didn't know what to think: George Graham Rice had been spotted taking afternoon tea at the Hotel Chatham.

It turned out the rumor was true. Federal inmate No. 33135-A was supposed to be locked up in Atlanta. But Judge Knox had granted Rice permission to prepare for his tax evasion trial. Because the financial records George claimed he needed to see were so voluminous, Knox had no choice but to let the prisoner come to New York to view them rather than ship a warehouse full of paperwork to the prison.

"There are between fifty and sixty tons of evidence and records that I must go through," Rice had argued. "Unless I can get it, I am hobbled, shackled, helpless and locked in a cell, robbed of the evidence I expect will clear me."

Rice won a transfer to a federal holding facility near Manhattan. The court order specifically stated he could examine records for two and a half hours each week in his attorney's office. But at some point, the marshal entrusted to escort him had been incentivized to loosen the leash, and GG began strolling about Manhattan as he liked. This resulted in a judicial scolding for the marshal and curtailed privileges for Rice once the scandal hit the papers.

George, double chinned and potbellied atop pipe-stem legs, didn't appear to be missing too many meals while on his free pass from prison. After being rebuked by Judge Knox, he joked with reporters that preparing for a tax trial in New York was better than what they had him doing in Atlanta—squinting to sew buttons in the penitentiary tailor shop. When the press asked about his alleged $15 million in hidden assets and the scores of creditors suing him for it, GG brushed aside the folly with a dismissive "Ghouls, ghouls—nothing but ghouls!"

Even Theramutis Ivey, George's teenage bride from 1895, had jumped on the lawsuit bandwagon. Described as "elderly, penniless and ill," Ivey was going after Rice for $800 in monthly alimony. She claimed that he had promised to pay her $10,000 in 1920 for agreeing not to contest the divorce he filed in Reno but that George never followed through with the money.

By the end of 1930, unemployment was estimated at six million. Starving Americans were eating cardboard. No one trusted banks.

Former Wall Street kingpins were reduced to selling apples on street corners outside the very exchange where they once traded millions. Shipwreck Kelly ascended a flagpole atop the Paramount Building to raise money for disabled veterans, but hardly anyone looked up. Discouraged, he climbed down when volunteers passing the hat beneath him in Times Square could only raise $13 in thirteen days.

At least Babe Ruth was still extraordinary. The larger-than-life slugger belted forty-nine homers in 1930, even though the Yankees didn't win the pennant. When asked about his exorbitant salary ($80,000) eclipsing the U.S. president's ($75,000), the Bambino shrugged and replied, "I had a better year than Hoover."

By 1931, even ardent teetotalers were beginning to question the ridiculous amount of money the government was spending to enforce Prohibition. Why not legalize liquor and tax it? But the war against booze marched on. The overcrowded federal penitentiary in Atlanta could no longer handle the glut of convicted bootleggers, so the government began to outsource prisoners. Word got around that by paying $1,000 bribes, inmates could arrange for transfers to low-security military bases.

That July, George and 250 well-connected felons served their sentences in the sun and salt air of Fort Wadsworth on Staten Island, where they lived in officers' quarters with little supervision. "Work is practically unknown," the incredulous *Boston Globe* reported. "At night the strains of dance music float over the water from Midland Beach Amusement Park to lull the prisoners to sleep." The exposé ended GG's vacation, and everyone got shipped back to Atlanta.

Rice returned to New York on September 2, 1931, for his income tax trial. An additional eight years of prison was at stake.

George would once again be acting as his own attorney. The judge had granted permission for him to prepare his defense under guard in the courthouse until he got locked up in the detention center at 8:00 each night. Katherine was permitted to act as his legal secretary. When a re-porter for the *New York World-Telegram* glimpsed the sixty-one-year-old con artist holding hands with his twenty-eight-year-old bride as they pored over documents in the gloaming of an empty courtroom, he was intrigued enough to ask for an interview.

"This is a love story," the piece began, "telling of a young woman's devotion to an old man whom the world has branded as one of the most sinister swindlers alive."

The reporter described the beautiful Katherine as shiningly loyal to a husband more than twice her age: "His skin has a prison pallor. His eyes, behind the thick-lensed spectacles, have lost some of their fire. His hands tremble as he runs through his papers."

But as Rice talked about his wife and the certainty of winning his freedom, he regained his animated spark:

No matter what others think of me, [Katherine] thinks I am good. When I was sent to Atlanta in November 1929, she could have deserted me. She moved to Atlanta to be near me. She lived in a room by herself for nineteen months, alone and helpless, just so she could visit me for thirty minutes every two weeks. . . .

In my time I've spent $4 million in attorneys. . . . I can't afford an attorney now. I have two young men helping me. I'll pay them someday. I had thirty-three attorneys in my last case. None of them is willing to help me now. . . .

Do you know what [this case] has cost me to date? Exactly $541. And I am making better progress than if I had a dozen lawyers. . . .

It's a holiday anyway. . . . I feel like a new man here. I can even object to things. . . . And I can look over and see my sweet wife.

When the trial opened in October 1931, the gleam of battle shone in GG's eyes from behind pince-nez glasses. Wearing a smart blue serge suit and gray silk tie, Rice put the prosecution on defense right away by demanding the return of all his seized ledgers and records. He filed motions for 125 witness subpoenas, with all expenses to be picked up by the government because he was broke. George, rumored to be hiding millions, even asked the court for a daily allowance for subway fare and a cup of coffee for Katherine.

Rice's repeated claims of poverty succeeded in rattling the federal prosecutor. Instead of trying to prove Rice had evaded taxes, he became bent on establishing how George had access to hundreds of thousands of dollars Katherine recently made in stock trades. Over nine days, the trial devolved into an argument over whether Rice was hiding money or not. "I have spent millions on lawyers and I lost," GG confided to the jury in his impassioned three-hour summation. "Now I fight alone, with my wife, and I am sure I will be acquitted."

The verdict was unanimous—not guilty.

George wept.

If the crying jag was an act, it was his most convincing courtroom performance ever.

Rice had sixteen months remaining on his fraud sentence after beating the tax rap. Half a year into the final leg of his prison stay, he got a new cell mate—Public Enemy No. 1.

On May 4, 1932, Al Capone began an eleven-year sentence at the Atlanta federal penitentiary. The Feds, unable to get anyone to testify against him for extortion and murder, had nailed Capone for tax evasion. In contrast to George's low-key trial, Al's had been a spectacle: His underlings handed out $1,000 bills to prospective jurors, and Capone hosted all-night parties for everyone connected with the case, including famous actors who showed up in the gallery to study him for the inevitable movie about his life. When Capone arrived in Atlanta, he took over the prison by buying off the warden and tipping guards like bellhops.

Al had his "suite" redecorated with plush carpeting, furniture, fresh linens, and a radio. It was rumored he even had luxuries like a telephone and silk underwear. Seeking highbrow companionship (or perhaps, like Rothstein, a mentor), Capone asked Rice to move in with him.

George was old enough to be Al's father but must have viewed Capone's invitation as the proverbial offer he couldn't refuse. The two shared a loathing of government and a zeal for gambling but were complete opposites in manners and style. Capone, thirty-three, was grossly overweight, ravaged by syphilis, and suffering from cocaine withdrawal. He had a piggish, scarred face and a sallow complexion and sweated profusely while constantly picking at his facial lesions. But Al treated you right if he liked you, and right away he got George reassigned from sewing in the tailor shop to running the prison library. The ruthless brute and the gentleman grifter ended up spending many congenial evenings together, kibitzing about Wall Street or quietly reading Capone's private set of *Encyclopaedia Britannica*.

Rice would recall his cell mate as a "fine fellow" after the Feds eradicated Capone's influence by transferring him to Alcatraz. "I'd take Al's word quicker than anybody on the stock exchange," George quipped. Rice particularly admired Capone's ambition to get out of whiskey running and monopolize the dairy industry: Milk was legal, every mother in America fed it to her kids, and the potential for marking up the price was obscenely—if not criminally—high. "Honest to God," Capone would carp, "we've been in the wrong racket all along."

George completed his sentence and was released on March 17, 1933. The first thing he and Katherine did was take a drive along the seacoast. George probably noticed right away that skirt lengths had plummeted in line with stock prices.

Some criminals have difficulty adjusting to life after prison, overwhelmed by the sudden freedom. Rice faced a substantially different challenge: getting by with so few suckers left to swindle in the dearth of the Great Depression.

America's speculative landscape had been razed, but GG couldn't resist the dark, lucrative world of confidence hustling; it was all he knew. Piecing together the remnants of his sucker list, he handpicked two hundred names to breezily inquire if old friends were "meeting the challenges of the New Deal."

Four years after the crash of 1929, America was still sifting the economic wreckage. Politicians convened endless federal hearings, largely for the purpose of hanging blame on scapegoats. One senator likened the drawn-out proceedings to a circus. The mockery bottomed out when the tycoon J. P. Morgan Jr. was on the stand and had an actual circus dwarf plopped in his lap by a Ringling Brothers publicist. Photographs of the startled billionaire with the grinning, pint-sized performer atop his knee circulated around the world. The juxtaposition of farce and austerity became emblematic of the nation after its fall.

On May 27, 1933, President Franklin Delano Roosevelt signed the Truth in Securities Act into law. In crafting the first national set of blue-sky statutes, members of Congress had cited Rice's misdeeds as a catalyst for consumer protection.

George found it preposterous that trading stocks based on confidential information was now considered fraud. He was trying to break back into securities promotion, but his name and reputation were now liabilities. To land with a "live" company whose stock might benefit from his manipulation, Rice had to call in a favor whose seeds he had sown decades ago.

In 1906, GG had invited Kermit Roosevelt, the son of the then president, Teddy, to the Gans-Nelson fight for a weekend of debauchery. Twenty-seven years later, Kermit was a depressed alcoholic who also happened to be the confidant cousin of the newly elected commander in chief. Perhaps acting on a tip from FDR that Prohibition would soon be repealed, Kermit got himself appointed to the board of Atlas Tack, a Boston company that manufactured small metal products, and secured contracts to provide 4.5 million bottle caps to meet the anticipated demand of breweries. On the strength of this news, George talked Kermit into hiring him to spike the Atlas stock price, which had started 1933 trading at $1.50.

Fueled by Rice's puffery and well-planted newsletter tips, Atlas Tack rocketed to $34.

Two weeks after Prohibition ended on December 5, 1933, insiders took gigantic profits, and the stock collapsed to $10.

George likely made a heap of money but was apparently so concerned about being caught that he paid a visit to the New York attorney general, just to preemptively deny any involvement with the wild price fluctuations.

In January 1934, GG launched a new financial paper called *Rice's Financial Watch-Tower*. Its intent, he claimed, was to attack Wall Street cronyism without boosting any of his own stocks. To create the illusion that he was objective, George dangled a $5,000 reward to anyone who could prove he had ownership in any securities the publication touted. "This is going to be absolutely clean," he vowed. "No advertising. No promotions. Sound financial advice and relentless support of the president."

Rice had taken a pauper's oath upon leaving prison, but he and Katherine welcomed press guests into their sixteen-room Manhattan apartment for the *Watch-Tower*'s launch party. In high spirits, GG boasted how he wrote the entire sheet himself, dictating columns every fifteen minutes to a stenographer, taking breaks only to sip coffee and light another stogie.

One of the journalists in attendance was an up-and-coming reporter for the *New York World-Telegram*. A. J. Liebling would blossom into one of the twentieth century's most gifted essayists, and the concept of a hustler in decline captivated him. Decades later, after everybody had forgotten about Rice, Liebling would continue to reference him, long after he first profiled George in a January 26, 1934, column:

> *Rising from his chair, the hawk-nosed Mr. Rice swayed above white spats, as contagiously optimistic as the days when he ran Maxim & Gay's horse race tipping service. . . .*

"I am sixty-four years old now," said Mr. Rice, who has alter-nated fortunes and jail terms for forty years, "and I felt for the six remaining years of the span allotted to me by the Lord I could not be happy without an outlet for my warm thoughts. . . . So if I get a few thousand subscribers I can earn a living. It's all I want. . . ."

Full-jowled, roseate and plump, his fine white hair and a pair of rimless spectacles [made] him appear almost respectable. . . . Here Mr. Rice flashed his most phosphorescent smile. . . .

"I have no vices. I am devoted to my wife. I used to like a glass of champagne, but (he placed a hand on the region of heartburn) my doctor forbids it. My only indulgence is an occasional cigar. . . ."

"Isn't it a wonderful story? Me, after all I've been through, com-ing back as the only honest financial writer in town."

From 1935 on out, it was hit and run for Rice. Mostly run.

In September 1935, George accepted, then quickly sold, twenty-eight hundred shares of International Silver & Gold Corporation as compensation for authoring a series of fawning pieces about the stock.

In January 1936, Rice bought twelve thousand shares of Texas Oil & Land Company at an under-market price. He boosted the stock relentlessly in the *Watch-Tower,* then made a killing by dumping it at substantial profit.

In the spring of 1936, George executed a series of below-market buys of Sonotone Corporation before cashing out a whopping sixty thousand shares—a classic Ricecakes "pump and dump."

Just as GG had told countless co-conspirators in four decades of stock swindling, if you're stealing suckers blind, you'd better expect to take heat.

Rice's federal probation officer had only been requiring him to check in on an every-now-and-then basis. But by the fall of 1936, George's stock manipulating was getting so blatant that the chief probation officer of the Southern District of New York ordered him in to explain suspicious transactions that securities regulators had been tracking.

Rice ignored the summons and failed to appear.

On November 17, 1936, George's probation was revoked and a federal judge issued a warrant for his arrest. "Bad Boy Rice at It Again— Vanishes as Prison Yawns," blared the headline in the New York *Evening Post*.

Rice was now facing five years behind bars just for violating probation. If caught, he knew he would also be tried for his market-rigging misdeeds. At sixty-six, George would die in prison if convicted. He and Katherine bolted into hiding—this time, the Feds feared, for good.

The elusive Rice did not resurface in the news until *The Sun* reported on April 19, 1937, that the Feds had suddenly become "intensely interested, and there is a real hunt on." Some of George's old-time dynamiters had been active, and there was a rumor linking him anew to his accomplice turned enemy William Jarvis in Boston, who was mired in his own legal woes for violating the Truth in Securities Act. *The Sun* likened Rice to the Old Faithful geyser, noting he was "overdue" for an eruption.

The chase went quiet until December 17, 1938, when the price of Atlas Tack fell precipitously, just as it had in 1933. Word on the Street was that insiders had pulled off a seven-figure coup by unloading massive amounts of manipulated shares.

Within forty eight hours, securities authorities seized phone records that traced a barrage of dynamiters' calls to 126 Newbury Street in Boston. The office at that address was leased to an attorney who had recently defended Jarvis, but Jarvis was now in prison. When investigators tried to pin down the whereabouts of Atlas's director, Roosevelt, they learned Kermit had the alibi of being hospitalized during the time his firm's shares went into free fall. He claimed to know nothing about the suspicious price plunge.

By connecting the expert dynamiting to the most common denominator in Jarvis's and Roosevelt's criminal histories, law enforcement officials had a pretty clear idea of whose name should appear on the search and arrest warrants.

"Faint footsteps of George Graham Rice, the biggest and baddest Wolf of Wall Street, were being tracked yesterday by investigators on the trail of 'stocketeers' who last Friday took more than $1 million from sucker traders," the New York *Daily News* reported. "State Securities Bureau sleuths picked up Rice's obscured scent, they thought, in Boston."

On December 20, 1938, almost ten years to the day George was sentenced to federal prison, authorities stormed into the rogue brokerage on Newbury Street to take the sixty-eight-year-old Rice by force.

If the agents pounded on the door before kicking it in, the echo in the office should have been the dead giveaway that they were too late.

The stock ticker lines had been cut, the phones had been ripped out and removed, and there wasn't a shred of useful paperwork left in the drafty, abandoned office. The only evidence was that of a sudden, disorderly departure.

If the investigators had discerning noses, they might have detected the faint, lingering aroma of fine cigar smoke—the kind from luxuriously fragrant perfectos that a man of confidence might enjoy as he placed bets with a leveraged edge and raked in his winnings with a defiant smirk.

EPILOGUE

When the bedridden, seventy-three-year-old Jacob Simon Herzig died in obscurity in a modest Upper West Side apartment at 3:40 A.M. on October 24, 1943, not a single newspaper ran his obituary.

Not that anyone would have recognized him by that name. It had been fifteen years since the Jackal of Wall Street was front-page news. Even though he swindled an estimated $500 million over five decades ($6 billion in today's dollars), the alias "George Graham Rice" barely registered with anyone under age forty at the time of his death.

"How different the death of the swindler!" Captain Barabbas Whitefeather wrote in his 1839 *Hand-Book of Swindling*. "He makes no irreparable gap in society—not he! He agonizes neither man nor woman nor child; not a tear is dropped at his grave—not a sigh rises at the earth rattling upon his coffin. Must not a conviction of this be the sweetest consolation to the dying swindler? Think of his end and . . ."

Whitefeather never finished that sentence. He was a confidence hustler writing about the death of confidence hustlers, and he died before he could complete the manuscript.

Given his flair for showmanship and an egotistical craving for the spotlight, it's amazing how successfully GG managed to stay hidden in the final five years of his life.

Rice's 1938 near miss with authorities in Boston was the last legitimate lead the Feds had as to his whereabouts. After an initial frenzy to act on his arrest warrant, the intensity of the chase petered out. The pursuit of a septuagenarian probation violator was apparently not a high priority as America became embroiled in fighting a second world war.

Where did George and Katherine live? How much cash did they stash before they went underground? Did the con artist extraordinaire retreat to some far-flung outpost, or was Rice brazenly hiding in plain sight?

Eight decades after his disappearance, answers to such questions are hard to come by. As GG would have put it, "The public demands to be mystified."

The death certificate for Jacob Simon Herzig yields only a few hazy clues: He died from unspecified natural causes in the presence of Katherine. The physician who documented his death had been caring for him since November 1942, and he wrote that he last saw Jacob alive at 10:00 P.M. the previous evening. The couple had been living at 10 West Eighty-Fourth Street for sixteen months, or at least that's what Katherine told the doctor. She wasn't quite sure of her husband's exact date of birth, so the certificate was off by one year. As far as the doctor knew, the deceased's occupation was "writer."

Jacob lived out his final months in a narrow four-story brownstone cut up into ten apartments with a handful of smaller rooms for lodgers. The 1940 census gives an idea of the types of people who lived in the building: A physician and an architect occupied two of the units, but otherwise the residents were working-class housekeepers and waitstaff and blue-collar tradesmen. It's a given that Herzig would have lied to census takers if he was there at the time of the enumeration, but even if we account for aliases, there was no pairing of an older man with a much younger wife at that address in 1940. So perhaps the couple first lived in more upscale dwellings and only later ended up at 10 West Eighty-Fourth as their funds ran low.

Jacob was interred in the Herzig family mausoleum at Linden Hill Jewish Cemetery in Ridgewood, New York. He either had gotten back into his family's good graces or outlived the relatives who had disowned him. Fronted by polished marble pillars and the green patina of an ornate copper *H,* the chamber occupies a prominent spot near the cemetery entrance, on a rise with a view of the Manhattan skyline, not far from the tomb that houses the founder of the Bloomingdale's department store. Through glass clouded by time, it is possible to make out Jacob's name on one of the markers. An empty crypt is at his side, never to be occupied.

Herzig/Rice left no will, according to Surrogate's Court of New York County. Jacob/George was never one for disclosing his assets, and he would not have wanted to create a paper trail. If there was any money left, Katherine almost certainly ended up with it—by either George's specific instruction, a sense of self-entitlement, or the fact that there was no one else to take it.

The few known descriptions of Katherine attest to her radiant loyalty. But considering the company George kept, it is not difficult to imagine she too might have had darker, hidden motives. Katherine could very well have been conning her sugar-daddy husband, or at least tolerating him until payoff arrived in the form of George's last breath. Maybe Katherine walked away filthy rich to start a new life at age forty. Maybe she held on too long and got nothing except a life on the run while having to play nursemaid to a dying liar.

Katherine's demise is even more difficult to trace than George's. Once she became a widow (assuming they were even legally married in the first place), Katherine could have changed her name, remarried, or moved far away—maybe even all three. A search of ancestry records requires guessing at her birth year and the mixing and matching of all known variations of her names (Katherine, Catherine, and Kathryn paired with Herzig and Rice). The result is a maze of dead ends that yields no cogent explanation of where she ended up.

The 1936 arrest warrant for Rice is now in the possession of the

National Archives. Its front cover is stamped with an April 13, 1944, authorization to vacate the probation violation, thereby voiding the warrant. This indicates the Feds didn't find out about George's death until nearly six months after it occurred.

The "golden age" of grifting ended up dovetailing seamlessly with Rice's life span. Although the core concepts of swindles from that era are destined to live in perpetuity, the social opportunities to pull them off were changing by the 1940s. Americans started traveling more by automobile, which meant the days of chatting up marks in Pullman cars were long gone. Information had sped up (radios were superfluous, and soon everyone would own a television), so if someone like the King of the Fakirs tried to travel the countryside trotting out the same swindles in each burg, the villagers would be armed with advance warning of his scams—and possibly shotguns.

"Relatively few confidence men end their lives as wealthy men," David Maurer wrote in *The Big Con* in 1940. Maurer once asked an old-time grifter what becomes of con men in their autumn years.

"They just dry up and blow away" was the laconic answer.

As he wound down his life in hiding and quite likely broke, GG couldn't resist planting one final clue that he was lurking far beneath the radar, still taking the pulse of the mining-stock marketplace—and very much self-aware of his legacy.

The March 1939 edition of *Mining and Metallurgy* floated a breezy query along the lines of "Whatever happened to George Graham Rice?" while wisecracking about his anything-goes high jinks during the Wild West mining boom of the early twentieth century.

The publication had not really expected an answer. But six months later, *Mining and Metallurgy* received a lone response from a loyal reader.

The sincere, almost-believable tone makes the correspondence seem plausible. But when you read it as a sly attempt at geographic misdirection—and consider that the writer's alias does not match any real name listed in city directories at that time—there is no doubt who penned the upbeat reply the magazine was suckered into printing: "It was not long before we had a note from a Milwaukee reader, J. V. Stayoke, saying that George is now the owner of one of the finest cabarets in Milwaukee, working hard and happy as a lark."

NOTES AND SOURCES

This book began in 2011, when I was researching modern-day con artistry for a freelance assignment and got sidetracked by an archived *Time* magazine clipping from 1934. The article profiled a past-his-prime grifter named George Graham Rice, portraying him as America's most nefarious swindler. Despite my fascination with the shadow world of confidence hustling, I had never heard of him. A quick skim of the Internet revealed that in the twenty-first century, hardly anyone else had either.

It gnawed at me: If Rice was once considered such an iconic figure, why had his legacy all but evaporated? Over the next four years, I aimed to find out. The deeper I dug, the more compelling GG's tale became.

Between 1900 and 1930, Rice's exploits were front-page news nationwide. But by the Great Depression, America's sumptuous pool of suckers had dried up, and muckraking newspapermen were writing about a fresh crop of villains.

Part of Rice's allure today can be attributed to our fascination with criminals from earlier eras. In the early twentieth century, con artists were widely reviled as ruthless predators. Back then, being a "hustler" didn't at all conjure up the sort of dashing "sharpie in a fedora" imagery the way we might envision a 1920s con man now. The haze of nostalgia and the passage of time have lent an aura of mystery to the dark art of confidence hustling. My goal with this book is to bring a vivid slice of it back to life.

My initial interest in con artistry was sparked in 2007 when I stumbled upon a copy of David Maurer's *The Big Con: The Story of the Confidence Man and the Confidence Game* in a secondhand bookstore in Vermont. Maurer's 1940 tome is the be-all and end-all book about the history and inner workings of confidence swindling. Without *The Big Con,* I would not have had a keen interest in the lore of grifting, and I relied heavily on Maurer's psychological profiling of con artists when trying to interpret the behavior of Rice and other swindlers of his era.

The original *My Adventures with Your Money*—Rice's 1913 autobiography—was my primary source for George's formative years as a hustler. A century after its publication, I would like to think that Rice would be amused (or at least appreciate from a grifter's point of view) that St. Martin's Press and I have chosen to "liberate" his original title for a retelling of his life's events.

GG probably would not, however, have approved of my attempts to verify and correct his numerous exaggerations, half-truths, and outright lies. Although Rice's memoir was imperative to helping me reconstruct his life between 1901 and 1911, many of the tales he tells must be read as egotistic, one-sided accounts penned by a master of persuasion. I have attempted to balance his side of the story with objective news accounts from that era whenever possible.

Dan Plazak's *A Hole in the Ground with a Liar at the Top: Fraud and Deceit in the Golden Age of American Mining* (2006) was the only book I came across that attempts a complete time line of Rice's life. Plazak's version was helpful to me not only for filling in chronological gaps but for illustrating how our styles varied with regard to emphasizing certain aspects of Rice's overall arc.

To get an "immediate aftermath" feel for what it was like to live through America's rollercoaster Roaring Twenties run-up and subsequent stock market crash, I relied on three books that were published shortly after those events: Frederick Lewis Allen's *Only Yesterday: An Informal History of the 1920's* (1931), Watson Washburn and Edmund S. De Long's *High and Low Financiers: Some Notorious Swindlers and Their Abuses of Our Modern Stock Selling System* (1932), and Proctor W. Hansl's *Years of Plunder: A Financial Chronicle of Our Times* (1935). All three are liberally cited in the notes below.

Clips from the New York News Media Morgues, courtesy of the Briscoe Center for American History, University of Texas at Austin, were a valuable source of information. Any undated or unsourced clips that I note came from this collection.

All dialogue, thoughts, and ideas that appear between quotation marks in this book are sourced below.

1. Confidence Man

2 "Buy me a drink": George Graham Rice, *My Adventures with Your Money* (Boston: Gorham Press, 1913), 11–18.

5 Maxim & Gay: Ibid., 11–45; A. J. Liebling, *The Honest Rainmaker: The Life and Times of Colonel John R. Stingo* (Garden City, N.Y.: Doubleday, 1953; repr., San Francisco: North Point Press, 1989), 95–108. Rice and Stingo essentially tell the same racetrack stories, but both play fast and loose with regard to the accuracy of horse names and race dates. Within this book, horse race results are only cited specifically when those details could be corroborated by official *Daily Racing Form* statistics archived by Keeneland Library, Lexington, Kentucky. In the Silver Coin and Annie Lauretta races, for example, Rice and Stingo both recall the principal horses correctly, but the correct names of other horses in these races that I have inserted come from *Racing Form* archives.

6 "It looked puny": Rice, *My Adventures,* 14.

7 "Finally, the money came": Ibid., 17.

9   Jacob Simon Herzig was born: There is conflicting documentation about Jacob Simon Her-
    zig's birth date, but June 18, 1870, appears correct. Herzig's death certificate lists his date
    of birth as June 18, 1871. But that date is superseded by his inclusion as an infant member
    of the Herzig household in the 1870 census and is backed up by various penal documents
    that list an age (but not a specific birth date) for Herzig/Rice.

9   King of the Fakirs: J. B. Costello, ed., *Swindling Exposed: From the Diary of William B.
    Moreau, King of Fakirs; Methods of the Crooks Explained; History of the Worst Gang That
    Ever Infested This Country; Names, Locations, and Incidents; A Volume of Intense Interest;
    Truth Stranger Than Fiction* (Syracuse, N.Y.: J. B. Costello, 1907), 138–41.

12 When the Austrian immigrants: 1870 census, 6th District, 14th Ward, New York, N.Y., 28;
    1880 census, Supervisor's District 1, Enumeration District 539, New York, N.Y., 2; Watson
    Washburn and Edmund S. De Long, *High and Low Financiers: Some Notorious Swindlers
    and Their Abuses of Our Modern Stock Selling System* (Indianapolis: Bobbs-Merrill, 1932),
    16–18; Louis Guenther, "Pirates of Promotion," *World's Work*, Oct. 1918, 584–91, and Nov.
    1918, 29–33; Albert Lord Belden, *The Fur Trade of America and Some of the Men Who Made
    and Maintain It* (New York: Peltries, 1917), 224–26; "George B. Herzig Enters New Field,"
    American Furrier, Oct. 1922, 39; "Charles S. Herzig, Mining Expert, Dies," *New York Times*,
    Nov. 19, 1926.

15 "If the public thought": Rice, *My Adventures*, 26.

15 By 1889, Jacob had begun: Inmate records and biographical registers from Elmira Refor-
    matory (ser. B0141, no. 4018) and Sing Sing Prison (ser. B0143, box 11, vol. 29, 499), both
    courtesy New York State Archives. These documents also provide specific dates for Her-
    zig's jail admissions and release dates from 1890 through 1900.

16 The "Elmira system": "Elmira, Nation's First Reformatory," accessed June 7, 2013, www
    .correctionhistory.org/html/chronicl/docs2day/elmira.html; Cyndi Banks, *Punishment in
    America: A Reference Handbook* (Santa Barbara, Calif.: ABC-CLIO, 2005), 225.

16 "Escapes, violence, gangs": Marilyn D. McShane and Frank P. Williams, eds., *Encyclope-
    dia of American Prisons* (London: Taylor & Francis, 1996), 627–29.

17 "They come to me at interview": Alexander Pisciotta, *Benevolent Repression: Social Con-
    trol and the American Reformatory-Prison Movement* (New York: New York University
    Press, 2012), 55.

18 "coney catching": "London and the Development of Popular Literature: Robert Greene's
    Social Pamphlets," accessed June 11, 2013, bartleby.com/214/1604.html.

18 "To make one's way": Edward J. Balleisen, "Private Cops on the Fraud Beat: The Limits of
    American Business Self-Regulation, 1895–1932," *Business History Review* (Spring 2009): 114.

18 "Knight of Every Order": *The Hand-Book of Swindling by the Late Captain Barabbas White-
    feather*, ed. John Jackdaw (London: Chapman and Hall, 1839).

18 "For the last few months": "Arrest of the Confidence Man," *New York Herald*, July 8, 1849.

19 "A crow thieves": Edgar Allan Poe, "Diddling," in *The Works of the Late Edgar Allan Poe*
    (New York: Redfield, 1856), 257.

19 By the time Herman Melville: Herman Melville, *The Confidence-Man: His Masquerade*
    (New York: Dix, Edwards, 1857).

19 "gold brick swindle": "The Gold Brick Swindle," *New York Times*, May 4, 1881.

19 "green goods game": "The Sawdust Swindle," *New York Times,* Jan. 22, 1873.

20 "whose cupidity overcomes": Allan Pinkerton, *Thirty Years a Detective: A Thorough and Comprehensive Exposé of All Grades and Classes* (New York: G. W. Dillingham, 1900), 70.

20 An 1860 survey: Karen Halttunen, *Confidence Men and Painted Women: A Study of Middle-Class Culture in America, 1830–1870* (New Haven, Conn.: Yale University Press, 1982), 7.

20 "There's a sucker born every minute": Bill Ryan, "Sorting Myth from Reality: Was Barnum Wronged?," *New York Times,* Jan. 9, 1994.

21 "Why, it would just make you giddy": Costello, *Swindling Exposed,* 146.

21 By 1880, popular publications were jammed: Ibid., 145–46.

21 "What they were Heaven only knows": Ibid., 146.

22 "The kindergarten of the forger": Ibid., 220.

23 "The methods by which I collected": David W. Maurer, *The Big Con: The Story of the Confidence Man and the Confidence Game* (Indianapolis: Bobbs-Merrill, 1940; repr., New York: Anchor Books, 1999), xvii.

24 "The impetus": Ibid.

24 True confidence swindlers: Ibid., 1–4.

25 "Confidence games are cyclic phenomena": Ibid., 313.

26 "Confidence men trade upon certain weaknesses": Ibid., 314.

26 Just before his Elmira stint was up: "Married Another on Train," *Meriden (Conn.) Journal,* Nov. 5, 1910; Guenther, "Pirates of Promotion," Oct. 1918, 585.

28 Superintendent Brockway, it seems: It's an educated guess that Rice's skull injury was the result of a blow by Brockway. Writing in his autobiography about events in 1907, Rice mentions a "cyst, of fifteen years' growth," that originated during his stay at Elmira (*My Adventures,* 170). His comrade Colonel Stingo also noted in *Honest Rainmaker* an "extraordinary bump, or protuberance, on the pointed end of his cranium."

29 Within weeks, every sizable newspaper in New York: "More About Brockway's Paddle," *New York Times,* Nov. 12, 1893; "Elmira's Modern Inferno; Tales of Shocking Brutality at the Reformatory," *New York Times,* Nov. 18, 1893; "Annual Report of the State Reformatory at Elmira," in *Documents of the Senate of the State of New York,* vol. 4 (New York State Legislature, 1895); "Elmira Reformatory Investigation," *Cyclopedic Review of Current History* 4 (1895): 613.

29 "unlawful, unjust, cruel": Michael Newton, *Prison and the Penal System* (New York: Chelsea House, 2010), 28–29.

30 Sixteen months: "Herzig His Own Lawyer," *New York World,* Nov. 10, 1894.

31 "The young rascal": "A Young Adept in Forgery," *Philadelphia Record,* Nov. 11, 1894.

31 "He was no sooner released": "Arrested for Many Forgeries," *New York Times,* Nov. 11, 1894.

32 Erected in the style: "The Lost 1838 Egyptian Revival 'The Tombs,'" accessed June 8, 2013, www.daytoninmanhattan.blogspot.com/2011/07/lost-1838-egyptian-revival-tombs.html.

32 "Such treatment of dogs": *Annual Report of the Prison Association of New York for the Year 1895* (New York: Prison Association of New York, 1896), 78–79.

32 "strange young woman": "Herzig, the Alleged Forger, in Court," *New-York Tribune,* March 8, 1895.

32 "I know that I am under indictment": "Herzig, the Alleged Forger, a Poor Witness," *New-York Tribune,* March 10, 1895.

33 "An educated criminal": "Herzig Sentenced for Forgery," *New York Times,* April 20, 1895.

33 Sing Sing prisoners: Timothy J. Gilfoyle, *A Pickpocket's Tale: The Underworld of Nineteenth-Century New York* (New York: W. W. Norton, 2011), 44–58.

34 "represented all that was vile": Frederick Howard Wines, *Punishment and Reformation: A Study of the Penitentiary System,* ed. Winthrop David Lane (New York: Crowell, 1919), 394.

35 The grim procession to the train station: [Prisoner] Number 1500, *Life in Sing Sing* (Indianapolis: Bobbs-Merrill, 1904), 1–12.

37 "When the train arrived at Yonkers": "Married to Convict Herzig," *New York World,* April 20, 1895.

38 "Hypnotism is said": "Miss Ivey Thinks She Was Svengallied into Marrying a Convict," *Norfolk Virginian,* May 1, 1895.

39 Choosing words that stung: "Rice, in Prison, Sued for a Separation," *New York Times,* Feb. 16, 1930.

39 Learning he had been tricked: "Mabel Gilmore Awarded Alimony," *Morning Telegraph,* Feb. 8, 1902.

39 Auburn Prison: "Served Time Here; Rice as Herzig Was First Editor of Star of Hope," *Auburn (N.Y.) Democrat Argus,* Oct. 4, 1910.

41 "Miss Frances Drake": "The Theatre," *Rochester (N.Y.) Democrat and Chronicle,* Dec. 24, 1894.

42 "I burst into tears": "How Mrs. Rice Learned Husband Was Ex-convict," *New York World,* Oct. 10, 1910.

43 A devastating tidal wave: Liebling, *Honest Rainmaker,* 98.

43 Capsized ships: Nathan C. Green, ed., *Story of the 1900 Galveston Hurricane* (1900; Gretna, La.: Pelican, 2000), 254–56.

44 "My offense": "Half Has Not Been Told About Galveston," *Kentucky New Era,* Sept. 27, 1900.

45 accepted a $5,000 offer: Liebling, *Honest Rainmaker,* 98.

45 "When my pass was taken": "Half Has Not Been Told About Galveston."

45 "It was a 'beat'": Rice, *My Adventures,* 11.

45 With part of his $5,000 windfall: Liebling, *Honest Rainmaker,* 99.

46 He got the hotel beat writer: "Prominent Arrivals at the Hotels," *New-York Tribune,* Nov. 5, 1900.

46 "loafing": Rice, *My Adventures,* 11.

46 After making a big splash: Ibid., 11–45; Liebling, *Honest Rainmaker,* 95–108, 117.

46 "provoked some sensation": Liebling, *Honest Rainmaker,* 102.

47 "handy with a needle": Ibid., 102

49 "We used in our big display advertising": Rice, *My Adventures,* 20.

50 "Got to hand it to you": Ibid., 25.

51 "A GIGANTIC HOG-KILLING": Ibid., 27–29.

52 "The whole enterprise": Ibid., 37.

53 "It was taking candy": Ibid., 36.

53 "Recklessly and improvidently": Ibid.

54 "The spectacle": "May J., at 100 to 1, First," *New York Times*, Oct. 31, 1902.

54 "The office was thronged": Rice, *My Adventures*, 30.

55 "I could not tolerate": Ibid., 31.

55 "He became crazed": Liebling, *Honest Rainmaker*, 104.

56 "Wait a minute": Rice, *My Adventures*, 37–38.

57 Belmont laced into Rice: Ibid., 42–43.

58 "The gain we will reap": Ibid., 41.

58 "Maxim & Gay Co.": *Daily Racing Form*, July 23, 1902.

58 "SPECIAL NOTICE": *Wichita Daily Eagle*, March 1, 1903.

59 "a dangerous practice": Liebling, *Honest Rainmaker*, 104.

59 "My exchequer was low": Rice, *My Adventures*, 43.

59 After the *Daily America* lost: "Amelia Bingham Sues an Editor," *New York World*, April 15, 1903; "Amelia Bingham Accepts Apology," unsourced news clip, May 2, 1903; "Daily America's Suit; Dissolution of the Publishing Company Wanted by the Directors," *New York Times*, April 23, 1903.

60 "I did not hear from Mr. Whitney": Rice, *My Adventures*, 44.

60 "The schemes are always fraudulent": "War on Tipsters Wages Fiercely," *Washington Times*, March 13, 1904.

60 In June, District Attorney Jerome: "Arrest Maxim & Gay Man," *New York Sun*, June 12, 1903; "Graham Rice Arrested," *New York Times*, June 12, 1903; "Fraud Order Against Maxim & Gay Company," *St. Louis Republic*, Dec. 18, 1903; "Maxim & Gay Company Under the Official Ban," *San Francisco Call*, Dec. 18, 1903.

61 "Having lost the *Daily America*": Rice, *My Adventures*, 44–45.

2. Gold Without Digging for It

63 George would have been well acquainted: Maurer, *Big Con*, 109–10.

64 "Broadly speaking": Proctor W. Hansl, *Years of Plunder: A Financial Chronicle of Our Times* (New York: Smith and Haas, 1935), 28–29.

65 Everyday swindling was so topical: "Get Rich Quick Promoters," *Wichita Daily Eagle*, Feb. 4, 1905; "To Swindle Mrs. Roosevelt," *Philadelphia Record*, July 27, 1904; "Cassie Chadwick, 1904," accessed Jan. 2, 2014, museumofhoaxes.com/hoax/archive/permalink/cassie_chadwick; "The Unrivaled Efforts of the St. Louis Detective Department Have Made the World's-Fair City Anything but a 'Mecca for Crooks,'" *St. Louis Republic*, Oct. 30, 1904; *Judicial and Statutory Definitions of Words and Phrases* (St. Paul: West, 1904), 2:1421.

65 References to swindling abounded: *New-York Tribune*, Dec. 11, 1904.

66 "Your honor": *Salt Lake City Broad Ax*, July 23, 1904.

67 "I had never visited": Rice, *My Adventures*, 46–48.

67 William J. Arkell: Pierre Berton, *The Klondike Fever: The Life and Death of the Last Great Gold Rush* (New York: Basic Books, 2003), 115; "W. J. Arkell in Straits," *New York Times*, April 8, 1906.

71 "After breakfast, which consisted": Rice, *My Adventures*, 48–50.

71 Tonopah was decidedly a sellers' market: Robert D. McCracken, *Tonopah: The Greatest, the Richest, and the Best Mining Camp in the World* (Tonopah, Nev.: Nye County Press, 1990), 26–50; Russell R. Elliott, *Nevada's Twentieth-Century Mining Boom: Tonopah, Goldfield, Ely* (Reno: University of Nevada Press, 1966), 3–77.

74 This was why Macdonald: Rice, *My Adventures,* 50–51.

75 "Tradition said that men": Ibid., 54.

76 Even so, its evolution: Elliott, *Nevada's Twentieth-Century Mining Boom,* 3–80; Frederick Leslie Ransome and George H. Garrey, *The Geology and Ore Deposits of Goldfield, Nevada* (Washington, D.C.: Government Printing Office, 1909), 14–20; Dan Plazak, *A Hole in the Ground with a Liar at the Top: Fraud and Deceit in the Golden Age of American Mining* (Salt Lake City: University of Utah Press, 2006), 255–58.

76 "thereby eliminating the delay": Rice, *My Adventures,* 52–53.

77 When George ran out of cigars: Ibid., 53–63.

78 "He wanted technical mining stuff": Ibid., 53.

78 "Honest Tom": Helen S. Carlson, *Nevada Place Names: A Geographical Dictionary* (Reno: University of Nevada Press, 1974), 144.

78 "I wrote what I considered": Rice, *My Adventures,* 53.

79 "There was an indefinable something": Ibid., 52–53.

79 "Why, you ought to be spending": Ibid., 55.

79 "The most remarkable feature": Ibid., 56.

80 "Within two months": Ibid., 55.

80 "Here fully seventy-five percent": Ibid., 61.

81 "Here was an opportunity": Ibid., 54.

81 "Tens of thousands of people": Ibid., 56.

81 "The mining stocks": Ibid., 61–62.

81 "the Henry Ford of the speculation game": Wilbur S. Shepperson, *East of Eden, West of Zion: Essays on Nevada* (Reno: University of Nevada Press, 1989), 52.

82 "Human-interest stories": Rice, *My Adventures,* 58–59.

82 "I felt confident": Ibid., 59.

82 "I was head of the news bureau": Ibid., 58.

82 By 1905, Goldfield's mining stocks: Ibid., 62.

83 "I had passed through": Ibid., 94.

83 "I resolved": Ibid.

83 "I was an enthusiast": Ibid., 56.

84 "Never in my life": Ibid., 59.

84 "I went about my business": Ibid., 89.

84 Even as Goldfield was thriving: Ibid., 63–83; "The Bullfrog Mining District," accessed Jan. 2, 2014, legendsofamerica.com/nv-bullfrogdistrict.html; "Inside History Shoshone Deal," accessed Jan. 2, 2014, rhyolitenevada.com/news_archives/rhyolite-nevada-and -bullfrog-mining-district-news-archive/inside-history-shoshone-deal-75.html.

85 "to believe that when": Rice, *My Adventures,* 65.

85 "to help along my enthusiasm": Ibid., 64.

85 "turned out to be": Ibid.

85 "at figures which netted me": Ibid., 65.

85 "the powerful magnet": Ibid.

85 "I've seen many gold rushes": Richard E. Lingenfelter, *Death Valley and the Amargosa* (Berkeley: University of California Press, 1988), 204.

86 "Mr. Schwab at once": Rice, *My Adventures,* 66–67.

87 "welcher who pleads": Lingenfelter, *Death Valley and the Amargosa,* 237.

87 "Mr. Schwab, at the time": Ibid., 72–73.

88 "It is acknowledged": Ibid., 57.

88 "I had a youthful past": Plazak, *Hole in the Ground,* 258.

89 "If faro were honestly played": Robert Frederick Foster, *Foster's Encyclopedia of Games* (New York: F. A. Stokes, 1897), 490.

90 "Faro is a hard-hearted monarch": John Nevil Maskelyne, *Sharps and Flats: A Complete Revelation of the Secrets of Cheating at Games of Chance and Skill* (New York: Longmans, Green, 1894), 214.

90 "When a man is idiot enough": Ibid., 212.

91 "It is indeed strange": Maurer, *Big Con,* 180.

91 "It's the only game in town": William Norman Thompson, *Gambling in America: An Encyclopedia of History, Issues, and Society* (Santa Barbara, Calif.: ABC-CLIO, 2001), 205.

91 Faro was the pastime: Rice, *My Adventures,* 77.

91 "I found myself gossiped": Ibid., 83.

91 got taken for $300,000: "Just a Little Game," *Los Angeles Herald,* April 1, 1907.

91 "I bought blankets": Rice, *My Adventures,* 78.

92 "The Stray Dog": Ibid.

92 "There was great excitement": Ibid.

92 "A few days later": Ibid., 79.

92 "I was again in funds": Ibid., 83.

92 Lawrence M. Sullivan: "Larry Sullivan: Boxer, Politician, Con Artist, Shanghai Man," accessed Jan. 28, 2014, offbeatoregon.com/1212e-larry-sullivan-shanghaiing-legend .html.

93 "Put that money in a sack": Rice, *My Adventures,* 84.

93 "At this juncture": Ibid., 85.

94 "Right now I've got a whole carload": Plazak, *Hole in the Ground,* 259.

94 "We've just struck six feet": Rice, *My Adventures,* 97–98.

96 At 5:12 A.M., the most devastating earthquake: D. G. Doubleday to unknown recipient, telegram, May 12, 1906, accessed Jan. 28, 2014, oac.cdlib.org/view?docId=hb8c60097j &brand=oac4&doc.view=entire_text.

96 "The San Francisco Stock Exchange": Rice, *My Adventures,* 99.

97 "For two months": Ibid., 100.

97 "Castle-building": Ibid., 112–13.

99 "Seizing a box of cigars": *Salt Lake City Truth,* June 30, 1906, 8–9.

102 Shanghai Larry pined for: William Gildea, *The Longest Fight: In the Ring with Joe Gans, Boxing's First African American Champion* (New York: Farrar, Straus and Giroux, 2012), 1–132; Charles Samuels, *The Magnificent Rube: The Life and Gaudy Times of Tex Rickard* (New York: McGraw-Hill, 1957), 96–126; Colleen Aycock and Mark Scott, *Tex Rickard:*

Boxing's Greatest Promoter (Jefferson, N.C.: McFarland, 2012), 63–74; Elliott, *Nevada's Twentieth-Century Mining Boom,* 83–84; Rice, *My Adventures,* 113–19.

104 "probably the greatest boxer who ever lived": H. L. Mencken, *Heathen Days: Mencken's Autobiography, 1890–1936* (Baltimore: Johns Hopkins University Press, 2006), 96.

104 "abysmal brute": Jack London, "Brain Beaten by Brute Force," *San Francisco Examiner,* Sept. 10, 1905.

105 "All coons look alike": Gildea, *Longest Fight,* 56.

106 "an offer from Neromus": J. Dee Kille, *United by Gold and Glory: The Making of Mining Culture in Goldfield, Nevada, 1906–1908* (ProQuest, 2008), 84.

106 "Prize-fighting suited": Rice, *My Adventures,* 114.

106 "good nigger": Gildea, *Longest Fight,* 15.

107 "If you lose": Colleen Aycock and Mark Scott, *Joe Gans: A Biography of the First African American World Boxing Champion* (Jefferson, N.C.: McFarland, 2008), 159.

107 "If I had any money": Gildea, *Longest Fight,* 16.

108 "Are you willing": Samuels, *Magnificent Rube,* 104.

108 "Bring home the bacon": "The Meaning and Origin of the Expression: Bring Home the Bacon," accessed April 6, 2014, phrases.org.uk/meanings/bring-home-the-bacon.html.

109 "I'm four-flushing": Rice, *My Adventures,* 114–15.

109 Siler and Sullivan argued back and forth: Ibid., 114–16.

112 "announcer Sullivan's attempt": Ibid., 119.

112 "Butt him": "Joe Gans vs. Battling Nelson Fight," accessed April 16, 2014, eastsideboxing.com/weblog/news.php?p=11052&more=1.

113 "It was a vicious trick": Samuels, *Magnificent Rube,* 125.

113 "This doesn't look like the cinch": Rice, *My Adventures,* 117.

115 "He went down in sections": Gildea, *Longest Fight,* 120.

115 "Now, Siler, you saw": Rice, *My Adventures,* 117.

115 "Gentlemen, the referee declares": Ibid., 118.

115 "It was as clear": Gildea, *Longest Fight,* 121.

115 In Nelson's hometown: "Result Causes a Riot in Nelson's Home Town," *San Francisco Call,* Sept. 4, 1906.

115 In New York, dozens of accounts: "Almost a Lynching After Gans's Victory," *New York Times,* Sept. 5, 1906.

116 "excess of joy": "Result Causes a Riot in Nelson's Home Town."

117 "The securities": Rice, *My Adventures,* 156.

118 "It was a pet belief": Ibid., 164.

118 Existing only on maps: Ibid., 133–42; Lingenfelter, *Death Valley and the Amargosa,* 333–36.

118 "the monumental mining-stock swindle": Rice, *My Adventures,* 142.

118 "Greenwater is situated": Ibid., 133.

119 "The fact that Mr. Schwab": Ibid., 134.

119 "blood raw": Ibid., 135.

119 "Did I fall for Greenwater": Ibid., 139.

119 "Greenwater, a rich man's camp": Ibid., 132.

120 John Grant Lyman: "John Grant Lyman Reported Missing," *St. Louis Republic*, March 23, 1901; "Dr. J. Grant Lyman Is Here Once More," *New York Times*, Jan. 11, 1911; "Lyman Asks Return to Western Prison," *New York Times*, Feb. 27, 1916; Rice, *My Adventures*, 104–9; Guenther, "Pirates of Promotion," Oct. 1918, 590; Lingenfelter, *Death Valley and the Amargosa*, 332–33.

122 "Bullfrog Rush had not yet been listed": Rice, *My Adventures*, 106.

122 "I have formed here in Goldfield": Ibid.

122 "Governor Sparks, who is the best friend": Ibid.

123 "If you move a finger": Ibid., 107.

123 "Dr. Lyman was tall as a poplar": Ibid.

123 "In a second": Ibid.

123 "Several clerks who followed him": Ibid.

124 "Conscience had made a coward": Ibid., 108.

124 He was forced to run apology ads: *Milwaukee Journal*, Nov. 9, 1906.

124 "By this time": Rice, *My Adventures*, 170.

125 "I departed from Goldfield": Ibid., 177.

3. Blue Skies and Bucket Shops

126 "My reward": Rice, *My Adventures*, 178.

126 "Had I kept out": Ibid., 174.

127 "Wherever I went": Ibid., 180–81.

127 New York Curb Exchange: S. S. Huebner, *Stocks and the Stock Market* (Philadelphia: American Academy of Political and Social Science, 1910), 21–23; Jerry W. Markham, *A Financial History of the United States: From Christopher Columbus to the Robber Barons, 1492–1900* (Armonk, N.Y.: M. E. Sharpe, 2002), 241–43; "The Curb Market Deserts the Curb," *Literary Digest*, July 9, 1921; "New Curb Market Building at Greenwich Street and Trinity Place to Cost About $1,300,000," *New York Times*, Dec. 5, 1920.

131 "Goldfield had been the mining emporium": Rice, *My Adventures*, 181.

132 "It seemed quite apparent": Ibid., 194.

132 "I was as full of spirit": Ibid., 181.

132 "I was enthused": Ibid., 194.

132 *Nevada Mining News:* Richard E. Lingenfelter, *The Newspapers of Nevada: A History and Bibliography, 1854–1979* (Reno: University of Nevada Press, 1984), 187.

133 Rice crossed paths with Larry Sullivan: Samuels, *Magnificent Rube*, 128–29; Plazak, *Hole in the Ground*, 262; Rice, *My Adventures*, 195–205; "L. M. Sullivan Arrested on Mining Stock Deal," *San Francisco Call*, June 6, 1907; "Larry Sullivan Falls Out with His Partner," *San Francisco Call*, Aug. 6, 1907.

134 panic of 1907: Hansl, *Years of Plunder*, 86–89; "The Panic of 1907 & the History of the Banking System," accessed June 19, 2014, theglobalmovement.info/wp/the-panic-of-1907 -the-history-of-the-banking-system; "The Panic of 1907," accessed June 19, 2014, ritholtz .com/blog/2007/11/the-panic-of-1907-book-excerpt/; Markham, *Financial History of the United States*, 29–32.

134 "The panic of 1907 was brought about": "Wants 1907 Panic Inquiry," *New York Times,* Aug. 22, 1911.

135 In Nevada, labor unrest: Elliott, *Nevada's Twentieth-Century Mining Boom,* 130–44; Rice, *My Adventures,* 212–18.

135 "The governor, [an] honest": Rice, *My Adventures,* 216.

135 "Even at the moment": Ibid., 217.

135 "Prices of listed Nevada issues": Ibid., 209–10.

136 Because Rawhide: Ibid., 218.

136 Legitimate gold discoveries: Ibid., 218–31.

136 "gold with a little rock in it": Ibid., 220.

136 "The scenes enacted in Rawhide": Ibid., 259.

137 "When Rawhide was born": Ibid., 226.

137 "graveyard of a million blighted hopes": Ibid., 176.

137 "CHURCH CLOSED": Samuels, *Magnificent Rube,* 132.

137 "Why should not the American public": Rice, *My Adventures,* 220.

137 "kaleidoscopic maelstrom of humanity": Ibid., 259.

137 "Champagne was the common beverage": Ibid., 259–60.

138 In America, sex as an overt selling tool: Tom Reichert, *The Erotic History of Advertising* (Amherst, N.Y.: Prometheus Books, 2003), 46–79.

138 "a young woman of dazzling beauty": Rice, *My Adventures,* 240–41.

139 Her novels—scandalous at the time: Ibid., 232–36.

139 "Nothing would attract more attention": Ibid., 232–33.

140 "Would you like to sin": Lori Landay, *Madcaps, Screwballs, and Con Women: The Female Trickster in American Culture* (Philadelphia: University of Pennsylvania Press, 1998), 76.

140 "The men were coatless and grimy": Rice, *My Adventures,* 233–34.

141 "This was followed by hollow groans": Ibid., 234.

142 "A fire alarm was rung in": Ibid., 235–36.

142 "I have traveled from Budapest": "Elinor Glyn Plays Faro," *New York Times,* May 29, 1908.

143 Nathaniel Carl Goodwin: Nat C. Goodwin, *Nat Goodwin's Book* (Boston: Gorham Press, 1914), 293–302; Rice, *My Adventures,* 208–11, 223–24; "A Gilded Fool in Earnest," *New York Times,* Oct. 23, 1892; "Nat C. Goodwin Dies of Apoplexy," *New York Times,* Feb. 1, 1919; " 'Nat' Goodwin, Almost a Great American Actor," *Literary Digest,* Feb. 15, 1919, 88–92.

144 "Although I made but little money": Goodwin, *Nat Goodwin's Book,* 297.

145 "How much capital": Rice, *My Adventures,* 209.

145 "turned the tables": Ibid.

145 "One of my partners": Goodwin, *Nat Goodwin's Book,* 299.

145–46 "guards were maintained": Rice, *My Adventures,* 221–22.

146 "It was as exciting": Goodwin, *Nat Goodwin's Book,* 297.

147 Around 9:00 A.M., a gust blew: "Big Mining Camp Swept by Flames," *New York Times,* Sept. 5, 1908.

148 Rawhide Coalition, at twenty-five cents per share: *Boston Daily Globe,* Nov. 15 and Dec. 5, 1908.

148 Rawhide Coalition clawed its way: Rice, *My Adventures,* 277–87.

150 "wholly insolvent and irresponsible": "Sues Nat Goodwin's Company," *New York Sun*, Dec. 5, 1908.

150 "ore, as they call it": "Notes on Rawhide, Nevada," *Mining and Scientific Press*, March 28, 1908, 124.

151 Around noon on December 10: "Prices of Rawhide Hit Hard," *New York Sun*, Dec. 11, 1908.

151 "without any evidence of willingness": "Slump in Rawhide Coalition," *New York Times*, Dec. 11, 1908.

152 "a word from Mr. Goodwin": Ibid.

153 Bernard H. Scheftels: Rice, *My Adventures*, 288–97.

154 "Before the Scheftels corporation was in business a month": Ibid., 290, 296.

155 "bucket shop": Washburn and De Long, *High and Low Financiers*, 215–16; Leo Katcher, *The Big Bankroll: The Life and Times of Arnold Rothstein* (New York: Harper, 1959), 182–84.

156 "If you want to learn": "The Bucket Shop Man's View," *Ticker and Investment Digest*, Feb. 1910, 172.

157 Investors should have been able: Guenther, "Pirates of Promotion," Nov. 1918, 30.

158 "*both* parties to the trade intended": *Documents of the Senate of the State of New York* (New York State Legislature, 1910), 29–31.

158 "You hear a hue and a cry": Rice, *My Adventures*, 268.

158 "The 'kitty,' or 'rake-off' ": Ibid., 267.

159 "only carried out": Ibid., 315.

159 Ely Central: Ibid., 315–40; "A New Scheme to Hook Suckers," *Engineering and Mining Journal*, Nov. 6, 1909, 931–35; "Curb Lambs Caught by Ely Central," *New York Times*, Nov. 10, 1909.

159 "Their credit was assailed": Rice, *My Adventures*, 317.

160 "The prospect fairly took": Ibid., 319.

160 "to take advantage of": Ibid., 320.

160 "all the speculating world": Ibid., 321.

161 "I asked Captain W. Murdoch Wiley": Ibid., 333–35.

162 "The professional selling": Ibid., 322.

162 "pointing conclusively": Ibid.

163 "shameful attempt to inveigle": "New Scheme to Hook Suckers," 931.

163 "Savage attack": Rice, *My Adventures*, 334.

163 "All the New York papers": Ibid., 324.

164 "The air was surcharged": Ibid., 324–25.

164 "anyone who bought": "Ely Central in Rawhide Act," *New York Sun*, Nov. 9, 1909.

165 "It was a proud moment": Rice, *My Adventures*, 328–29.

165 "I got busy": Rice, *My Adventures*, 329–30.

165 "It was formal notice": Ibid., 336.

166 In order to make money: "Million in Margins Gone at Scheftels," *New York Times*, Oct. 1, 1910; "Rice Letters Show Scheftels Took in $5,000 a Day," unsourced news clip, Oct. 10, 1910; Rice, *My Adventures*, 336–46.

166 "I have formed": Ibid., 335.

166 "He stalked scowlingly": Ibid., 336.

167 "Scores of these letters": Ibid., 338.

167 The panic was a boon: "Halley's Comet 100 Years Ago," *Denver Post,* May 26, 2010.

168 Rice insisted on private telegraph wires: "Reading Telegrams in Scheftels Trial," *New York Times,* Nov. 1, 1911; "'Squawk Sheet' Used Against Scheftels," *New York Times,* Nov. 15, 1911; "Rice's Ely Central Boom," *New York Times,* Dec. 13, 1911.

169 "He held the market in his hand": "Scheftels Counsel Speaks of Enemies," *New York Times,* Nov. 4, 1911.

169 "The information was reliable": Rice, *My Adventures,* 340.

170 At 2:00 P.M. on August 19: "Rumor Starts Riot on Broad St. Curb," *New York Times,* Aug. 20, 1910; "Riot in Brokers' Office," *New-York Tribune,* Aug. 20, 1910; "Scheftels Firm Backer Waves $1,000 Bill to Stay Crowd," unsourced news clip, Aug. 20, 1910.

170 "I want my money": "Scheftels & Co. Stormed by Throng of Customers," unsourced news clip, Aug. 20, 1910.

170 "new even to the Curb": "Scheftels's Checks Good," *New York Times,* Aug. 21, 1910.

171 "When Mr. Rice was asked": "Checks, After All, Good," *New-York Tribune,* Aug. 21, 1910.

171 "The strain was great": Rice, *My Adventures,* 344.

171 "The sureties never qualified": Ibid., 345.

172 One by one, plainclothes detectives: "Federal Raid on B. H. Scheftels Co.," *New-York Tribune,* Sept. 30, 1910; "Government Raids B. H. Scheftels & Co.," *New York Times,* Sept. 30, 1910; "Inspectors Trailing Head of Bucket Shop," *Washington Times,* Sept. 30, 1910; "Rice Gives Himself Up," *New-York Tribune,* Oct. 1, 1910; "Nat Goodwin Is Placed on Rack," *San Francisco Call,* Oct. 4, 1901; "Rice Surrenders," *Toledo Blade,* Oct. 6, 1910; Rice, *My Adventures,* 346–53.

172 Scarborough, thirty-four: "The Author of the Lure," *Theatre,* Oct. 1913, 124–25.

174 "That settled it": Rice, *My Adventures,* 347.

174 "When he got his first peep": Ibid., 349.

175 "I walked across": Ibid., 347.

176 "Glad to see you going": "Government Raids B. H. Scheftels & Co."

176 "No prize fight": "Federal Raid on B. H. Scheftels Co."

176 "My attention was attracted": Rice, *My Adventures,* 348.

178 "looked as cool and bland": "Rice Gives Himself Up."

178 "I know him well": *Marion* (Ohio) *Daily Star,* Sept. 30, 1910.

180 "First one may ask": C. M. Keys, "The Get-Rich-Quick Game," *World's Work,* March 1911, 14116–18.

180 "It is the end": "End Long Crusade on Bucket Shops," *Washington Herald,* Dec. 16, 1910.

181 "Many state blue sky laws": "Chasing the Devil Around the Stump: Securities Regulation, the SEC and the Courts," accessed Sept. 16, 2014, sechistorical.org/museum/galleries/ctd/ctd02d_limits_blue.php.

182 "Very few ventured": "Gossip of Wall Street," *New York Sun,* Dec. 24, 1910.

182 "old-time jollification": "'Change Christmas Riot," *New-York Tribune,* Dec. 24, 1910.

183 "The year has been rotten!": "High Jinks Rule in Wall Street," *Washington Herald,* Dec. 24, 1910.

4. Jackal of Wall Street

184 George Graham Rice would have his day: "Admits Bigamy to Foil Wife's Suit," *New York Times,* Nov. 5, 1910; "Divorces Ex-convict Rice," *New York Times,* Feb. 1, 1911; "Mrs. Rice Gets Divorce," *Boston Globe,* Feb. 1, 1911; "Would Drop Rice Divorce Suit," *New York Times,* June 11, 1912.

184 "When this man wants anything": Unsourced news clip, Oct. 10, 1910.

185 "I am only one of the innumerable dupes": *Boston Globe,* Feb. 1, 1911.

185 "Mrs. Rice sat in court": Ibid.

186 More than a year after his arrest: "Chips on Shoulders at Scheftels Trial," *New York Times,* Dec. 15, 1911; "Scheftels Trial Halted," *New-York Tribune,* Dec. 22, 1911; "Reports Bribe Offer in Scheftels Trial," *New York Times,* Dec. 22, 1911; "Rice Rearrested in Scheftels Case," *New York Times,* Dec. 28, 1911; "Scheftels Trial Ended at Last by Pleas of Guilty," *New York Evening World,* March 7, 1912.

186 "Scheftels' Clique Goes to Jail": "Scheftels Jurors, Closely Quizzed, Selected Slowly," *New York American,* Oct. 11, 1911.

187 "Not a syllable of evidence": "Using a Court Year on Scheftels Trial," *New York Times,* March 3, 1912.

188 "I have been played for a sucker": "Jurors Forced to Live Here on Just $1.50 a Day," *New York Times,* Nov. 23, 1911.

189 "I would consider myself lacking": "George Graham Rice Dismisses Lawyers," *New York Times,* Jan. 18, 1912.

189 "There isn't a man": "Rice Makes His Own Plea," *New York Times,* Jan. 19, 1912.

190 "Didn't you tell Rice": "Whiskers' Value, $20,000," *New York Times,* Feb. 23, 1912.

191 "If the negotiations": "Hint of Compromise in Scheftels Trial," *New York Times,* March 7, 1912.

191 "B. H. Scheftels & Co. did nothing": *Virginia Law Register* 17, no. 12 (April 1912): 971.

192 "Many will think": Ibid., 972.

192 "the mountain labored": "The 'Blue Sky' Law" *Mining and Scientific Press,* March 16, 1912, 497.

192 "It was said by some": "Rice Pleads Guilty," *New-York Tribune,* March 8, 1912.

192 Blackwell's Island: "Before Rikers, Blackwell's Was DOC's Island Home," accessed Sept. 26, 2014, http://www.correctionhistory.org/html/chronicl/nycdoc/html/blakwel1.html.

193 His new lawyers: "Graham Rice a Bankrupt," *New York Times,* May 21, 1912.

193 "in various lines": *The New York Supplement* (St. Paul: West, 1916), 536–38.

193 sparked interest from a publisher: *Reports of Cases Heard and Determined in the Appellate Division of the Supreme Court of the State of New York* (Albany, N.Y.: Banks, 1916), 170:728–30.

193 "In his articles Rice made himself appear": "Lawson's New Fad, the Reform," *Financial World,* Sept. 12, 1912, 12.

193 "Two societies here": "Rice Is Anxious to War on Wall St.," unsourced news clip, Oct. 12, 1912.

194 George, thinking he had bought: Candice Millard, *The River of Doubt: Theodore Roosevelt's Darkest Journey* (New York: Knopf Doubleday, 2009), 8–9.

195 "the most illuminating book": *Educational Review*, May 1912.

195 "In boyhood": Rice, *My Adventures*, 8–10.

196 "the spicy confessions": *Life*, Oct. 9, 1913, 616.

196 "Rice is not only a good story-teller": *Smart Set*, Oct. 1913, 158.

196 the term "con artist" first appeared: "Coin Matchers of Times Square Are Doing Rushing Business," *New York Times*, Nov. 9, 1913.

196 Arnold Rothstein: Katcher, *Big Bankroll*, 1–369; David Pietrusza, *Rothstein: The Life, Times, and Murder of the Criminal Genius Who Fixed the 1919 World Series* (New York: Basic Books, 2011); Michael Alexander, *Jazz Age Jews* (Princeton, N.J.: Princeton University Press, 2003), 40–44.

198 "the first mining company": Guenther, "Pirates of Promotion," Oct. 1918, 591.

198 On the morning of June 28, 1914: "How Bad Directions (and a Sandwich?) Started World War I," accessed Oct. 1, 2014, http://www.npr.org/templates/transcript/transcript.php ?storyId=285893848.

199 "The resourceful Rice": "The Lobster Palace, the Tango, and Rice," *Financial World*, July 18, 1914, 20.

199 For forty-eight hours: William L. Silber, "What Happened to Liquidity When World War I Shut the NYSE?," *Journal of Financial Economics* 78, no. 3 (2005): 685–701; Roy C. Smith, *The Global Bankers* (Washington, D.C.: Beard Books, 2000), 21–23; "Odds Favor Long War," *New York Times*, March 27, 1915.

200 "The textile industry": Hansl, *Years of Plunder*, 115.

201 "Soon all corporate profits": Ibid., 100.

201 Nigger Lips: "Babe Ruth and the Issue of Race," accessed Oct. 1, 2014, http://www .baberuthcentral.com/the-humanitarian/babe-ruth-and-the-issue-of-race-bill-jenkinson/.

202 "Nationwide Insanity": *Lewiston (Maine) Herald*, Oct. 6, 1915.

202 Even Henry Ford: "Henry the Farmboy—War Profits," accessed Oct. 1, 2014, http://www .queencitymodelaclub.com/id363.html.

202 nicknamed dynamiters: Guenther, "Pirates of Promotion," Nov. 1918, 30. Hansl, *Years of Plunder*, 129–31.

203 "The 'dynamiter' or veteran 'loader'": "The Crooks in White Collars," *Life*, Oct. 14, 1957, 165.

204 As combat intensified: "Brokers in a Feud over Curb Stocks," *New York Times*, Oct. 5, 1910.

204 "Hungry-eyed brokers": "Swann to Summon Brokers Rice Names," *New York Times*, Oct. 6, 1916.

204 "The bucket shop crowd": Ibid.

205 "Blood Flows, Price Soars": "Brokers' Fists Fly in Curb Stock Feud," *New York Times*, Oct. 7, 1916.

205 "The open-air mart exists": "Brokers Again Use Fists on Broad St.," *New York Times*, Oct. 8, 1916.

205 Other dealers were embracing: Washburn and De Long, *High and Low Financiers*, 63–65.

206 "Prominent philanderer. Age 72": These are composite descriptions culled from index cards cited in ibid., 282–83.

208 "The man who kept a tight grip": Frederick Lewis Allen, *Only Yesterday: An Informal History of the 1920s* (New York: John Wiley & Sons, 1931), 171.

208 "Do not waste the power": Guenther, "Pirates of Promotion," Nov. 1918, 30.

209 "I note your further": Guenther, "Pirates of Promotion," Oct. 1918, 584.

209 "Rice's game is to paint": Ibid., 586.

211 The authorities smashed in: "G. G. Rice Held on Mail Fraud Order," *New York Sun,* July 30, 1918; "Two Grand Juries Sift Rice's Deals," *New-York Tribune,* July 31, 1918.

211 "What do you mean": "Huge Swindle Is Charged to Graham Rice," *New-York Tribune,* July 30, 1918.

212 "the worst crook on Wall Street": "Geo. Graham Rice Is Held On $4,000," *New York Sun,* July 31, 1919.

212 If they were snooping around: "A False Armistice," *New York Sun,* Nov. 10, 2004.

213 "Nothing is too good": Allen, *Only Yesterday,* 6.

214 Rothstein's motivation to help: Katcher, *Big Bankroll,* 181–93.

215 "Curiously, advancing prices": Hansl, *Years of Plunder,* 120.

215 When the trial opened: *New York Supreme Court Case on Appeal, The People of the State of New York v. George Graham Rice,* 3:1001–589; "Rice Faces Eight More Charges," *New-York Tribune,* Jan. 10, 1920; "Graham Rice Assails Prosecutor," *New York Times,* Jan. 16, 1920.

216 "I believe that you are absolutely controlled": *New York v. Rice,* 1021.

216 "[Insiders] are on the destructive side": Ibid., 1025.

216 "Rothstein held lawyers in peculiar esteem": Katcher, *Big Bankroll,* 167.

5. Vortex of Decadence

218 "lifting skirts far beyond": Allen, *Only Yesterday,* 68.

220 New York officials broke ground: *New York Times,* Dec. 5, 1920.

221 "The drastic Volstead Act": "Rice, Nevada Booster, with Us," *Nevada State Journal,* April 4, 1920.

222 "My son": "Capra Shoots as He Pleases," *Saturday Evening Post,* May 14, 1938.

222 "It is fair to ask": "At It Again," *New-York Tribune,* Aug. 23, 1920.

222 "Rice may have done many questionable things": "Broken Hills Excitement," *Mohave County Miner,* July 17, 1920.

222 "the pot is so actively boiling": "An Old Game with a New Angle," *Engineering and Mining Journal,* Nov. 13, 1920.

222 "it would not take much": "Rice, Who Made a Million and Still Went to Prison, Sure He'll Win This Time with Aid of Wife Alone," *New York World,* Oct. 21, 1931.

223 On December 11, 1920: "G. Graham Rice Seeks Divorce," *Reno Evening Gazette,* Feb. 5, 1921.

223 "Officials are wondering": "Officials Worried," *Bismarck (N.D.) Tribune,* Feb. 17, 1921.

224 "I challenge you": "Rice Sends Wire to Coast Officer," *Deseret News,* July 15, 1921.

225 the charges were dropped: "Charges Against Rice Dismissed," *Ogden (Utah) Standard-Examiner,* Jan. 31, 1922.

225 "From now on": *New York Mail,* Sept. 7, 1921.

227 "Propaganda . . . permeated": Hansl, *Years of Plunder,* 187.

228 Alvin "Sailor" Kelly: "Body of 'Shipwreck' Kelly Lies Unclaimed in Morgue," *Sarasota Herald-Tribune,* Oct. 13, 1952; "About New York," *Spartanburg (S.C.) Herald,* Oct. 5, 1933.

228 Idaho Copper Corporation: *Idaho Copper Corporation v. Campbell,* Circuit Court of Appeals, 9th Cir., unsourced court document dated Aug. 20, 1928, accessed Oct. 20, 2014, leagle.com/decision/192886027F2d833_1573; *Rice et al. v. United States,* Circuit Court of Appeals, 2nd Cir., unsourced court document dated Nov. 4, 1929, accessed Oct. 20, 2014, leagle.com/decision/192972435F2d689_1481.xml/RICE%20v.%20UNITED%20 STATES.

228 On July 2, 1924, the appellate division: "Court Sets Aside Rice's Conviction," *New York Times,* July 3, 1924; "Rice Wins Plea for New Trial," unsourced news clip, July 3, 1924.

228 *Wall Street Iconoclast:* Washburn and De Long, *High and Low Financiers,* 26–27; Dan Krier, *Speculative Management: Stock Market Power and Corporate Change* (Albany: State University of New York Press, 2005).

229 the Boston Curb: "The Boston Curb," *Pittsburgh Press,* Feb. 20, 1928.

229 "There is not a thread": "Filth from Doorstep," *Time,* Nov. 26, 1934.

229 GG rented an office in Boston: Washburn and De Long, *High and Low Financiers,* 29–34; National Archives Criminal Case File C53-663, *United States v. Jacob Simon Herzig,* U.S. District Court for the Southern District of New York, Records of District Courts of the U.S., Record Group 21; "Rice, Editor, and 2 Indicted in Jump of Copper Stock," *New York Evening Post,* Jan. 17, 1928; "Rice Again Indicted for Stock Frauds," *New York Times,* Jan. 18, 1928; "Boston Broker Tells of Rice Stock Deals," *New York Times,* Nov. 17, 1928.

231 Walter Harvey Weed: Plazak, *Hole in the Ground,* 283–85.

232 "There is nothing here": *Rice et al. v. United States.*

232 "The ore is spectacular": Ibid.

232 "Behind every one of those lights": Liebling, *Honest Rainmaker,* 97.

232 "The rich man's chauffeur": Allen, *Only Yesterday,* 237–38.

234 Suckers essentially conned themselves: Washburn and De Long, *High and Low Financiers,* 15; Maurer, *Big Con,* 105–7.

235 "At that time": Maurer, *Big Con,* 116.

235 "That match cost him $100,000": Ibid., 112.

235 Colombia Emerald Development Corporation: Plazak, *Hole in the Ground,* 281–82; *New York v. George Graham Rice, Also Known as Jacob S. Herzig, Wall Street Iconoclast, Inc., and Rose McKernan,* New York Supreme Court, unsourced court document dated Nov. 18, 1927, accessed Oct. 20, 2014, sechistorical.org; Criminal Case File C53-663.

237 Better Business Bureau: Balleisen, "Private Cops on the Fraud Beat," 117–60.

237 "By the admission": Ibid., 152.

238 "I have been informed and believe": *New York v. Rice et al.*

238 They hired nine lawyers to gut: "Call Martin Act Unconstitutional," *New York Times,* Feb. 12, 1926.

238 "Sell any stock you own": Criminal Case File C53-663.

240 farmer in South Dakota: Washburn and De Long, *High and Low Financiers,* 32–34.

241 "the wildest frenzy of hero worship": "Why We Mob Heroes," *Popular Science Monthly,* Sept. 1927, 24.

241 "I swing big": Wilborn Hampton, *Babe Ruth: A Twentieth-Century Life* (New York: Penguin, 2009), 189.

241 "Hundreds of passersby": "Flagpole Rooster," *Time,* June 20, 1927.

242 "To many it seemed": Hansl, *Years of Plunder,* 145.

242 "If three-million-share days": Ibid., 140.

242 In New York, Winter continued: *New York v. Rice et al.;* "Jared Flagg Dies at Fraud Inquiry," *New York Times,* Aug. 27, 1926; "Martin Act Upheld as Constitutional," *New York Times,* Oct. 12, 1926.

244 That morning in western New York:: "Rice Indicted for Larceny," *New York Times,* Sept. 21, 1927.

244 "he will be designated as a special deputy": "Keyes Winter Quits Fraud Bureau," *New York Times,* Sept. 21, 1927; *New York v. Rice et al.*

244 In November, Idaho: "Receiver for Idaho Copper," *New York Times,* Nov. 27, 1927; "Rice's Activities Curbed by Court," *New York Times,* Dec. 17, 1927.

245 A subsequent audit: Katcher, *Big Bankroll,* 189–90.

245 In the first week of December: Allen, *Only Yesterday,* 121–31.

246 By the middle of January: Washburn and De Long, *High and Low Financiers,* 34–35.

247 stocks continued to trade at zany prices: Allen, *Only Yesterday,* 243–46; Hansl, *Years of Plunder,* 178.

248 "turn to the financial pages": Paul Adomites, *Babe Ruth: His Life and Times* (Lincolnwood, Ill.: Publications International, 1995), 159.

249 "We shall soon": "Senator Bruce Finds Little to Favor in Hoover Speech," *New York Times,* Aug. 28, 1928.

249 Perhaps the truest barometer: Ron Chepesiuk, *The War on Drugs: An International Encyclopedia* (Santa Barbara, Calif.: ABC-CLIO, 1999), 209–10. Also: Katcher, *Big Bankroll,* 1–9, 321–33; Kevin Cook, *Titanic Thompson: The Man Who Bet on Everything* (New York: Norton, 2010), 99–121.

250 "Tell them to keep their shirts on": Cook, *Titanic Thompson,* 120.

251 "I'll take care of it myself": James McManus, *Cowboys Full: The Story of Poker* (New York: Farrar, Straus and Giroux, 2009), 191.

251 "Gimme a dime": accessed Oct. 19, 2014, http://www.spdermnk.com/images/books /northwest_fly_fishing_book.pdf.

252 When the trial began: "Rice Put on Trial; 11 Picked for Jury," *New York Times,* Nov. 14, 1928; "Trial of Rice Opens on Fraud Charges," *New York Times,* Nov. 15, 1928; "Boston Broker Tells of Rice Stock Deals," *New York Times,* Nov. 17, 1928; "Rice's Methods Revealed," *New York Times,* Nov. 28, 1928; "Rice Opens Defense in Idaho Copper Case," *New York Times,* Dec. 4, 1928; "Rice Found Guilty on Fraud Charges," *New York Times,* Dec. 15, 1928; "Rice Gets Four Years in Stock Swindle," *New York Times,* Dec. 22, 1928; "Rice's Coats in Dispute," *New York Times,* Dec. 27, 1928.

253 "This man, the tool of the bucket shops": "Fake Promoter Imprisoned on Fraud Charges," *St. Petersburg Times,* Dec. 22, 1928.

253 "Rice formerly was a spectacular figure": "Rice Found Guilty on Fraud Charges."

254 "the outstanding incident": "Finds Check in Year to Stock Frauds," *New York Times,* May 20, 1929.

255 The hits kept coming: "Rice Is Now Accused of Income Tax Fraud," *New York Times*, March 8, 1929; "Rice Loses Plea for New Trial," *New York Times*, April 11, 1929; "Seeks to Curb Rice in New Stock Deal," *New York Times*, Sept. 22, 1929.

255 No one knew it at the time: Allen, *Only Yesterday*, 243–80.

257 "Under my very window": Tim McNeese, *The Great Depression, 1929–1938* (New York: Infobase 2010), 26.

257 "We have examined them all": *Rice et al. v. United States.*

257 George applied to the U.S. Supreme Court: "Rice's Conviction as Tipster Upheld," *New York Times*, Nov. 5, 1929; "G. G. Rice Missing as Writ Is Denied," *New York Times*, Nov. 9, 1929; "Rice Not Missing; At His Hotel Here," *New York Times*, Nov. 11, 1929; "Rice Imprisoned for Stock Fraud," *New York Times*, Nov. 12, 1929; "Rice Going to Prison," *Time*, Nov. 25, 1929; "Rice Asks Trial Review," *New York Times*, Feb. 1, 1930.

258 "faultlessly attired": "George Graham Rice to Be Sent to Atlanta," *Providence Evening Tribune*, Nov. 11, 1929.

259 "I'll show all of you!": Washburn and De Long, *High and Low Financiers*, 37.

6. Vanishing Act

260 In the aftermath of the big bull: Hansl, *Years of Plunder*, 272–73.

260 Rice had been spotted: "Court Allowed Rice Brief Trips to Hotel," *New York Times*, Jan. 22, 1930; "Court May Halt Rice's Trips from Cell," *New York Evening Journal*, Jan. 22, 1930; "Judge to Probe Rice Jail Exits," *New York American*, Jan. 23, 1930.

261 "There are between fifty and sixty tons": "Rice Goes on Trial in Income Tax Case," *New York Times*, Oct. 20, 1931.

261 "Ghouls, ghouls": "Graham Rice Mum About $15,000,000," unsourced, undated news clip.

261 "elderly, penniless and ill": "Train Bride Seeks Balm Following Sentence," *Milwaukee Sentinel*, Feb. 22, 1930.

262 Discouraged, he climbed down: " 'Shipwreck' Kelly Causes Job 'Crisis,'" *New York Times*, Dec. 14, 1930.

262 "I had a better year": William B. Mead and Paul Dickson, *Baseball: The Presidents' Game* (New York: Walker, 1997), 59.

262 "Work is practically unknown": "Federal Felons Buy Transfers," *Boston Globe*, July 11, 1931.

262 Rice returned to New York: "Rice Here for Income Tax Trial," *New York Times*, Sept. 3, 1931; "Rice, as Counsel, Wins Point at Trial," *New York Times*, Oct. 21, 1931; "Rice Acquitted After Defending Self in Tax Case," *New-York Tribune*, Oct. 30, 1931; "Jury Acquits Rice in Income Tax Case," *New York Times*, Oct. 30, 1931.

263 "This is a love story": *New York World-Telegram*, Oct. 21, 1931.

264 "I have spent millions on lawyers": "Jury Acquits Rice of Income Tax Evasion," *New York American*, Oct. 30, 1931.

264 George wept: "Convict Lawyer Wins Own Case," *St. Petersburg Evening Independent*, Oct. 30, 1931.

264 he got a new cell mate: "Capone's Complaining Makes Him Unpopular with Prison Mates," *Rochester (N.Y.) Evening Journal*, Jan. 24, 1933.

265 "I'd take Al's word": A. J. Liebling, "Rice Back from Prison with 'Phosphorescent Mind' to Run Paper Exposing Bankers in Glass Houses," *New York World*, Jan. 26, 1934.

265 "Honest to God": John Madinger, *Money Laundering: A Guide for Criminal Investigators* (Boca Raton, Fla.: CRC Press, 2006), 130.

266 "meeting the challenges": "Rice Resumes," *Time*, Jan. 29, 1934.

266 The mockery bottomed out: John Faber, *Great News Photos and the Stories Behind Them* (New York: Dover, 1978), 55–56.

266 Perhaps acting on a tip: "Uncomfortable Tack," *Time*, Jan. 1, 1934; "George G. Rice Is Back at Old Stand," *New York Sun*, Jan. 13, 1934; "George Graham Rice Launches New Paper," *Deseret News*, Feb. 1, 1934.

267 "This is going to be absolutely clean": Liebling, "Rice Back from Prison."

269 George's probation was revoked: Petition of Revocation of Probation and Order for Issuance of Bench Warrant C 53-663, U.S. District Court, Southern District of New York, No. 17, 1936; "Bad Boy Rice at It Again—Vanishes as Prison Yawns," *New York Evening Post*, Nov. 20, 1936; "Faces Return to Cell," *New York Herald*, Nov. 21, 1936; "G. G. Rice Sought on Parole Charge," *New York Times*, Nov. 21, 1936.

269 "intensely interested": "George Graham Rice Overdue for New Eruption," *New York Sun*, April 19, 1937.

270 "Faint footsteps of George Graham Rice": "Rice Trailed as Raider on Atlas Stock," *New York Daily News*, Dec. 20, 1938.

Epilogue

271 "How different the death": *Hand-Book of Swindling*, 81–82.

272 The death certificate: Certificate of Death No. 23110 (Jacob Herzig), Department of Health, Borough of Manhattan, New York, N.Y., stamped Oct. 24, 1943.

272 Jacob lived out his final months: 1940 U.S. Federal Census, Supervisor's District 1, Enumeration District 31-801, New York, N.Y., Sheet No. 8B.

274 "Relatively few confidence men": Maurer, *Big Con*, 208–13.

274 "Whatever happened to George Graham Rice": *Mining and Metallurgy*, March 1939, 166; Sept. 1939, 417.

ACKNOWLEDGMENTS

Without the support of friends and family, this book would be nothing more than a jumbled collection of notes and news clippings. I owe lots of people unpayable debts of gratitude for helping to turn what began as a brain spark into reality.

A big thanks to Michael Flamini, my editor at St. Martin's Press, for his enthusiasm straight from the proposal stage. Michael has the rare gift of being able to shape a story arc and give it direction, then step back to allow the author to bring it to life. Once we completed the manuscript, the St. Martin's creative team fine-tuned it into a fully realized book that I could be proud of. The result of their collaborative efforts, to me, was like putting on a pair of glasses to see something you thought you knew well, but with sharper clarity.

I had a fortuitous detour en route to writing *My Adventures*. In the spring of 2011, I was introduced to the literary agent David R. Patterson with the hope that he would represent a different book I was researching on an entirely separate topic. David underscored that he wanted to represent me as an evolving author, but with tact and grace he opened my eyes to the benefits of deviating from my original book pitch. I took his advice and embraced the risk of switching ideas, and only because of that did I discover the forgotten corner of con artistry that became the backbone of *My Adventures*. I'm looking forward to many more leaps into the unknown with David, who is now with the Stuart Krichevsky Literary Agency.

I am continually astounded at how genuinely and tirelessly my family and friends champion my work. I am especially grateful to members of the Thornton, Shislo, Raymond, Esper, and Blizard families. At a young age, my parents, Sandra and Paul, instilled in me a zeal for writing, and they still encourage it every day. My sister, Kathy, and my nieces, Abbey and Kelly, are the rocks that keep our family grounded. Special thanks to my exceptional friends Terry Bean and Demetri Papas for a ceaseless supply of camaraderie and counterpoint.

I've saved the best for last—my wife, Dena. Her loyalty knows no bounds, and my appreciation, respect, and love for her go beyond words. Baby, you're the greatest!